Fiscal and Welfare Impacts of Electricity Subsidies in Central America

DIRECTIONS IN DEVELOPMENT
Public Sector Governance

Fiscal and Welfare Impacts of Electricity Subsidies in Central America

Marco Antonio Hernández Oré, Luis Álvaro Sánchez, Liliana D. Sousa, and Leopoldo Tornarolli, Editors

WORLD BANK GROUP

Contents

Boxes

Figures

Tables

Foreword

Policy makers considering tax increases or spending cuts in the context of fiscal consolidation efforts typically face demands from important segments of the population who argue that, before increasing taxes or cutting spending in general, the government should assess the quality of public spending. It is common sense that the public sector should implement all possible savings by cutting inefficient expenses before requesting additional efforts.

Nevertheless, when we reflect on the quality of public spending, there are many questions—some of which require refined technical analyses to provide an answer—that come to mind: Do the resources reach the intended beneficiaries? Is public spending having the expected impact? Is this good value for the money? Do we have alternatives that may achieve similar results in a more efficient way? Does the intervention have any undesirable secondary impact?

This book, by my colleagues Marco Hernández, Luis Álvaro Sánchez, Liliana Sousa, and Leopoldo Tornarolli, focuses precisely on these questions in the context of electricity subsidies in the countries of Central America. I am sure that policy makers and practitioners alike will be able to make good use of its findings, because it identifies efficiency gains that will allow fiscal resources to be generated without infringing on social and development goals.

One of the basic findings of the analysis is that a significant proportion of electricity subsidies in Central America is inefficiently targeted, with the bulk going to higher-income households. Given the limited fiscal space in the region and the major needs of the countries in terms of social services and physical infrastructure, this book reaches the conclusion that electricity subsidies are an important missed opportunity.

A second key finding is that direct subsidies significantly reduce expenditures on electricity for the poorest 40 percent of households in most countries and thus contribute to reducing poverty. This is very much welcomed, taking into account the levels of poverty prevailing in Central America, but this result is achieved with a high level of inefficiency because wealthy households receive a large proportion of the subsidies, including households at the top of the income distribution.

Building on this, the book presents a number of scenarios that would contribute to improving the welfare of families living in poverty, while at the same time reducing fiscal spending without inflicting excessive costs on higher-income households. In other words, there are win–win situations for policy makers to consider.

I am sure that readers familiar with subsidy reforms will recognize that this analysis, while very useful, does not guarantee successful reform. For this reason, the authors take the analysis further and reflect on the analytical tools and data needed to engage in the necessary discussion of these important yet politically complex reforms, including clear leadership. Because electricity subsidies are neither social assistance nor electricity policy, they become, in many cases, political orphans that lack a champion. This could be taken as an invitation to the ministries of finance, which are well positioned to define the fiscal implications and opportunity costs of these subsidies, to take leadership on this front.

We believe this volume, *Fiscal and Welfare Impacts of Electricity Subsidies in Central America*, is a valuable contribution to the regional debate on the quality and efficiency of public spending at a time when several countries are facing fiscal pressures that will require consolidation. As a development institution, we at the World Bank are committed to enriching, supporting, and learning from this debate, which is critical to the design of policies conductive to enhancing the welfare of the population.

J. Humberto López
Director of Strategy and Operations,
Latin America and the Caribbean
Former Country Director, Central America
The World Bank

Acknowledgments

We are most grateful to the contributors to this book for their efforts in preparing the various versions of the manuscript. The team worked under the overall guidance of J. Humberto López (director of strategy and operations for Latin America and the Caribbean, and former country director for Central America), Pablo Saavedra (practice manager, Macroeconomics and Fiscal Management Global Practice), Oscar Calvo-Gonzalez (practice manager, Poverty and Equity Global Practice), and Manuela Francisco (practice manager, Macroeconomics and Fiscal Management Global Practice, and former program leader for Central America).

We are indebted to Maryam Ali-Lothrop and Sean Lothrop, who provided excellent research and editorial assistance during the production of this study. The team would also like to thank a number of colleagues who provided useful comments and advice, in particular Anabela Abreu, Laura Berman, Luis Constantino, Melisa Fanconi, Thomas Flochel, Homa-Zahra Fotouhi, Mariano Gonzalez, Fernando Im, Odile Johnson, Juan Jose Miranda, Martin Ochoa, Laura Maria Oliveri, Sameer Shukla, Giorgio Valentini, and Fabrizio Zarcone, as well as our peer reviewers, Guillermo Beylis, Anna Fruttero, and David Reinstein.

The team is especially grateful to the authorities of Costa Rica, El Salvador, Guatemala, Honduras, Nicaragua, and Panama, who provided invaluable knowledge, data, and advice. We also thank the individuals who gave generously of their time to meet with the team and share their thoughts. In particular, the study benefited from fruitful exchanges with citizens of all Central American nations, including government officials, civil society stakeholders, and representatives from development agencies.

We gratefully acknowledge funding from the Energy Sector Management Assistance Program (ESMAP) for the production of this study.[*]

---

* ESMAP—a global knowledge and technical assistance program administered by the World Bank Group—assists low- and middle-income countries in increasing their know-how and institutional capacity to achieve environmentally sustainable energy solutions for poverty reduction and economic growth. ESMAP is funded by Australia, Austria, Denmark, Finland, France, Germany, Iceland, Japan, Lithuania, the Netherlands, Norway, Sweden, Switzerland, the United Kingdom, and the World Bank Group.

About the Editors and Contributors

Marco Antonio Hernández Oré is program leader and lead economist for the Western Balkans at the World Bank. At the time of writing, he was a senior economist in the Macroeconomics and Fiscal Management Global Practice of the World Bank. His areas of expertise include macro-fiscal policy, economic growth, and political economy.

Ewa Korczyc is an economist in the Macroeconomics and Fiscal Management Global Practice of the World Bank. Her areas of expertise include macro-fiscal policy and economic growth.

Laura Olivera is a research analyst in the Macroeconomics and Fiscal Management Global Practice of the World Bank. Her areas of expertise include macroeconomics and financial programming.

Luis Rizo Patrón is a consultant on mineral and energy economics, natural resource management, and financial programming.

Luis Álvaro Sánchez is a consultant and adviser on macroeconomics, growth, economic analysis, strategy, evaluation, and innovation.

Liliana D. Sousa is an economist in the Poverty and Equity Global Practice of the World Bank. Her areas of expertise include labor economics and household economics.

Leopoldo Tornarolli is a senior researcher at the Centro de Estudios Distributivos, Laborales y Sociales (CEDLAS) of Universidad Nacional de La Plata, Argentina. He is codirector of the Socio-Economic Database for Latin America and the Caribbean (SEDLAC), a joint project of CEDLAS and the World Bank. His areas of expertise include labor economics and the empirical analysis of social issues.

Executive Summary

All countries in Central America provide direct electricity subsidies to a majority of residential consumers, in some cases benefiting close to 80 percent of the population. In general, these subsidies entail substantial fiscal costs for countries that are already facing tight budget constraints. Approximately 1 percent of Central America's aggregate gross domestic product is spent subsidizing residential electricity consumption, an amount comparable to what these countries spend on education and social assistance. Moreover, governments rarely set hard budget constrains for these subsidies, resulting in unexpected budget impacts.

This book answers key questions regarding residential electricity subsidies in Central America. In particular: How do the subsidy mechanisms function in each country? What are their fiscal costs? How effective have these subsidies been in easing the burden of electricity expenditures on poor households? How efficiently has this spending reached households in need, and what factors drive this effectiveness? What are the reform options?

The main message of this book is that there is considerable scope for improving the efficiency of electricity subsidies in Central America by better targeting them to low-income households. More specifically, most countries in the region have the opportunity to significantly reduce the fiscal costs of electricity subsidies without imposing significant costs on households, particularly poor households.

Over the last two decades, Central American countries have undertaken many electricity subsidy reforms. Sometimes they have introduced new subsidy mechanisms with the intention of decreasing the burden of rising oil prices on households. Other times they have reformed existing mechanisms when the fiscal burden imposed by these subsidies became unsustainable. At the moment, with slower global growth and less-favorable financing conditions, policy makers need to think about solutions not only on *what* to reform but also on *how* to reform. For this, it is imperative to have solid analytical underpinnings that distinguish the trade-offs that policy makers face.

What have Central American governments accomplished with electricity subsidies? On the one hand, electricity subsidies have helped reduce the burden of electricity costs on the lowest-income groups. On the other hand, however, current electricity subsidy schemes are inefficient at targeting resources to low-income households. Efficiency in targeting is measured as the share of total subsidies that low-income households receive using a uniform benchmark across the six countries—namely, the poorest 40 percent of the income distribution. In all countries in Central America, for every dollar spent subsidizing electricity consumption, less than 40 cents goes to the poorest 40 percent of the population.

Why are electricity subsidies inefficiently targeted? The analysis identifies and quantifies four factors that together determine the degree of targeting efficiency of these subsidy mechanisms. Two are found to increase efficiency. First, the eligibility criteria in each country are more likely to exclude high-income households. Second, depending on the design of subsidy schemes, the average subsidy amount received per kilowatt-hour consumed is typically higher for lower-income consumers. The other two factors, however, reduce efficiency. First, households that are not connected to the power grid (which are disproportionately likely to be poor) do not benefit. This factor is less relevant for urban areas, where access to electricity is relatively high, but remains a concern in rural areas. Second, the largest driver of inefficiency in targeting is that higher-income households consume more subsidized electricity than lower-income households.

From this analysis, two key lessons stand out. First, "design matters"; the thresholds to determine household eligibility and the depth of subsidies determine most of the efficiency of targeting. Second, although schemes in all countries rely on electricity consumption as a proxy for income, the relationship between income and consumption is imperfect. This introduces *errors of inclusion* and *errors of exclusion*; the subsidy scheme covers some higher-income households (i.e., they are included), and some poor households are excluded. Therefore, policy makers need to identify alternative targeting strategies that do not rely only on the amount of electricity consumed.

The fiscal costs of electricity subsidies have fallen since 2012, aided by reforms in some countries but mostly driven by falling oil prices. Where they have been undertaken, reforms have addressed some but not all of the concerns that this study raises. El Salvador, for instance, eliminated a subsidy scheme targeted to higher consumption (100–300 kWh) that benefited mostly middle- and higher-income groups in the population. Honduras reduced eligibility thresholds for its main subsidy while preserving a subsidy for smaller consumers. Nevertheless, despite recent policy efforts, there is much room for improving the efficiency of electricity subsidies. Simulations in this study show that gains can be made across the board in all countries: affordability can be increased for low-income households, and fiscal costs can be reduced by generating efficiency gains that come mostly from curbing errors of inclusion.

To best assess potential reforms, countries would benefit from stating explicitly the objectives of electricity subsidies and the fiscal resources available to fund these. For example, are subsidies meant to support households living in or close to poverty, or are they expected to support a larger segment of the population? This information is essential to design a scheme that reaches the target population and achieves the stated objectives. Given the level of subsidies in place today, in some countries, a rapid adjustment of the current schemes would imply sharp changes in tariffs, which could be difficult for households to absorb. For this reason, this study also illustrates options for a gradual approach to reforming electricity subsidies.

In line with the literature on subsidies, this book calls for integrating residential electricity subsidies and social assistance programs within a common conceptual framework. From a practical perspective, subsidies can be integrated into social assistance programs by using these programs as a mechanism to identify beneficiaries and distribute subsidies with greater accuracy. Viewing subsidies and other types of assistance within a single framework helps address errors of exclusion and inclusion.

The benefit of using complementary social assistance rosters depends on their quality and design. When they are able to identify low-income households and have national coverage, they can substantially enhance the efficiency in targeting electricity subsidies. As such, improving rosters and criteria for eligibility would lead to significant returns in terms of spending efficiency. Other approaches can also lead to improved targeting; for example, Honduras excludes high-income neighborhoods from eligibility for its more generous electricity subsidy.

Governments may soon face rising generation costs. In the past, the authorities responded by implementing subsidies to soften the effect on households, in turn generating increases in the beneficiary population and fiscal costs. Over the long term, the best option is to avoid exposure to cost increases by developing a generation mix that can adapt to changes in oil prices, such as shifting toward renewable energy. Recurrent shifts in the cost of production can be further managed with financial instruments to hedge the risks. Using direct subsidies to manage the impact on residential consumers results in a counterproductive reallocation of risk and costs and discourages needed investments, both by households and the electricity sector. In this context, this study seeks to provide Central American policy makers with the analytical foundations necessary to comprehensively appraise the costs and benefits of their residential electricity subsidy mechanisms and design effective reform strategies that reflect their unique circumstances and policy priorities.

Fiscal and Welfare Impacts of Electricity Subsidies in Central America
http://dx.doi.org/10.1596/978-1-4648-1104-3

Abbreviations

ARESEP	Autoridad Reguladora de los Servicios Públicos
CA	Central America
CAESS	Compañía de Alumbrado Eléctrico de San Salvador
CEDLAS	Centro de Estudios Distributivos, Laborales y Sociales
CEL	Comisión Ejecutiva Hidroeléctrica del Río Lempa
CEQ	commitment to equity
CIS	Commonwealth of Independent States
CRI	Costa Rica
DEOCSA	Distribuidora de Electricidad de Occidente, Sociedad Anónima
ENCOVI	national survey of living conditions
ENEE	Empresa Nacional de Energía Eléctrica
ENEL	Empresa Nicaragüense de Electricidad
ENV	living standards survey
ESI	energy subsidy impulse
ESMAP	Energy Sector Management Assistance Program
FACE	Energy Compensation Fund (Fondo de Compensación Energética)
FET	Fondo de Estabilización Tarifaria
FTO	Fondo Tarifario de Occidente
GDP	gross domestic product
GST	goods and services tax
GTM	Guatemala
HFO	heavy fuel oil
HND	Honduras
IBT	increasing block tariff
ICE	Instituto Costarricense de Electricidad
IMF	International Monetary Fund
INDE	Instituto Nacional de Electrificación
INE	Instituto Nicaragüense de Energía
IRHE	Instituto de Recursos Hidráulicos y de Electrificación

kWh	kilowatt hour
LAC	Latin America and the Caribbean
MENA	Middle East and North Africa
MWh	megawatt hour
NIC	Nicaragua
OECD	Organisation for Economic Co-operation and Development
PAN	Panama
R&D	research and development
SEDLAC	Socioeconomic Database for Latin America and the Caribbean
SIGET	Superintendencia General de Electricidad y Telecomunicaciones
SLV	El Salvador
TPI	targeting performance indicator
VAT	value-added tax
VDT	volume-differentiated tariff
WEO	World Economic Outlook
WTO	World Trade Organization

CHAPTER 1

Overview

Marco Antonio Hernández Oré, Luis Álvaro Sánchez, and
Liliana D. Sousa

Most countries in Central America spend an important share of their public resources on subsidizing residential electricity consumption. Between 2011 and 2014, Central American countries spent a combined US$1.3 billion per year on electricity subsidies, or 1 percent of the region's aggregate gross domestic product (GDP). Subsidy spending in Central America declined to approximately US$1.1 billion in 2015, following a steep drop in international oil prices and the implementation of subsidy reforms in some countries, but the fiscal cost of energy subsidies remains high, particularly given the low revenue-to-GDP ratios in the region. In the context of tight fiscal constraints, electricity subsidies come at a high opportunity cost in terms of public investment and social services; even the most conservative estimates indicate that spending on electricity subsidies exceeds spending on flagship social programs and in some countries rivals spending on health and education.

Although these subsidies make electricity more affordable for some poor households, most benefits go to higher-income households. Electricity subsidies reduce total spending of households in the bottom 10 percent of the income distribution in Central America by 4 percent on average, but subsidy mechanisms benefit wealthier households more than their poorer counterparts. For every US$1 of public spending in Central America on electricity subsidies, less than 40 cents goes to the poorest 40 percent of the population. Because of weaknesses in their ability to target households according to income level, electricity subsidy regimes are an inefficient tool for reducing poverty and promoting distributional equity.

The policy challenge for Central American countries is to implement politically viable reforms that reduce fiscal costs while protecting the well-being of their most vulnerable residents. Since being introduced in the mid-1990s, electricity subsidy regimes have become firmly entrenched in all Central American countries. The wide coverage of these benefits—providing noticeable monetary benefits to a majority of households—makes it difficult to eliminate them because they enjoy popular support. Decades of piecemeal reform efforts have intensified the complexity of subsidy regimes without significantly reducing spending on electricity subsidies.

This is the first study to assess the fiscal and welfare implications of electricity subsides in Central America and to simulate policy options aimed at improving the efficiency of spending. The analysis begins by outlining the key design features of and institutional arrangements for residential electricity subsidies in the six countries of Central America: Costa Rica, El Salvador, Guatemala, Honduras, Nicaragua, and Panama. It then presents a detailed assessment of their fiscal costs; implications for household welfare, including poverty reduction; the factors explaining their distributional and equity effects; and simulations of potential policy reforms and their implications. The focus of the study is on residential subsidies because these account for the largest share of electricity (and energy) subsidies in Central America. The study also touches on a number of related concerns. However, given the complexity of the topic, it is unable to fully address topics such as the environmental consequences of subsidies and the risks that subsidies pose to the financial sustainability of electric utilities (box 1.1).

Box 1.1 Other Relevant Considerations

Although this study's focus on the fiscal cost, efficiency, and design characteristics of residential electricity subsidy regimes in Central America allows for a thorough analysis of these topics, it necessarily omits related concerns that have important implications in the regional context. Some of these topics include the political economy of electricity subsidies, their environmental impact, the regulatory challenges they entail, and their effect on competitiveness. These subjects are explored in detail elsewhere in the international literature (annex 1A).

Political economy can be a formidable obstacle to reform, especially when subsidies benefit a large or politically powerful constituency. The World Bank is evaluating the experience of several countries that have reformed electricity subsidies to better understand their strategies for managing the political economy of the reform process (e.g., Inchauste and Victor 2017). Although this topic was not studied in detail—and a thorough analysis of the political economy of each country would easily be a stand-alone study—this report includes empirical analysis of the distribution of costs and benefits under different reform scenarios.

This study only briefly considers the environmental effect of electricity subsidies, another key area for further analytical work. Subsidizing electricity can increase energy consumption and be a disincentive to increasing energy efficiency, with negative environmental consequences. This is especially true for countries that rely on fossil fuels for power generation. The environmental cost of carbon-based power is an urgent concern in the global community in its attempt to meet the United Nations Sustainable Development Goals. A brief discussion of some of the environmental concerns and related research is included in annex 1B.

Electricity subsidies have complex implications for the management and regulation of the electricity sector. Untargeted subsidies are regressive and distortionary, and how best to integrate subsidy design and regulation is an open question. The price distortions of subsidies can imply artificially high demand and, simultaneously, inadequate funding of the energy sector to provide the necessary infrastructure to meet this demand.

box continues next page

Box 1.1 Other Relevant Considerations *(continued)*

Electricity subsidies can influence the competitiveness of goods and services, especially when they affect prices in the commercial and industrial sectors. Although, in some cases, residential electricity subsidies may indirectly influence commercial and industrial electricity prices though cross-subsidies between sectors, in all six Central American countries, this effect is marginal. Costa Rica, for example, technically imposes a cross-subsidy between sectors, but its influence on commercial and industrial electricity prices is negligible. Although the present study does not explore competitiveness, this would play a central role in an analysis of commercial and industrial electricity subsidies.

Finally, the analysis included in this study does not account for behavioral responses to changes in electricity pricing. Estimates for pre- and postsubsidy spending and simulations of potential changes in policy in this study are based on the observed level of electricity consumption of each household under the price regime in effect at the time of the survey. Results from the literature find that consumers adjust their demand for electricity in response to price changes (e.g., Ito 2014), but without adequate price-elasticity estimates for electricity consumers in Central America, much of the analysis in this study is based on a benefit-incidence methodology that assumes no changes in demand.

The payoffs for reforming electricity subsidies are substantial. The analysis demonstrates that, in each Central American country, reforming electricity subsidy policies could generate substantial fiscal savings while maintaining or even enhancing their welfare effects. We estimate that, by reducing leakages to higher-income households, reforms could reduce fiscal costs by 30–50 percent without increasing poverty. Even so, any shift in the distribution of subsidy benefits—even if it makes the system more progressive and pro-poor—will have negative implications for some households, in particular those in the middle class. Policy makers must be sensitive to these concerns and properly acknowledge and address the costs of reform. That said, an overarching message of this study is that a combination of progressive tariffs and targeted fiscal transfers can reduce poverty and achieve distributional equity and macroeconomic stability objectives more efficiently than residential electricity subsidies.

This study contributes to the international literature on the economic and social effects of electricity subsidies and to policy research on the efficiency of public spending in Central America. For the first time in the region, it estimates household-level subsidy benefits for the six countries of Central America using comparable household survey data combined with pricing and financial information obtained from electric companies. Building on this new database and details of the region's subsidy mechanisms, the study estimates direct and indirect fiscal costs of electricity subsidies and the distribution of benefits across income groups. It presents a comparable measure of efficiency of targeting for each country and assesses the contributions of four drivers of efficiency: access to electricity, coverage by subsidies, the quantity of subsidized electricity that households consume, and the depth of benefits.

Fiscal and Welfare Impacts of Electricity Subsidies in Central America
http://dx.doi.org/10.1596/978-1-4648-1104-3

Finally, it simulates a common set of reform scenarios that highlight the trade-offs that policy makers face.

The recent drop in global oil prices presents an opportunity to reform electricity subsidy mechanisms with minimal impact on the current distribution of benefits. Low oil prices have helped bring tariffs closer to cost-recovery levels, so undertaking reforms now would result in less fiscal pressure when international oil prices rise. In this context, this study seeks to provide Central American policy makers with the analytical foundations necessary to comprehensively appraise the costs and benefits of their residential electricity subsidy mechanisms and to design effective reform strategies that reflect their unique circumstances and policy priorities.

Key Findings

Residential Electricity Subsidies Impose Substantial Fiscal Costs in Countries that Are Already Facing Tight Budget Constraints

Residential electricity subsidies represent important fiscal costs in Central America. With the exception of Costa Rica, all of the countries in the region finance their electricity subsidy regimes from public resources, at fiscal costs ranging from 0.31 percent of GDP in Guatemala to 1.57 percent of GDP in Nicaragua (figure 1.1).[1] Although most countries offer residential and nonresidential electricity subsidies, in all cases except Costa Rica, residential subsidies are by far the largest component of the total fiscal cost. Within the residential sector, Costa Rica uses above-cost tariffs for high-volume consumers to finance a cross-subsidy to low-volume consumers. It also uses a limited degree of cross-subsidization between the commercial and residential sectors. Such a system requires only a modest fiscal outlay, because the use of a cross-subsidy lowers the fiscal cost of Costa Rica's subsidy regime to near zero.

Overall, Central American countries spent an average of 1 percent of their combined GDP on electricity subsidies between 2012 and 2015, only modestly above the average of 0.8 percent for Latin America and the Caribbean (LAC). However, due to the region's relatively low level of public spending, electricity subsidies accounted for a larger share of public expenditures in Central America than in LAC. Electricity subsidies in Central America represented 4.2 percent of total public spending during the period, far above the LAC average of 3.0 percent. Because most Central American countries were running substantial deficits in the early 2010s, the cost of electricity subsidies relative to domestic revenues was even higher (figure 1.2), and electricity subsidies were responsible for just over one-third of the region's aggregate fiscal deficit.

Despite the recent decline in global oil prices, the fiscal cost of electricity subsidies is comparable to that of other major public expenditure items. Guatemala spends as much on electricity subsidies as it does on its two largest social assistance programs combined. In Nicaragua, the cost of electricity subsidies dwarfs spending on secondary education. In Honduras, more is spent on electricity subsidies than on postsecondary education (figure 1.3).

Figure 1.1 Fiscal Cost of Electricity Subsidies, by Country, as a Percentage of Gross Domestic Product, 2012–15 Average

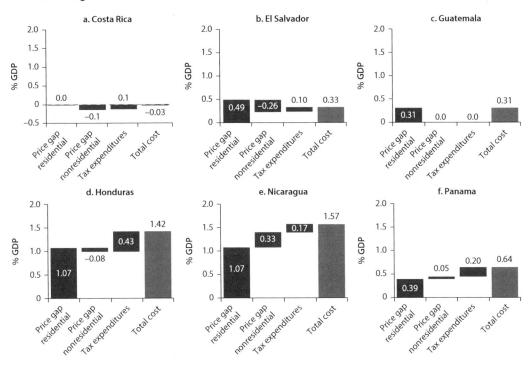

Source: World Bank elaboration based on data obtained from country authorities.
Note: The estimates for Honduras derived using the price-gap approach were augmented with the cost of direct subsidies to the residential sector in 2014–15. For details, see chapter 3.

Figure 1.2 Spending on Electricity Subsidies, by Country, as a Percentage of Gross Domestic Product and Tax Revenues, 2012–15 Average

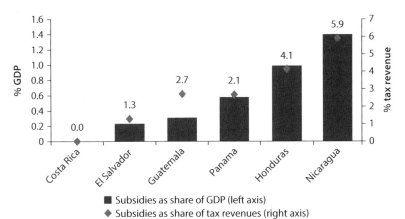

Source: World Bank elaboration based on data obtained from country authorities and data from the International Monetary Fund World Economic Outlook Database (October 2016).
Note: Electricity subsidy estimates were derived using the price-gap approach and reflect residential and nonresidential subsidies. (Tax exemptions were not included.)

Fiscal and Welfare Impacts of Electricity Subsidies in Central America
http://dx.doi.org/10.1596/978-1-4648-1104-3

Figure 1.3 Public Spending on Electricity Subsidies, Cash-Transfer Programs, Education, and Research and Development in Central America as a Percentage of Gross Domestic Product, 2011–13 Average

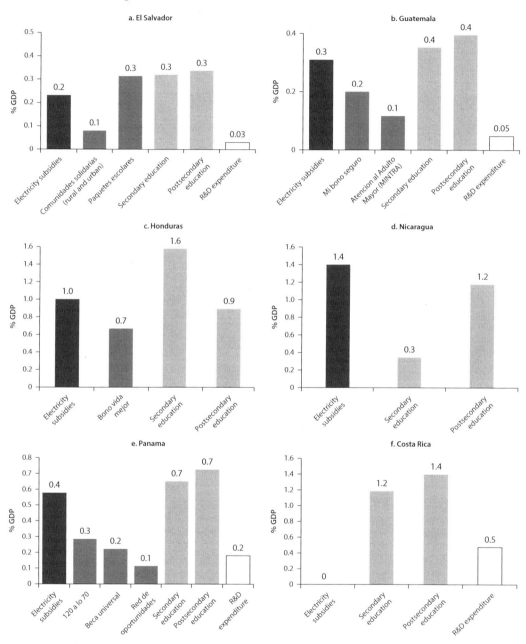

Source: World Bank elaboration based on the World Bank's Atlas of Social Protection Indicators of Resilience and Equity database.
Notes: Data on spending on R&D refers to 2011 and was derived from the World Bank World Development Indicators database. Electricity subsidy estimates are derived using the price-gap approach and reflect residential and nonresidential subsidies. Labels in this figure reported in Spanish are specific social programs in each country. R&D = research and develoment.

In addition to their explicit subsidy regimes, all countries in the region except Guatemala subsidize electricity consumption through preferential tax rates. Residential electricity consumption is fully tax exempt in Costa Rica and Nicaragua below certain thresholds, and reduced rates are applied to consumption above these thresholds. The majority of residential consumers in Honduras pay no taxes on electricity; and in El Salvador, fuels used for electricity generation are tax exempt.

Nontechnical losses are another significant source of indirect subsidies. Nontechnical losses arise from unmetered connections, billing fraud, and non-payment. From an economic perspective, electricity that is not paid for is effectively fully subsidized, but nontechnical losses are distinct from other types of subsidies in that they result from administrative failures rather than any deliberate policy. Nevertheless, nontechnical losses can impose substantial costs that paying consumers or the government must bear. Even if nontechnical losses are eventually covered, they can adversely affect the financial standing of electricity companies and may discourage private investment in the electricity sector. Nontechnical losses are particularly large in Honduras, Nicaragua, and El Salvador.

Residential Electricity Subsidies Make Electricity More Affordable for Poor Households, but Structural and Policy-Design Factors Affect Their Targeting Efficiency

Electricity subsidies in Central America make electricity more affordable for lower-income households. In the region as a whole, electricity subsidies reduce spending of households in the bottom decile of the income distribution by 4 percentage points of household income and by 0.5 percentage point in households in the top decile (figure 1.4).[2] This varies by country. For example, in the absence of subsidies, an average Honduran household in the bottom income quintile would spend an average of 8.3 percent of its income on electricity. With subsidies, this expense decreases to 4.3 percent, an increase in their household budget of 4 percent. Costa Rica's electricity subsidies generate a modest benefit, reducing electricity spending from 6.2 to 5.9 percent of household income in households in the lowest income quintile.

In every country in Central America, electricity subsidies are inefficiently targeted, resulting in most going to higher-income households. Comparing the share of subsidy benefits that accrue to the bottom 40 percent of the income distribution with the share that accrues to the top 40 percent reveals the regressivity of their distribution, the magnitude of which varies according to country (figure 1.5). This regressivity is particularly notable in Nicaragua and Panama, where for every US$1 spent on subsidies, the wealthiest 40 percent receive approximately 56–57 cents, and the poorest 40 percent receive only 24–25 cents. The distribution of subsidies in El Salvador and Costa Rica is also regressive, although the degree of regressivity is lower; for every US$1 spent, the wealthiest 40 percent receive 43–45 cents, and the poorest 40 percent receive 35–37 cents.

Figure 1.4 Electricity Spending as a Share of Household Income in Central America, by Income Decile, 2016

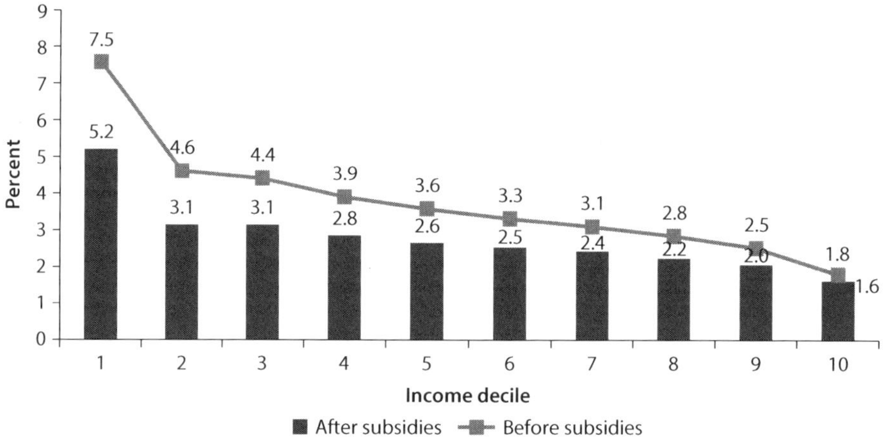

Source: World Bank elaboration using SEDLAC (CEDLAS and the World Bank).
Note: This calculation includes all households, including those without electricity.

Figure 1.5 Percentage of Subsidies Received by Households in the Top and Bottom 40 Percent of the Income Distribution

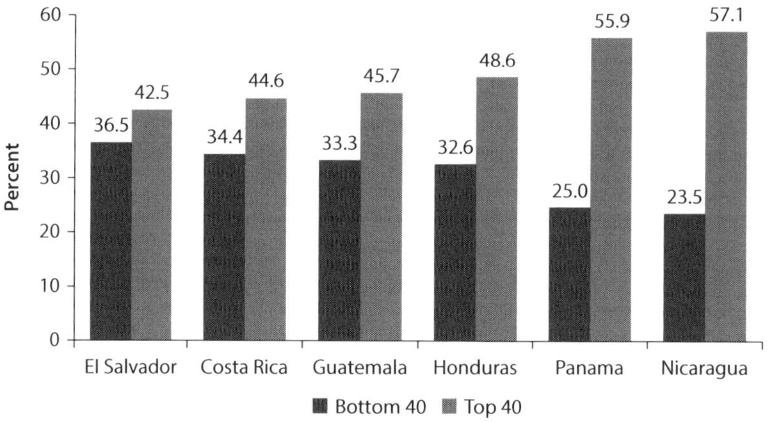

Source: World Bank elaboration using SEDLAC (CEDLAS and the World Bank).

What explains the differences in subsidy targeting efficiency between countries? The efficiency of a subsidy policy depends on two key questions: *Who receives subsidies?* and *How much do they receive?* These two questions frame the analysis needed to understand the determinants of electricity subsidy targeting. A number of factors, including electrification rates and the extent to which subsidy policies include or exclude households, determine who receives subsidies. On the other hand, how much households receive depends on consumption patterns and the generosity of the benefits.

Fiscal and Welfare Impacts of Electricity Subsidies in Central America
http://dx.doi.org/10.1596/978-1-4648-1104-3

In this study, we explore these two questions by analyzing four factors: access to the electricity grid, coverage of subsidy mechanisms, subsidy depth (subsidy amount per unit of electricity consumed), and the amount of subsidized electricity consumed.

The first factor is the share of households connected to the electricity grid. Only households connected to the electricity grid benefit from electricity subsidies. Of the poorest 40 percent, the share of unconnected households ranges from 32 percent in Nicaragua to less than 2 percent in Costa Rica. Because low-income households are more likely to be unconnected, the exclusion of these households automatically reduces the progressivity of subsidy benefits.

The second factor is the coverage of households across the income distribution. The eligibility criteria of the subsidy mechanisms determine coverage. In Central America, as elsewhere, electricity subsidies are typically allocated based on consumption thresholds that exclude higher-volume consumers. For example, in Costa Rica, households receive a subsidy for the first 200 kilowatt hours (kWh) per month that they consume. In Honduras, one of the subsidy mechanisms is limited to households that consume 75 kWh or less, whereas another mechanism provides discounted electricity to households consuming more than 800 kWh per month. As a result, Honduras's subsidy schemes reach almost all households connected to the grid. High coverage rates like the one in Honduras (figure 1.6) are a sign of inefficient targeting. El Salvador and Guatemala cover fewer wealthy households than Honduras does because the thresholds used in these countries are much lower: 99 kWh per month in El Salvador and 100 kWh per month in Guatemala.

Figure 1.6 Share of Households with Electricity That Received Subsidies, 2016

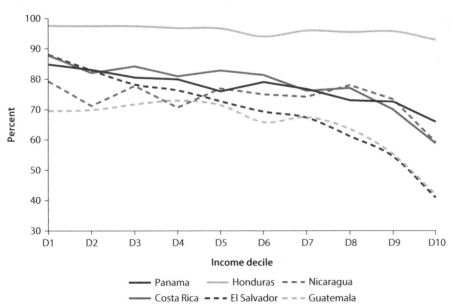

Source: World Bank elaboration using SEDLAC (CEDLAS and the World Bank). This figure is limited to households connected to the electricity grid.

Fiscal and Welfare Impacts of Electricity Subsidies in Central America
http://dx.doi.org/10.1596/978-1-4648-1104-3

These two factors determine which households receive subsidies, and hence the "errors of inclusion" and "errors of exclusion" of the residential subsidy policies. The key challenge inherent in electricity subsidy mechanisms in Central America is that they identify beneficiaries based on their level of electricity consumption; but consumption is not a perfect proxy for income. Using consumption as a proxy for income leads to errors of inclusion, in which high-income households receive subsidies, and errors of exclusion, in which low-income households do not receive subsidies. In many cases, consumption thresholds are set too high to exclude a significant proportion of higher-income households, resulting in errors of inclusion that drive the regressive allocation of subsidy benefits. On the other hand, the high poverty rate among households that lack electricity access exacerbates errors of exclusion. In Guatemala and Nicaragua, countries with high poverty rates and low electrification rates, more than one-fifth of the population of each country consists of individuals living on less than US$4 per day who are excluded from receiving subsidies (figure 1.7).[3] There is a clear trade-off between reducing errors of exclusion and inclusion; by increasing eligibility thresholds, more poor households are covered, but so are more wealthy ones.

The third factor is the generosity of the subsidy mechanism, known as the "depth" of the subsidy. More depth indicates a larger discount on electricity consumption. In most countries in the region, the different subsidy mechanisms provide distinct levels of discounts in an effort to provide deeper discounts for lower levels of electricity consumption. As a result of its direct subsidy, Honduras's depth of subsidies is relatively high for low-income consumers (figure 1.8). For those who receive electricity subsidies, the poorest decile receives, on average, a subsidy of more than US$0.11 per kWh, substantially higher than the US$0.03 that the wealthiest 10 percent receive. Costa Rica, on the other hand, provides the same average subsidy of US$0.02 per kWh consumed for the first 200 kWh per month for all households.

Figure 1.7 Estimated Errors of Inclusion and Exclusion Based on US$4 per Day Poverty Line

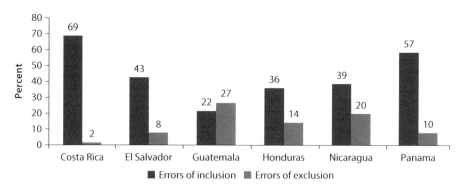

Source: World Bank elaboration using SEDLAC (CEDLAS and the World Bank). Errors of inclusion and exclusion are reported as a percentage of the total population. For example, Costa Rica's errors of exclusion (households living on less than US$4 per day that did not receive subsidies) account for 2 percent of the national population.

Fiscal and Welfare Impacts of Electricity Subsidies in Central America
http://dx.doi.org/10.1596/978-1-4648-1104-3

Figure 1.8 Average Subsidy per kWh of Subsidized Electricity, by Income Decile, 2016

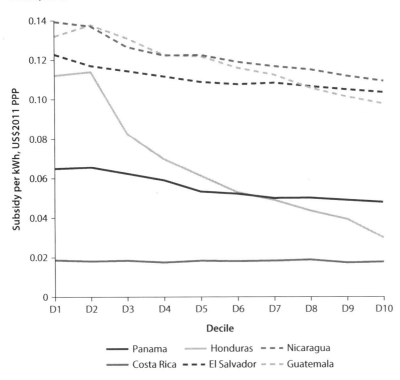

Source: World Bank elaboration using SEDLAC (CEDLAS and the World Bank). This figure is limited to households that receive subsidies.

Efficiency of targeting can be increased by increasing the relative depth of subsidies for households that consume less electricity.

The fourth factor is the amount of subsidized electricity that households across income groups consume. This study identifies this as the leading factor driving the inefficiency of targeting. Higher-income households receive a disproportionate share of subsidies because they consume more subsidized electricity. For subsidy beneficiaries in Nicaragua and Honduras, households in the wealthiest 10 percent consume more than double the amount of subsidized electricity as those in the poorest 10 percent (figure 1.9). This error can be reduced by using lower inclusion thresholds. In Guatemala, the country with the most compact consumption rate distribution, the difference in consumption between the first and tenth deciles is just over 12 kWh per month, a fraction of the 191 kWh difference in Honduras and the 113 kWh difference in Panama. Although in most countries, the subsidy that low-income households receive is deeper than what high-income households receive, greater electricity consumption in higher-income households skews the total distribution of subsidies in their favor.

Fiscal and Welfare Impacts of Electricity Subsidies in Central America
http://dx.doi.org/10.1596/978-1-4648-1104-3

Figure 1.9 Electricity Consumption of Subsidy Beneficiaries, by Income Decile, 2016

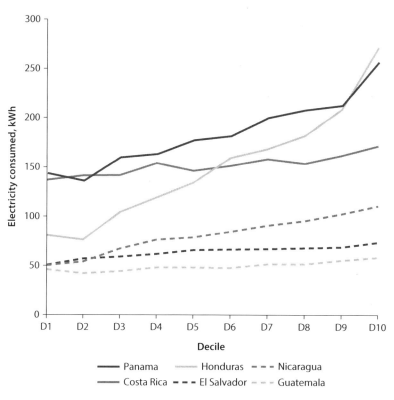

Source: World Bank elaboration using SEDLAC (CEDLAS and the World Bank). This figure is limited to households that receive subsidies.

To assess the extent to which each of these four factors contributes to the overall distribution of subsidies, this study used a diagnostic tool—referred to in this study as the targeting performance indicator (TPI)—to systematically compare subsidy mechanisms. The importance of these four factors varies from country to country, according to the subsidy mechanism, and over time. For the countries of Central America, this study measures each of these factors using independent ratios. For example, the fourth factor (amount of subsidized electricity consumed) is estimated as the average that a given target group (e.g., the poorest 40 percent) consumes divided by the average that the entire population consumes. Based on the literature on subsidies, the TPI is a simple way of combining these four factors into one measure.[4] A TPI score greater than 1 means that the target group receives a subsidy benefit that is greater than its share in the total population and hence indicates a more progressive distribution of benefits.

What does the TPI tell us? The TPI for electricity subsidy benefits in each of the four lowest-income deciles is less than 1 in every country in Central America. El Salvador's TPI for households in the bottom 40 percent is the highest in the region (0.91), yet this indicates that households in the bottom 40 percent of the income distribution still receive only 91 percent of what they would receive under a neutral distribution of benefits. Meanwhile, the bottom 10 percent of households in Nicaragua and Panama have the lowest TPI scores (0.40 and 0.30, respectively), indicating that they receive less than half what they would receive under an untargeted neutral distribution (table 1.1).

The TPI score can be decomposed into each of the four factors to better understand how these interact to determine the overall distribution of benefits (figure 1.10). In all Central American countries, two factors always increase the share of subsidies that reach households in the bottom 40 percent of the income distribution: the depth of the subsidy and the coverage rates. Deeper subsidies to households in the bottom 40 percent directly increase the share of subsidies they receive, and the contribution of coverage rates reflects the extent to which the consumption thresholds successfully reduce errors of inclusion. Conversely, low electrification rates completely exclude a share of poor households in each country. In all countries, the single biggest driver of inefficiency in targeting is the higher rates of electricity consumption in wealthier households.

Table 1.1 Targeting Performance Indicator Scores for Four Target Groups, 2016

Target group	Costa Rica	El Salvador	Guatemala	Honduras	Nicaragua	Panama
Poorest 10%	0.77	0.79	0.70	0.73	0.40	0.30
Poorest 20%	0.80	0.85	0.73	0.77	0.45	0.43
Poorest 30%	0.84	0.88	0.79	0.79	0.54	0.54
Poorest 40%	0.86	0.91	0.83	0.81	0.59	0.62

Source: World Bank elaboration using SEDLAC (CEDLAS and the World Bank) and data obtained from country authorities.

Figure 1.10 Factors That Determine Targeting Performance for the Poorest 40 Percent of Households

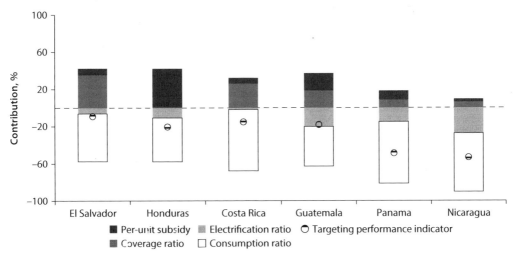

Source: World Bank elaboration using SEDLAC (CEDLAS and the World Bank) and data obtained from country authorities.

Fiscal and Welfare Impacts of Electricity Subsidies in Central America
http://dx.doi.org/10.1596/978-1-4648-1104-3

Simulating the Effects of Electricity Subsidy Reforms Can Offer Insight into the Advantages and Disadvantages of Alternative Strategies

In light of the identified weaknesses in the region's current electricity subsidy policies, the report simulates the impact of various reform scenarios. These simulations reveal that improving the design of subsidy regimes can deliver substantial fiscal gains while maintaining or even enhancing their positive impact on the welfare of lower-income households. Even so, considerable limitations remain when subsidies are allocated based on a household's level of electricity consumption.

Although many simulations are possible, this study included five scenarios, with their relative effectiveness assessed against a set of outcome indicators designed to reflect their core policy objectives.[5] The first and second scenarios completely eliminate the fiscal burden. The third and fourth scenarios return 50 percent of the fiscal savings to residential consumers through alternative targeting mechanisms, including current public cash-transfer programs. The last scenario focuses on protecting the welfare of the poorest 40 percent of the population and estimates the fiscal cost necessary to achieve this.

The outcome of each reform scenario is judged according to four criteria: fiscal savings, targeting efficiency, poverty impact, and impact on households. The fiscal savings criterion measures the fiscal savings that each set of reforms generates. The targeting efficiency criterion assesses the distributional equity of spending, as measured using the TPI for households in the poorest 40 percent of the income distribution, and identifies the amount of subsidy benefits "leaked" to upper-income households, defined in all countries as those in the top 20 percent of the income distribution. The welfare criterion assesses the impact of the reforms on poverty as measured according to changes in the poverty rate using the international poverty line of US$4 per person per day. Finally, the impact on households assesses the reforms' impact on the distribution of benefits to middle-class households and households vulnerable to falling into poverty. This final criterion provides an estimate of the costs of reform that nonpoor households would bear. Results are reported in table 1.2.

The simulations begin with Scenario 1, in which residential electricity subsidies are eliminated entirely and replaced with a cost-reflective tariff for all consumers. This results in savings ranging from 0.31 percent of GDP in Guatemala to 1.07 percent in Honduras and Nicaragua. It also results in an increase in poverty of more than 2 percent in El Salvador and Nicaragua and increases between 0.5 and 1.2 percent for the remaining countries. The resulting rise in electricity costs for lower-income households and the increase in poverty rates underscore the extent to which electricity subsidies advance poverty and equity objectives, despite their limitations. At the same time, the relatively small effect on the household budgets of the middle class, an average of 35 cents per US$100 of household income, shows that the high spending allocated to these households through subsidies is a minor source of income for them.

The second scenario frees subsidy regimes from their dependence on the national budget by establishing a fully self-financing cross-subsidy. Under this

Table 1.2 Fiscal, Efficiency, Welfare, and Political Economy Results of Potential Reforms

Country	Current situation			Scenario 1: Cost recovery (flat tariff)			
		TPI	Poverty (US$4 per day)	Fiscal savings (% GDP)	TPI	Change in poverty (%)	Impact on budget of middle class (%)
SLV		0.91	31.4	0.49	n.a.	2.1	−0.32
GTM		0.83	59.8	0.31	n.a.	0.5	−0.13
HND		0.81	58.1	1.07	n.a.	0.6	−0.28
PAN		0.62	16.9	0.39	n.a.	1.2	−0.38
NIC		0.62	35.9	1.07	n.a.	2.3	−0.64

Country	Scenario 2: Cost recovery (progressive tariff)				Scenario 3: Partial recovery (progressive tariff)			
	Fiscal savings (% GDP)	TPI	Change in poverty (%)	Impact on budget of middle class (%)	Fiscal savings (% GDP)	TPI	Change in poverty (%)	Impact on budget of middle class (%)
SLV	0.49	0.91	1.0	−0.77	0.25	0.91	0.3	−0.39
GTM	0.31	0.83	0.6	−0.43	0.16	0.83	0.3	−0.21
HND	1.07	1.33	0.5	−0.70	0.54	1.33	0.2	−0.35
PAN	0.39	0.73	0.6	−0.39	0.20	0.67	0.2	−0.19
NIC	1.07	0.70	1.4	−1.15	0.53	0.63	0.6	−0.62

Country	Scenario 4: Scenario 2 + targeted cash transfers with transfer amount based on welfare needs				Scenario 5: Scenario 2 + targeted cash transfers equivalent to 50% of fiscal savings			
	Fiscal savings (% GDP)	TPI	Change in poverty (%)	Impact on budget of middle class (%)	Fiscal savings (% GDP)	TPI	Change in poverty (%)	Impact on budget of middle class (%)
SLV	0.22	1.18	−4.2	−0.71	0.25	1.16	−3.7	−0.72
GTM	0.08	0.98	−0.8	−0.40	0.16	0.95	−0.7	−0.38
HND	0.42	1.34	−0.4	−0.67	0.54	1.35	−0.4	−0.67
PAN	0.23	1.09	−2.6	−0.32	0.20	1.13	−3.1	−0.30
NIC*	0.49	0.89	−4.1	−1.01	0.53	0.88	−3.5	−1.02

Source: World Bank elaboration using SEDLAC (CEDLAS and the World Bank) and data from country authorities.

Note: Baseline values for leakage and poverty refer to the leakage rates estimated using 2016 tariffs and poverty rate estimated for 2014 (2015 in the case of Panama). Nicaragua's results for Scenarios 4 and 5 are based on quantity targeting rather than cash transfers because there is no dominant cash-transfer program in place. Change in poverty and impact on the budget of the middle class are reported as percent changes relative to their baseline values. Fiscal savings are estimated based on the average fiscal cost of residential subsidies from 2012 to 2015. TPI = targeting performance indicator.

scenario, each country's subsidized tariff structure for households consuming less than 100 kWh per month remains unchanged, but tariffs on households consuming more than 100 kWh are increased to cover the full cost of the subsidy. The tariff increases are undertaken is such a manner that the current structure is preserved. Thus, in some countries, households consuming more than 100 kWh per month will still be paying below cost. The fiscal savings are the same as under Scenario 1. This approach softens the impact on households in the low and middle ranges of income.

As shown under Scenario 2, implementing a cross-subsidy improves the targeting efficiency of each country's subsidy regime and its targeting efficiency.

Fiscal and Welfare Impacts of Electricity Subsidies in Central America
http://dx.doi.org/10.1596/978-1-4648-1104-3

The reform eliminates subsidies for low-income households consuming more than 100 kWh per month, increasing errors of exclusion, but by improving targeting efficiency by reducing the proportion of benefits accruing to wealthier households, it decreases errors of inclusion more than it increases errors of exclusion. Poverty rates increase under this scenario, although by less than they would if subsidies were eliminated entirely. Meanwhile, the middle class experiences a substantial cost increase ranging from 1.15 percent of their income in Nicaragua to 0.39 percent in Panama.

Under the third scenario, fiscal spending on electricity subsidies is reduced by 50 percent and the other 50 percent is financed through a cross-subsidy. By construction, this reduces fiscal savings by half. It mitigates the negative impact on lower-income households that errors of exclusion cause, but still results in higher poverty than the current systems. This scenario also reduces leakages to households in the top 20 percent of the income distribution, although less effectively than the second scenario, and the impact on the middle class is more modest.

The fourth reform scenario offsets the impact of the cross-subsidy used in the second scenario through targeted cash transfers with the objective of protecting the welfare of lower-income households. This is accomplished by estimating the total subsidy benefit that households in the bottom 40 percent of the income distribution receive under the current mechanisms and delivering an equivalent benefit through one of two subscenario targeting mechanisms. First, the transfers are targeted to households in the bottom 40 percent of the electricity consumption distribution. Second, the transfers are targeted to households who are beneficiaries of public cash-transfer programs. Table 1.2 reports the results using the second mechanism, except in the case of Nicaragua which does not have a dominant cash-transfer program. A key finding from this scenario is that the welfare goal can be accomplished while still generating significant fiscal gains. In this scenario, the fiscal savings differ according to mechanism and country, ranging from as little as 0.08 percent of GDP in Guatemala to as much as 0.49 percent in Nicaragua.

The fifth scenario takes the tariff structure as in the second scenario but returns to the households 50 percent of the fiscal savings through targeted transfers. It uses the same mechanisms as the fourth scenario, yet the amount of fiscal spending on subsidies is set based on a specified fiscal goal rather than a specified welfare goal. A key finding of this scenario is that, because the transfers were executed through each country's existing cash-transfer system, the magnitude of their poverty and equity impacts depend on the targeting efficiency of each transfer system. Hence, this reform would lead to larger reductions in poverty in El Salvador and Panama but not necessarily in Honduras and Guatemala.

Policy Directions

Considerable scope for further improvements in the design and impact of residential electricity subsidy designs is possible in Central American countries. Over the last three years, the fiscal costs of electricity subsidies have fallen in most of the countries, aided by policy reforms and the drop in the price of oil. Several governments have been reducing eligibility thresholds or eliminating some of the schemes introduced when production costs were increasing. These gains notwithstanding, there is room for substantial further improvements in the design of the incentive schemes to make electricity more affordable for poor households, lessen fiscal pressure, and protect the middle class. The study identified relevant options for each country. At the same time, the region's history of patchwork reforms highlights the need for a thorough, sustainable pricing strategy that considers the social needs and costs of subsidies and the resources that the energy sector needs to meet demand.

Lowering subsidy thresholds can increase the targeting efficiency of electricity subsidies but only if it reduces the magnitude of errors of inclusion more than it increases that of errors of exclusion. High consumption thresholds ensure that subsidies reach a larger share of the poor, but they also increase leakages to higher-income households. At the same time, high subsidy thresholds increase the amount of subsidized electricity that higher-income households consume more than lower-income households, the key driver of inefficiency in the electricity subsidy mechanisms of Central America. This reflects the fundamental weakness of using electricity consumption as a basis for social policy.

The simulations highlight the limitations of current mechanisms for targeting the distribution of their benefits. Although they are far from the only policy alternatives available for enhancing the efficiency and pro-poor impact of electricity subsidies, the simulated policy actions highlight the important trade-offs involved in electricity subsidy reform. Replacing current electricity subsidy mechanisms with a cross-subsidy augmented by cash transfers could yield simultaneous improvements in the fiscal cost, targeting efficiency, and pro-poor impact of subsidy policies across Central America yet impose politically difficult costs on middle-and higher-income consumers. Establishing a system of partial or full cross-subsidization could greatly reduce the fiscal burden of electricity subsidies and increase the progressivity of their distribution, although accomplishing this would require a substantial increase in the tariff rates applied to wealthier households. Moreover, identifying the appropriate level and targeting criteria for cash transfers requires weighing the equity and poverty objectives of each national subsidy regime against its fiscal cost.

Augmenting electricity consumption with other eligibility criteria can enhance targeting efficiency. Although a well-designed tariff structure that provides deep subsidies to low-volume consumers could, in principle, yield a progressive distribution of benefits, in practice, the positive correlation between electricity consumption and household income drives the regressivity of subsidy regimes in Central America. The simulations reveal that complementing quantity targeting with additional criteria such as participation in a national cash-transfer program can significantly reduce errors of exclusion and inclusion. Improved targeting efficiency can be used to deliver a larger share of benefits to lower-income households and alleviate the fiscal cost of electricity subsidies.

Fiscal and Welfare Impacts of Electricity Subsidies in Central America
http://dx.doi.org/10.1596/978-1-4648-1104-3

In each country, improving the balance between fiscal savings, targeting efficiency, and poverty reduction will depend on the priorities of domestic policy makers.

Further reforms would be improved by internal ownership of subsidies within the government and a clear statement of objectives with regard to target populations and the expected impact of the residential electricity subsidies. Although electricity subsidies were in principle introduced to ease affordability for low-income residential consumers, de facto electricity subsidies ended up subsidizing the consumption of higher-income households, in some countries reaching into the highest income levels. Moreover, tight budget constraints were never introduced, except in Costa Rica, where residential subsidies have been balanced financially using cross-subsidies. The consequence was the endogenous determination of the public budget resources used for subsidies, which then escalated to levels similar to key social expenditures such as social assistance, and even education in some cases. Clearly stated objectives regarding beneficiary populations and expected outcomes combined with tight budget constraints can help with evaluation of trade-offs in designs, tracking impact, and introducing modifications as required. At the same time, because subsidies are a combination of energy and social policy, they often fall outside the ownership of existing ministries. Because of their fiscal cost and the central role of the ministries of finance, these ministries may be in the best position to undertake the leadership necessary for implementing reforms (box 1.2). From a broader

---

Box 1.2 Reforming Subsidies: Lessons Learned from International Experience

International experience has revealed several key lessons for successfully reforming energy subsidies:[a]

- Identify groups that will be negatively affected by reforms. These groups should be the focus of a proactive outreach strategy, and some form of compensatory policy measure may be necessary to secure their support. For example, in the Dominican Republic, the creation of a program benefiting drivers of gas-fueled taxicabs complemented a reduction in subsidies for liquefied petroleum gas.
- Publicize the benefits of reforms, and ensure that reform efforts are credible. An analysis of fuel-subsidy reform in El Salvador found that, although the reform benefited most of the population, it was generally unpopular. This case underscores the importance of adopting an effective communication strategy to keep the public apprised of the reform process and its implementation, particularly when the benefits of reform are individually modest and diffuse. The study also determined that the government's perceived policy credibility had a major impact on public support for the reform program (Calvo-Gonzalez, Cunha, and Trezzi 2015).
- Recognize and address political economy challenges. In some cases, subsidy reform efforts may pit the interests of a highly motivated minority against those of a largely

box continues next page

Box 1.2 Reforming Subsidies: Lessons Learned from International Experience (*continued*)

apathetic majority. In other cases, reforming subsidies may involve reducing a modest but concrete benefit that a large segment of the population enjoys to advance an important but abstract policy goal, such as fiscal sustainability. Efforts to raise public awareness of the benefits of the reform program can help to build a broad-based consensus and overcome the resistance of entrenched interests.

• Ensure that the reform agenda enjoys sufficient support within the government. Successful reform efforts require significant political capital. In cases in which political support is limited, reformers can leverage opportunities, such as the inauguration of a new administration or the onset of a crisis, to accelerate the reform process.

• Improve targeted social assistance. Replacing subsidies with more accurately targeted forms of social assistance can often advance the same policy objectives at a lower fiscal cost. Including subsidy reform in a comprehensive social assistance strategy can help the government build political and popular support.

a. A recent World Bank study examined energy reforms in the Dominican Republic, Ghana, Indonesia, and Jordan, identifying key political economy considerations. Lessons from that study can help guide energy reform policies in Central America (Inchauste and Victor 2017).

---

perspective, a clear statement of objectives can facilitate agendas that incorporate or consider electricity subsidies as part of support for the poor. Inasmuch as direct electricity subsidies remain, perhaps they can be used to induce consumers to adopt efficiencies in the use of electricity.

The effectiveness of the targeting mechanisms supporting the electricity subsidy schemes would benefit from updating current rosters of beneficiaries or using alternative rosters, such as those used for public cash-transfer programs. This study has shown that, although the relationship between income and electricity consumption is positive, the fit is weak and therefore does not facilitate targeting populations (e.g., the poor or the poorest 40 percent) without incurring errors of inclusion and exclusion, with adverse consequences for efficiency and fiscal costs. Attempts to reduce errors of exclusion using high thresholds create high errors of inclusion and introduce considerable efficiency distortions. Therefore, this study concurs with other studies that emphasize the importance of improving the efficiency of targeting by using alternative strategies, including geographical targeting and using poverty rosters where they exist and are of good quality.

Fiscal savings from improving the targeting of electricity subsidies could be reinvested in the electricity sector to improve the quality of service, increase electrification, and reduce volatility related to electricity generation costs by diversifying the energy matrix through investment in green energy. Effective policies to reduce price volatility over the medium and long terms should focus on addressing volatile energy generation costs. Common structural reforms to reduce vulnerability to shocks in international oil prices include energy portfolio diversification from oil-fired power generation, investment in energy efficiency, and increased regional integration with countries endowed with more diversified supplies. These reforms can also boost the quality of service in the region, which is often spotty, with frequent blackouts resulting in greater costs and inefficiencies for households and businesses. Investing in renewable electricity sources and diversifying the regions' energy matrix is an important step for most countries in Central America, which are net importers of fossil fuels for thermal generation.

Finally, countries could be better prepared to manage potentially sharp increases in electricity production costs. This study has shown that most countries adjusted their electricity subsidy schemes in response to sharp increases in the cost of generating electricity induced by shifts in the price of oil or because of droughts, but such policy responses have resulted in large beneficiary populations, high fiscal costs, and inefficiency. Future increases in electricity production costs are likely and, with them, renewed concerns about affordability. Policy responses to new cost increases can be different from those of the past, aided by sharper policy objectives and improved mechanism designs. This study provides tools for the evaluation of trade-offs when considering policy changes needed in response to higher production costs.

Organization of the Study

Chapter 2 describes the evolution of electricity sectors and subsidy mechanisms in each of the six countries of Central America. Expanding access to electricity and rising consumption levels led to major sectoral reforms during the 1990s, yet electricity spending continued to increase rapidly in absolute terms and as a share of household budgets. Meanwhile, a major structural shift occurred in the regional energy mix. While Costa Rica moved decisively toward renewable energy, the other five countries increased their reliance on oil-based thermal generation, which increased their exposure to oil price shocks. Repeated price spikes created strong political pressure to use subsidies as a way to shield households from price volatility and reduce costs for lower-income consumers. This gave rise to a range of electricity pricing mechanisms and support schemes, which had complex effects on equity, efficiency, and poverty reduction.

Chapter 3 examines the fiscal impacts of electricity subsidies. Although Central American governments collect less revenue than comparable countries, almost all of them spend a substantial share of their budgets on electricity subsidies. The preferential tax treatment afforded to the electricity sector and the contingent liabilities that public utilities generate compound the fiscal cost of electricity subsidies. In the context of fiscal constraints, electricity subsidies come at a high opportunity cost in terms of public investment and social services. Reforming electricity subsidy schemes—or eliminating them altogether—could enable Central American governments to accelerate poverty reduction, rebuild fiscal buffers, and reinforce medium-term macroeconomic sustainability.

Chapter 4 assesses the distribution of benefits of electricity subsidies in terms of their ability to reduce the electricity costs of low-income households.

Electricity subsidies in each of the six Central American countries reduce the burden of electricity costs on low-income households, making electricity more affordable. Nevertheless, for every US$1 in electricity subsidies that households in the lowest income quintile receive, significantly more than US$1 reaches households in the highest quintile. This "leakage" of benefits to wealthier households reduces the welfare impact, and thus the efficiency, of scarce fiscal resources. Despite significant variations in energy prices and the design of different subsidy regimes, the distribution of electricity subsidies is regressive in every country in the region, although certain components of individual subsidy regimes are progressive, and examining them can yield important lessons for reforms.

Chapter 5 identifies why the subsidy mechanisms in Central America result in inefficient targeting and a regressive distribution of public spending. The efficiency of a given subsidy mechanism depends on two key questions: Who receives subsidies? and How much do they receive? To answer these questions, this chapter focuses on four factors, which taken together characterize the targeting performance of each mechanism. A key finding of this chapter is that one factor is primarily responsible for the inefficient targeting of Central America's electricity subsidy schemes: higher-income households consume more subsidized electricity.

Chapter 6 illustrates the broad trade-offs between reform strategies by simulating fiscal savings, efficiency gains, and welfare impacts of five prospective scenarios in each of the six countries in the region. The chapter explores reform options designed to manage the cost of subsidy regimes without reducing the welfare of lower-income households. The results show that, in each country, restructuring electricity subsidy regimes could reduce the fiscal cost of residential electricity subsidies and improve their targeting efficiency without reducing the welfare of lower-income households.

Summary of Results, by Country

Costa Rica

Costa Rica emerges as an outlier from various perspectives. Within Central America, it has a relatively low poverty rate and a high level of per capita electricity consumption. The electricity generation matrix is almost entirely renewable (mainly hydropower), and the bulk of the electricity sector is in the hands of the state. Because thermally generated electricity plays a negligible role, weather shocks, in particular droughts, rather than the volatility of the international price of oil, affect the cost of electricity production.

The design of Costa Rica's incremental block tariff (IBT) residential electricity subsidy mechanism is simple and transparent, with a single threshold set at 200 kWh per month. Subsidies provided to consumers who use less electricity are fully financed through cross-subsidies from those who use more. As a result, the state does not need to use resources to subsidize residential electricity consumption.

Although Costa Rica's electricity subsidy mechanism does not generate fiscal costs, its targeting efficiency is relatively low, with 65 percent of the subsidies going to the top 60 percent of the income distribution. Access to electricity is high across all income groups, and the coverage of the subsidy mechanism results in low errors of exclusion. The main challenge related to Costa Rica's subsidy mechanism is high errors of inclusion, because even the higher deciles benefit from subsidies. Since higher-income households consume considerably more electricity than eligible households in the lower deciles, households that are net contributors to the system are largely financing the middle levels of consumption.

The depth of the subsidy is relatively small (US$0.02 per kWh), and the impact on household electricity expenditures is negligible even for lower-income households. Hence, in terms of affordability, the electricity subsidy mechanism in Costa Rica has the lowest impact in the region. Simulations show that eliminating the subsidy would have a minor impact on the poverty rate, measured at US$4 per day, which would increase by 1 percent if a flat cost-recovery tariff were to replace the current system. Eliminating the subsidy would decrease the income of vulnerable households, those with incomes above the poverty line but not in the middle class, by the equivalent of 12 cents per US$100 of income while increasing the income of an average middle-class household by 1 cent per US$100 of income.

The bottom line: Costa Rica's "light" subsidy system does not present a fiscal challenge, but neither does it address potential concerns about affordability of electricity for poor households. Affordability concerns could be better addressed through income means–tested programs, such as cash transfers that are targeted at low-income households and are independent of electricity consumption levels. Lowering the current threshold would reduce errors of inclusion and hence increase targeting efficiency. The full elimination of the existing cross-subsidy system would have a limited impact on social welfare and the country's fiscal situation.

El Salvador

El Salvador's per capita income and average household electricity consumption fall in the middle of the group. The country unbundled generation, transmission, and distribution; opened the sector to private sector participation, especially in distribution; and set up a regulatory agency. Reliance on thermally generated electricity has grown gradually during the past decade, which has exposed the country to fluctuations in oil prices. The fiscal cost of residential electricity subsidies from 2012 to 2015 is estimated at 0.49 percent of GDP. Because the nonresidential sector partially subsidizes residential consumption, the impact on the public budget is lower (0.26 percent of GDP).

El Salvador operates a volume-differentiated tariff (VDT) scheme with two ranges. The lower range (0–49 kWh) has one of the best targeting performances in the region; 66 percent of the beneficiaries in this range are in the bottom 40 percent of the income distribution. The efficiency of targeting is lower for the second range (50–99 kWh), with only 33 percent of beneficiaries being part of the bottom 40 percent of the income distribution. That is, as one moves from the lower to the higher range, errors of inclusion increase, and with them the consumption of subsidized electricity by wealthier households, which reduces the progressivity of the subsidy. Until recently, the country operated a third range (100–300 kWh) that was regressive and channeled resources primarily toward higher-income households.

The depth of the subsidy is high according to regional standards (approximately US$0.12 per kWh), and it helps to increase affordability by reducing expenditures on electricity for lower-income households. Thanks to electricity subsidies, the share of household expenditure on electricity among poor households is similar to that of high-income households. It is estimated that eliminating the VDT subsidy scheme altogether would result in an increase of 2.1 percent in poverty, but implementing a cross-subsidy and returning half of the fiscal gains as targeted cash transfers would not only offset this negative impact but also reduce the poverty rate by 4.1 percent. That is, using information from the country's conditional cash transfer presents an opportunity to reduce leakages and generate fiscal savings without hurting poor households. As a result of implementing a cross-subsidy, the higher electricity price would reduce the budget of middle-class households by approximately 72 cents per US$100 of income.

The bottom line: El Salvador already has one of the most efficient electricity subsidy schemes in the region. Even so, it could improve targeting performance and achieve fiscal gains without increasing poverty rates. In particular, using a means-tested transfer program (such as the existing conditional cash-transfer program, which is relatively well targeted to the poorest households) and building on the relatively efficient first range of its VDT subsidy mechanism are solid foundations for increasing the affordability of electricity for lower-income households without imposing large fiscal costs.

Guatemala

Guatemala's residential electricity consumption and per capita income fall in the middle range of the region. There are private sector participation and a market for electricity generation in the electricity sector. The fiscal cost estimated using the price-gap approach for 2012 to 2015 was 0.31 percent of GDP. Guatemala is the only country in Central America that does not subsidize electricity consumption through preferential tax rates, which helps keep its fiscal costs relatively low.

Guatemala has a VDT scheme of electricity subsidies with three consumption blocks. The lowest range (0–60 kWh) is the most efficient of the three. Even so, it subsidizes households in the poorest 40 percent for only 92 percent of what they would receive under a neutral distribution. The other two consumption blocks are less likely to include households from the poorest 40 percent; for example, only 35 percent of beneficiaries in the 89- to 100-kWh per month consumption block belong to the poorest 40 percent. Guatemala's low electrification rates and incomplete geographic coverage of subsidy mechanisms exclude many poor households and hence undermine the country's ability to efficiently provide subsidies for low-income households. As a result, Guatemala has the highest errors of exclusion in the region for individuals living on less than US$4 per day;

27 percent of the population lives on less than US$4 per day but does not receive subsidies.

Even with high errors of exclusion, average electricity subsidies are the equivalent of a 1.5 percent increase in household income in the poorest decile. Elimination of the subsidies outright would increase poverty by 0.5 percent. Implementing a fully balanced cross-subsidy and returning 50 percent of the fiscal gains from reform through existing targeted crash-transfer programs would reduce poverty below its present level by up to 0.7 percent. More modest reforms, with the aim of protecting existing subsidies to the poorest 40 percent, would require higher spending that could reduce fiscal savings by 0.08 percent of GDP.

The bottom line: Guatemala's VDT with a low inclusion threshold results in fiscal costs and errors of inclusion below those of other countries in Central America. The two lower-consumption blocks of the VDT are less likely to cover low-income households and would benefit from improved targeting using a means-tested program to increase efficiency. Currently, subsidies are not available for all regions of the country, suggesting that, if subsidies are maintained, expanding access nationwide while reducing the threshold of coverage could improve its targeting performance and reduce errors of exclusion. Further improvements to current cash-transfer programs could help improve the efficiency of electricity subsidy reforms.

Honduras

Honduras's per capita income is among the lowest in the region, although its intensity of electricity consumption is higher than those of its peers. The country initiated institutional reforms, but a solid institutional framework has taken time to emerge. A large state-owned enterprise continues to play a dominant role in the sector. The fiscal cost estimated using the price-gap approach for 2012–15 was 1.07 percent of GDP. Subsidies to residential consumers account for the bulk of direct subsidies. Total subsidies are considerably higher that direct subsidies to consumers (1.65 percent) because of preferential tax treatments related to the production and consumption of electricity.

Honduras simultaneously applies an IBT mechanism and a direct cash transfer, both based on the volume of consumption.[6] These mechanisms provide subsidies to approximately 99 percent of households that are connected to the electricity grid. This is a result of the IBT's high implicit threshold, which results in discounts to households consuming up to 840 kWh. On the other hand, the direct cash transfer is one of the most efficiently targeted mechanisms in Central America, delivering an estimated 60 percent of its benefits to the poorest 40 percent. A key driver of this performance is its low 75 kWh threshold, which is further assisted by geographical targeting.

Both the direct cash transfer and the IBT are designed to provide deeper discounts for smaller consumers. The cash transfer provides a fixed direct payment to households under the threshold, which results in a full subsidy for lower levels of electricity consumption. As a result, the subsidy per unit consumed that accrues to the poorest 40 percent is higher than for the top 60 percent. Because poor households have lower electrification rates and many low-income households are covered through the transfer program's superior targeting, only 35 percent of IBT beneficiaries are in the poorest 40 percent. Even so, spending through the IBT scheme dominates the fiscal and efficiency measures of Honduras's electricity subsidies. The direct cash transfer is a small program by comparison; and therefore, despite its design advantages, it makes a limited contribution to the overall distribution of electricity subsidies.[7]

In part because of the depth of subsidies under the direct transfer, the impact of subsidies on household electricity expenditures of the lowest income deciles is considerable. Subsidies imply an increase in household budgets on the order of 4 percent. Although the subsidies cover almost all households, their removal would have minor effects on poverty. According to the simulations undertaken in this study, the elimination of both subsidy mechanisms would increase the poverty rate by 0.6 percent, but implementing a cross-subsidy and allocating 50 percent of fiscal costs to targeted cash transfers through the country's current transfer programs could reduce the poverty rate by 0.4 percent from its current level.

The bottom line: Honduras has made major gains in targeting efficiency with the reforms it has undertaken in recent years, but the potential for further gains in efficiency remains considerable. Its direct cash subsidy for households consuming less than 75 kWh per month can be the anchor that focuses electricity subsidies on poor households. Reform attention should focus on the much more expensive IBT with a view to strengthening its cross-subsidization by adjusting the thresholds and depths of discounts. Because of Honduras's high poverty rate, the IBT that would emerge after carefully simulating the changes should be combined with targeted transfers to soften the impact of reducing subsidies. Although recent reforms have improved the targeting of the country's social protection programs, fiscal savings from reforming electricity subsidies could be used to further strengthen these programs and expand support among poor households.

Nicaragua

Nicaragua is at the low end of the average consumption per household in the region. Like most of its neighbors, it has undertaken institutional reforms and depends largely on thermally generated electricity. The fiscal cost estimated using the price-gap approach for 2012–15 was 1.1 percent of GDP. Spending on residential subsidies plus direct subsidies to the nonresidential sectors and preferential tax treatment led to an overall fiscal cost of 1.6 percent of GDP.

Nicaragua has a VDT and an IBT subsidy mechanism. Both of these are inefficiently targeted, partially because of the country's low electrification rates among the poor. However, a bigger reason for Nicaragua's poor targeting efficiency are the thresholds (150 kWh per month), which are high relative to consumption levels of low-income households, leading to significant coverage of subsidies for higher-income households. In addition, Nicaragua's VDT is one of only two that provides deeper discounts for higher consumption levels.

Because higher-income households consume more electricity, these deeper discounts go disproportionally to wealthier consumers. In 2016, this mechanism delivered 79 percent of benefits to the top 60 percent of the income distribution.

Electricity subsidies increase the affordability of electricity for poor households. They translate into the equivalent of a 2.4 percent income boost for the poorest 20 percent. Elimination of all the electricity subsidies would increase poverty by 2.3 percent, one of the largest impacts on poverty in the region. Establishing a balanced cross-subsidy and distributing 50 percent of the current fiscal cost of the subsidy mechanisms to those consuming less than 100 KWh per month could help reduce poverty by 3.5 percent while reducing spending by 0.54 percent of GDP. This reform would lead to an increase in electricity costs of approximately US$1.02 per US$100 of income for the middle class. Nicaragua does not have a dominant cash-transfer program, so options to find alternative transferring mechanisms are more limited than in other countries.

The bottom line: There is ample room to improve efficiency, reduce fiscal costs, and help poor households. The lack of a dominant, means-tested social assistance program is an important constraint that must be factored into the reform design. The VDT and IBT both need attention. The performance of the VDT can be strengthened by lowering the threshold and introducing a fixed transfer to beneficiaries. Reforming the VDT's deeper discounts for higher consumption blocks is another important reform to consider. Although reducing the inclusion threshold of the VDT and the IBT can be used to target very poor households, the IBT as is can help soften the transition for households in the middle of the income distribution.

Panama

Panama is a high-middle-income country with high per capita consumption of electricity. Institutional reforms unbundling generation, transmission, and distribution have resulted in Panama having the highest level of private sector involvement in the region. Its dependence on thermal generation is also high for the region. The fiscal cost estimated using the price-gap approach for 2012–15 was 0.39 percent of GDP, and the total, including direct subsidies to the nonresidential sectors and preferential tax treatment, was 0.64 of GDP.

Panama has four residential electricity subsidy schemes. The subsidy provided to older adults is notably inefficient, delivering only 21 percent of benefits to the poorest 40 percent. As a result, the higher levels of consumption of the top 60 percent of the income distribution dominate in the allocation of this subsidy. The Fondo de Estabilización Tarifaria (FET), which accounts for 42 percent of all electricity subsidy expenditures, has a 500 kWh inclusion threshold and delivers only approximately 26 percent of subsidies to the poorest 40 percent. The Fondo Tarifario de Occidente (FTO) is also inefficiently targeted and provides higher subsidies to higher consumption blocks (e.g., providing a discount of approximately 31 percent to households consuming more than 750 kWh per month). The high consumption level of the wealthier households dominates the allocation of these three schemes. Panama's most efficient electricity subsidy is its VDT mechanism, which has an inclusion threshold of 100 kWh. At this relatively low threshold, close to 60 percent of subsidies still leak to the wealthiest 60 percent. Although electrification rates are high in Panama, the poorest deciles' lack of access to electricity undermines the progressivity of the country's electricity subsidies.

Subsidies increase the affordability of electricity, resulting in the equivalent of an increase of 2.2 percent in the household budget of those living on less than US$4 per day who benefit from subsidies. Because of Panama's low poverty rate, simulation results show that eliminating all subsidies would have a limited impact on poverty, increasing it by 0.2 percent. Implementing a cross-subsidy and distributing 50 percent of the current fiscal cost of the subsidy mechanisms through the country's existing cash-transfer programs could help reduce poverty by 3.1 percent. Using the cash-transfer programs, greater fiscal savings would be possible without affecting transfers to the poorest 40 percent.

The bottom line: Panama has the opportunity to make fiscal, efficiency, and inclusion gains through electricity subsidy reforms. The country's cash-transfer programs are strong enough to improve efficiency and protect poor households if subsidies are reformed. The VDT mechanism, which is focused on less than 100 kWh, is relatively well targeted and provides a basis on which to build. Cash transfers can be used to reduce errors of exclusion, including by extending the subsidy to cash-transfer beneficiaries that are not connected to the electricity grid. The FET and FTO result in leakages to higher-income households. Reducing the inclusion thresholds for both, and in particular addressing the regressive deeper discounts of the FTO subsidy for higher-consumption blocks, would yield large fiscal savings and improve targeting performance. The subsidy to older adults could be absorbed into the existing cash-transfer programs that target retirees.

Annex 1A: Relevant Literature on Electricity Subsidies and Their Impacts

Fiscal, Growth, Energy Prices
Araar and Verme (2016); Bacon et al. (2010); Clements et al. (2013); Coady et al. (2015); Devarajan et al. (2014); Di Bella et al. (2015); Ebeke and Lonkeng Ngouana (2015); ESMAP (2013); Fattouh and El-Katiri (2012); IEA, OPEC, OECD, and World Bank (2010); OECD (2013); Olivier, Ruggeri, and Trimble (2013); Trimble, Yoshida, and Saqib (2011); Vagliasind (2013)

Fiscal impacts	
Fiscal cost	Energy subsidies may impose significant fiscal costs through direct transfers to consumers or electricity companies to avoid high electricity tariffs or through forgone revenues due to the existence of some preferred tax rates or tax exemptions.
Effect on fiscal deficit	Energy subsidies could constitute a significant proportion of the public budget, in some cases comparable to the education and health budget.

table continues next page

Fiscal transparency	Energy subsidies are often not transparently accounted for because they are not fully recorded in government accounts. This means that some public resources are allocated without a full discussion of spending priorities.
Contingent liabilities	Energy subsidies are sometimes channeled through the government's commitment to cover the financial losses of electric utilities. Even when there is not an explicit guarantee, underfunding of public services creates an implicit contingent liability, in the sense that the government will most likely need to adjust the cost of providing essential public services.
Quasi-fiscal operations	Energy subsidies provided through quasi-fiscal operations (state-owned companies) tend to be less-transparent operations. Some governments reduce the profits of state enterprises along the value chain to avoid any increase in domestic tariffs, with consequences that may not be apparent for some years.

Growth and competitiveness

Discourage capital accumulation	Low subsidized energy prices may result in lower profits or outright losses for producers, making it difficult for state-owned enterprises to expand energy production and unattractive for the private sector to invest.
Discourage efficiency	Subsidies may create losses and a vicious cycle of poor service and high technical and nontechnical losses. A less-competitive, less-reliable electricity sector is a constraint on economic growth and poverty reduction.
Have a crowding-out effect on other public spending	Some countries spend more on energy subsidies than on services, such as public health or education, that have a greater effect on long-term development. Reallocating some of the resources through subsidy reform to more productive public spending could help boost growth over the long term.
Diminish competitiveness	Energy subsidies could stimulate monopolistic behavior in the energy production and distribution industry because of cost structure characteristics. As an industry with decreasing marginal costs, subsidies could increase the profits of the more competitive producer rather than boosting competition.
Create incentives for smuggling	If local prices are substantially lower than those in neighboring areas, there are strong incentives to smuggle products to higher-priced destinations. This increases illegal trade and decreases tax revenue because those goods or services are not taxed.

Energy value chain and prices

Transparency	The lack of transparency leaves room for speculation in the energy market and throughout the value chain, affecting the prices of goods and services and households' welfare. Transparent pricing mechanisms would encourage greater competition and efficiency, which would result in more affordable prices and rates.
Regulatory and institutional framework	Regulatory agencies in the energy sector value chain must be strong enough to ensure efficient outcomes that benefit the market and consumers. In countries where state monopolies participate in the whole value chain or part of it, self-regulation tends to be softer, discretionary benefits are imposed, and competitiveness and efficiency are discouraged.
Dependence on government transfers	An efficient energy sector requires significant investment throughout the value chain. Although generation is under the control of states, transmission and distribution tend to be in private hands; so, to maintain low tariffs, the absorption of state-owned generation companies' losses may not be enough to ensure the required investment in the whole industry. If tariffs do not fully cover costs, the cash flow that distribution companies generate may be insufficient to fully pay for generation and transmission.
Demand management	Maintaining subsidized prices at a time of rising international prices leaves the state with no ability to maneuver in the sector because consumption remains the same but at higher prices. Price variability relates to the type of generation and/or distribution of electricity, and does not entirely depend on electricity demand.

table continues next page

Household welfare and income distribution	
Arora et al. (2011); Balza, Espinasa, and Serebrisky (2015); Beylis and Cunha (forthcoming); Clements et al. (2013); Di Bella et al. (2015); Hassan et al. (2015); Torero, Alcazar, and Nakasone (2007)	

Household welfare

Inequality in the welfare of rural households	Energy subsidies can create a vicious circle when they are financed by squeezing the margins of public companies. This practice can affect energy companies' ability to sustain adequate investment, which makes them less profitable. This reduces investments in increased electricity coverage in rural communities, which limits the provision of other basic services, such as health and education.
Effect on rural households	Access to electricity in rural households reduces air pollution; improves health by allowing refrigeration, reducing food poisoning; improves access to cleaner water; reduces domestic fire-related accidents; increases access to major medical services; and increases education and improves culture by providing access to programs to communities through mass campaigns through the media.
Access to electricity for poor households	Using resources for nontargeted energy subsidies reduces funds for investment in other areas, such as electricity access for rural communities. The participation of women in the local economy decreases when electrification rates are lower.
Lack of access to information	Lower electrification in rural areas due to nontargeted subsidies decreases access to information through media such as television and radio.
Quality, continuity, and reliability of electric service	Quality and continuity of electrical service are critical to sustainable economic development. Without reliable service, households seeking access to electricity may use batteries or small generators, which are more expensive.

Income distribution

Inequity in allocation of subsidies	Nontargeted subsidies do not benefit poor and extremely poor households, especially those in rural areas, because most are not connected to the electrical system. Therefore, most subsidies benefit middle- and high-income households.
Employment opportunities for rural households	Energy subsidies may also worsen income distribution indirectly. By encouraging more energy-intensive economic activities, they reduce employment opportunities, especially in rural communities whose main productive activities are labor intensive.

Gender equality

Köhlin et al. (2011); Rebosio Calderon and Georgieva (2015)

Labor market for rural women	Rural electrification increases the percentage of female employment outside the home, especially for younger women, by increasing the amount of time that women have available.
Female empowerment	Rural electrification increases women's access to information about their rights and how to participate in the labor market.
Access to health and education for women	Electricity in the community can have positive effects on women. Access to light enables them to study and provides greater security in rural areas for those traveling to educational institutions and health facilities.

Energy overconsumption and environmental damage	
Badiani, Jessoe, and Plant (2012); Clements et al. (2013); Coady et al. (2015); Devarajan et al. (2014); Di Bella et al. (2015); Ebeke and Lonkeng Ngouana (2015); Guevara-Sangines (2006); IEA, OPEC, OECD, and World Bank (2010); Olivier, Ruggeri, and Trimble (2013); Stuggins, Sharabaroff, and Semikolenova (2013)	

Energy overconsumption

Discourage investment in renewable energy	Energy subsidies for nonrenewable technologies could cause excessive consumption of petroleum products, coal, and natural gas, reducing incentives for investment in energy efficiency and renewable energy.

table continues next page

Devaluation of the real cost of energy	Distorting the real cost of energy encourages inefficient energy consumption and promotes ignorance of the effect that it has on development and welfare. Energy subsidies make it difficult to build a culture of efficiency and energy saving.
Environmental damage	
Climate change and local pollution	Electricity subsidies increase the consumption of coal, natural gas, and other fuels because of excessive demand for electricity, contributing to carbon emissions, global warming, and local pollution.
Excessive exploitation of natural resources	Exploitation of oil, coal, and natural gas (natural resources), especially in rural communities, causes deterioration of the ecosystem and reduces availability of natural resource reserves. Below-cost electricity also reduces costs for groundwater extraction.

Annex 1B: Electricity Subsidies and the Environment

Although assessing the environmental effect of subsidies is outside the scope of this study, electricity subsidies have important environmental externalities that must be carefully weighed against potential reductions in poverty and gains in productivity. Artificially reducing electricity tariffs below the cost of production inevitably encourages inefficient consumption.

The most obvious environmental implication of subsidies is the pollution associated with increased electricity consumption. Although Central American countries generate an unusually large share of renewable energy, in all cases, thermal generation from hydrocarbon fuels (oil and natural gas) is the fastest-growing share of the energy mix. Increasing thermal generation has negative environmental implications, both local and global. To the extent that they increase the demand for energy and that this energy is generated using pollution-emitting fuels, subsidies increase carbon emissions, worsening pollution, smog, and global warming.[8] At the local level, oil and gas power plants generate substantial amounts of air pollution, and fuel spills are an ever-present risk. Central American urban centers have unhealthy levels of air pollution.[9] A recent International Monetary Fund study suggested that the elimination of energy subsidies, including electricity subsidies, could reduce premature deaths from local air pollution by 25 percent in Latin America by reducing local pollution from burning fossil fuels (Coady et al. 2015).

At the global level, thermal generation contributes to the unsustainable production of carbon emissions, accelerating a process of climate change to which Central American countries are especially vulnerable. At the same time, by artificially decreasing the price of electricity, subsidies can discourage investments in renewable energy and energy efficiency, encouraging the perpetuation of an environmentally costly energy matrix. In countries like Costa Rica, where investments have been targeted to renewable energy, the energy matrix is significantly less polluting than in the other countries, which rely heavily on fossil fuels.

Other environmental consequences of electricity subsidies are less obvious, such as their effect on water consumption. Electricity subsidies have been found to increase electric-powered irrigation, leading to groundwater depletion.[10]

Although the effect of subsidies on groundwater extraction has not been measured in Central America, the practice is common in the region. Cheaper electricity can also induce increase household water use by lowering the price of water.

Subsidies can also have positive environmental consequences by reducing the use of traditional fuels and inefficient technologies, in particular firewood and kerosene. The burning of firewood in inefficient wood stoves is associated with high levels of "black carbon," or soot, in the atmosphere, which can contribute to changes in rainfall patterns, including an increased intensity of droughts and floods.[11] The use of firewood and kerosene is also associated with indoor air pollution (which has important health consequences). Household electrification in northern El Salvador resulted in a 67 percent decrease in indoor air pollution and was associated with a 33–66 percent reduction in acute respiratory infections (Barron and Torero 2016). Even so, under certain conditions, including sustainable forest management, wood can generate lower greenhouse gas emissions than coal-powered electricity, especially if combined with efficient cooking stoves.[12]

Notes

1. These estimates are based on the cost of subsidies to residential and nonresidential consumers derived using the price-gap approach combined with the cost of tax expenditures from special electricity tax regimes.

2. As further discussed in chapter 4, this indicates a progressive distribution in relative terms, because subsidy benefits are a larger share of household income in lower-income households.

3. Throughout this study, we use the internationally comparable poverty line of US$4 per day adjusted for purchasing power parity. The resulting poverty rates differ from official poverty statistics.

4. A similar approach has been taken in the literature (e.g., Komives et al. 2007). The TPI used in this study is used to assess the quality of spending on electricity subsidies, but it can also be used to measure the quality of other types of spending.

5. Because of the significant difference between its subsidy mechanism and that of the other five countries, different simulation scenarios were used for Costa Rica.

6. The results in this study reflect the subsidy scheme in place as of April 2016. Reforms were undertaken in Honduras later in 2016, but not enough information was available to estimate their distributional effects.

7. The direct cash transfer program is also more difficult to implement as it requires payments through the country's social protection programs. As a result it was not fully implemented in 2016. The results in this study are based on full implementation.

8. For example, in India, where coal accounts for 55 percent of electricity generation, electricity generation accounts for 48 percent of greenhouse gas emissions (Badiani, Jessoe, and Plant 2012).

9. The capital cities of El Salvador, Honduras, and Guatemala have high levels of air pollution (with annual mean levels ranging from 56 µg/m^3 in Guatemala City to 77 µg/m^3 in San Salvador, well above the World Health Organization's guideline value

of 20 µg/m³). Levels in the capital cities of Panama (31 µg/m³) and Costa Rica (27 µg/m³) are also above the guidelines. Nicaragua is not included in this database. World Health Organization, Ambient Air Pollution Database, May 2016.

10. For example, in India (Badiani, Jessoe, and Plant 2012) and Mexico (Guevara-Sangines 2006). India has an estimated electricity price elasticity of –0.18; in response to lower electricity prices, farmers increase the planting of water-intensive crops (Badiani and Jessoe 2016).

11. For example, the combustion of solid biofuels (e.g., wood in cooking stoves) is the largest source of black carbon emissions in India: 42 percent, compared with 25 percent associated with emissions from fossil fuels and 33 percent associated with open burning (Venkataraman et al. 2005).

12. For example, a study in Norway found that firewood can have 3 percent to 49 percent lower greenhouse gas emissions than electricity, depending on wood type, transportation emissions, and stove efficiency (Raymer 2006).

Bibliography

Araar, A., and P. Verme. 2016. "A Comparative Analysis of Subsidy Reforms in the Middle East and North Africa Region." Policy Research Working Paper, World Bank, Washington, DC.

Arora, A., R. Chawla, A. Ghate, S. Indukuri, G. Jain, N. Mahal, S. Malhotra, and D. Sharma. 2011. "Improving Energy Access to the Urban Poor in Developing Countries." Energy Sector Management Assistance Program (ESMAP), World Bank, Washington, DC.

Bacon, R., E. Ley, M. Kojima, and L. Garrido. 2010. *Subsidies in the Energy Sector: An Overview.* Washington, DC: World Bank.

Badiani, R., and K. Jessoe. 2016. "Electricity Prices, Groundwater and Agriculture: The Environmental and Agricultural Impacts of Electricity Subsidies in India." Working Paper, University of California, Davis. http://kkjessoe.ucdavis.edu/Research Papers/BJ_ElectricityH2O.pdf.

Badiani, R., K. Jessoe, and S. Plant. 2012. "Development and the Environment: The Implications of Agricultural Electricity Subsidies in India." *Journal of Environment and Development* 21 (2): 244–62.

Balza, L., R. Espinasa, and T. Serebrisky. 2015. *Lights On: Energy Needs in Latin America and the Caribbean to 2040.* Washington, DC: Inter-American Development Bank.

Barron, M., and M. Torero. 2016. "Household Electrification and Indoor Air Pollution." MPRA Working paper, University of California, Berkeley.

Beylis, G., and B. Cunha. Forthcoming. *Energy Pricing Policies in Latin America and Carribean.* Washington, DC: World Bank.

Calvo-Gonzalez, O., B. Cunha, and R. Trezzi. 2015. "When Winners Feel Like Losers: Evidence from an Energy Subsidy Reform." Policy Research Working Paper 7265, World Bank, Washington, DC.

Clements, B., D. Coady, S. Fabrizio, S. Gupta, T. Alleyne, and C. Sdralevich. 2013. *Energy Subsidy Reform: Lessons and Implications.* Washington, DC: International Monetary Fund.

Coady, D., I. Parry, L. Sears, and B. Shang. 2015. "How Large Are Global Energy Subsidies?" IMF Working Paper 15/105, International Monetary Fund, Washington, DC.

Devarajan, S., L. Mottaghi, F. Iqbal, G. Mundaca, M. Laursen, M. Vagliasindi, S. Commander, and I. Chaal-Dabi. 2014. *MENA Economic Monitor: Corrosive Subsidies*. Washington, DC: World Bank.

Di Bella, G., L. Norton, J. Ntamatungiro, S. Ogawa, I. Samake, and M. Santoro. 2015. *Energy Subsidies in Latin America and the Caribbean: Stocktaking and Policy Challenges*. Washington, DC: International Monetary Fund. https://www.imf.org/external/pubs /ft/wp/2015/wp1530.pdf.

Ebeke, C., and C. Lonkeng Ngouana. 2015. "Energy Subsidies and Public Social International Monetary Fund Spending: Theory and Evidence." International Monetary Fund, Washington, DC.

ESMAP (Energy Sector Management Assistance Program). 2013. *Results-Based Financing in the Energy Sector: An Analytical Guide*. Washington, DC: World Bank.

Fattouh, B., and L. El-Katiri. 2012. "Energy Subsidies in the Arab World." Research Paper Series. United Nations Development Programme, New York.

Guevara-Sangines, A. 2006. "Water Subsidies and Aquifer Depletion in Mexico's Arid Regions." Human Development Occasional Papers (No. HDOCPA-2006-23). United Nations Development Program, New York.

Hassan, F., E. Penglis, G. Seferiadis, and M. Araya. 2015. *Transparency and Social Accountability in the Egyptian Power Sector*. MENA Energy Series. Washington, DC: World Bank.

IEA, OPEC, OECD, and World Bank. 2010/2011. *Analysis of the Scope of Subsidies and Suggestions for the G-20 Initiative Energy*. (Joint Report).

Inchauste, G., and D. Victor. 2017. *The Political Economy of Energy Subsidy Reform*. Washington, DC: World Bank.

Ito, K. 2014. "Do Consumers Respond to Marginal or Average Price? Evidence from Nonlinear Electricity Pricing." *American Economic Review* 104 (2): 537–63.

Köhlin, G. E. Sills, S. Pattanayak, and C. Wilfong. 2011. "Energy, Gender and Development: What Are the Linkages? Where Is the Evidence?" Policy Research Working Paper, World Bank, Washington, DC.

Komives, K., J. Halpern, V. Foster, Q. Wodon, and R. Abdullah. 2007. "Utility Subsidies as Social Transfers: An Empirical Evaluation of Targeting Performance." *Development Policy Review*, 25 (6): 659–79.

OECD (Organisation for Economic Co-operation and Development). 2013. *Analyzing Energy Subsidies in the Countries of Eastern Europe, Caucasus and Central Asia*. Paris: OECD.

Olivier, A., C. Ruggeri Laderchi, and C. Trimble. 2013. *Balancing Act: Cutting Energy Subsidies While Protecting Affordability*. Europe and Central Asia Reports. Washington, DC: World Bank.

Raymer, A. 2006. "A Comparison of Avoided Greenhouse Gas Emissions When Using Different Kinds of Wood Energy." *Biomass and Bioenergy* 30 (7): 605–17.

Rebosio Calderon, M., and S. Georgieva. 2015. *Toward Gender-Informed Energy Subsidy Reforms: Findings from Qualitative Studies in Europe and Central Asia*. Washington, DC: World Bank.

Stuggins, G., A. Sharabaroff, and Y. Semikolenova. 2013. *Energy Efficiency Lessons Learned from Success Stories*. Europe and Central Asia Reports. Washington, DC: World Bank.

Torero, M., L. Alcazar, and E. Nakasone. 2007. "Provision of Public Services and Welfare of the Poor: Learning from an Incomplete Electricity Privatization Process in Rural Peru." IDB Working Paper 221, International Development Bank, Washington, DC.

Trimble, C., N. Yoshida, and M. Saqib. 2011. "Rethinking Electricity Tariffs and Subsidies in Pakistan." World Bank, Washington DC.

Vagliasind, M. 2013. *Implementing Energy Subsidy Reforms: Evidence from Developing Countries.* Directions in Development Series. Washington, DC: World Bank.

Venkataraman, C., G. Habib, A. Eiguren-Fernandez, A. H. Miguel, and S. K. Friendlander. 2005. "Residential Biodules in South Asia: Carbonaceous Aerosol Emissions and Climate Impacts." *Science* 307 (5714): 1454–56.

World Health Organization. 2016. *Ambient Air Pollution Database, May.* http://www.who.int/phe/health_topics/outdoorair/databases/en/.

CHAPTER 2

The Electricity Sector in Central America and Its Subsidy Mechanisms

Marco Antonio Hernández Oré, Luis Álvaro Sánchez, Liliana D. Sousa, and Leopoldo Tornarolli

This chapter describes the power sectors and subsidy mechanisms in each of the six Central American countries. Expanding electricity access and rising consumption levels led to major sectoral reforms during the 1990s and a major structural shift in the regional energy mix. While Costa Rica moved decisively toward renewable energy, the region's other five countries increased their reliance on oil-based thermal generation, which intensified their exposure to oil price shocks. Throughout this period, electricity spending continued to increase rapidly in absolute terms and as a share of household budgets. Repeated price spikes created strong political pressure to use subsidies to shield households from price volatility and reduce costs for lower-income consumers. This gave rise to a range of electricity pricing mechanisms and support schemes, with complex implications for equity, efficiency, and poverty reduction.

Behind the Rise of Subsidies: Rising Electricity Consumption and Costs

Electricity access has expanded significantly in Central America since the 1970s; by 2015, 91 percent of Central Americans had electricity, compared with 34 percent in 1970 (figure 2.1). Although this process was not uniform across the region, overall improvements in electricity access were considerable. Costa Rica led the region, reaching near-universal access in 2015. Although its GDP per capita is significantly lower than Costa Rica's, El Salvador has also achieved widespread electrification, in part because of the country's relatively high degree of urbanization. Panama largely kept pace with El Salvador, despite its more dispersed population. Guatemala recorded the most dramatic improvement of any country over the period, and by 2015, its electrification rate was approaching those of Panama and El Salvador, despite having a larger share of its population living in rural areas. Although Honduras and Nicaragua continued to have the lowest electrification rates in the region at just over 80 percent, both registered major gains during the period.

Figure 2.1 Electrification Rates, 1970–2015

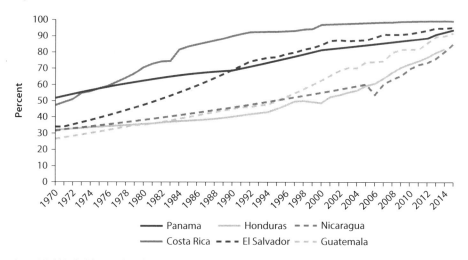

Source: World Bank elaboration based on Economics and Energy Information System—Latin American Organization of Energy (accessed November 2016).

Figure 2.2 Annual Electricity Consumption per Capita, 1970–2014

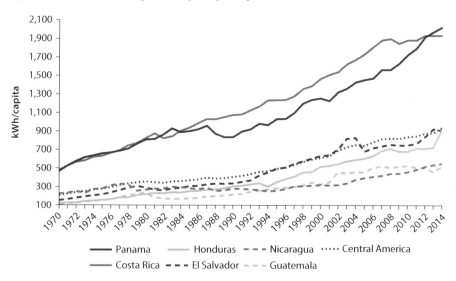

Source: World Bank elaboration based on Economics and Energy Information System—Latin American Organization of Energy (accessed November 2016).

As electrification rates rose, electricity consumption increased rapidly. Between 1970 and 1990, annual per capita electricity consumption in Central America almost doubled, rising from 207 kWh to 406 kWh (figure 2.2). It then more than doubled between 1990 and 2014, reaching 941 kWh in 2014. Consumption grew fastest in Honduras, El Salvador, and Guatemala, but Panama and Costa Rica experienced the largest increases in total consumption.

In the last 45 years, Honduras has experienced sustained growth in consumption, resulting in a total increase in per capita consumption of more than 600 percent. El Salvador and Guatemala, which had the lowest per capita consumption in 1970 (110 kWh), grew by 490 percent and 372 percent, respectively. Electricity consumption in Costa Rica increased by 302 percent, driven by expanding electricity access. Nicaragua had the lowest growth in the region (145 percent). Country-level variations notwithstanding, the dramatic overall increase in electricity consumption during this period posed new challenges to the electricity sector.

In the 1990s, several countries in Central America introduced ambitious institutional reforms designed to increase private participation in the production and distribution of electricity and enhance efficiency by introducing elements of private competition into the sector.[1] Competition was expected to result in incentives to increase the electricity supply and promote capacity expansion, leading to lower prices. Research in this area suggests that private ownership by itself does not generate substantive efficiency gains. For a heavily regulated natural monopoly such as the power sector (at least in transmission and distribution), other factors—such as effective regulation, quality of regulatory bodies, control mechanisms, and adequate planning—are needed. Combined with these, the increase in competition from privatization can reduce costs, lowering prices and increasing productive efficiency in the electricity sector (Michalet and Bouin 1991). Privatization and competition in the electricity sector, with effective regulation, also lead to growth in electricity output (Zhang, Kirkpatrick, and Parker 2008).

In most countries in Central America, generation, different combinations of transmission, and distribution elements of the electricity value chain were unbundled and partially privatized under the authority of a dedicated regulator.[2] The transformation of the electricity sector in El Salvador, Guatemala, Nicaragua, and Panama was especially profound, because these four countries shifted from vertically integrated, state-owned electricity companies to an unbundled structure with some private sector participation, mainly in generation and with different depth in transmission and distribution.[3] A number of structural challenges to privatization swiftly emerged: the small size of each national electricity market limited the scope for competition, investment financing proved difficult to acquire, and the quality of private management and public regulation varied from country to country.

As a consequence of significant growth in thermal generation during the early 2000s, nonrenewable energy sources account for a significant share of electricity generation in most Central American countries (figure 2.3), as a consequence of significant growth in thermal generation during the early 2000s (figure 2.4). A combination of factors resulted in the "carbonization" of the energy mix. In general, the small size and fragmentation of power grids in Central America prevented the installation of efficient units and technologies requiring scale to become feasible. Deficient planning led to the installation of emergency plants—mostly obsolete, inefficient, and polluting thermal units that were available in the market and could be made operational easily,

Figure 2.3 Share of Renewable and Nonrenewable Sources in Total Power Generation, 2011–15 Average

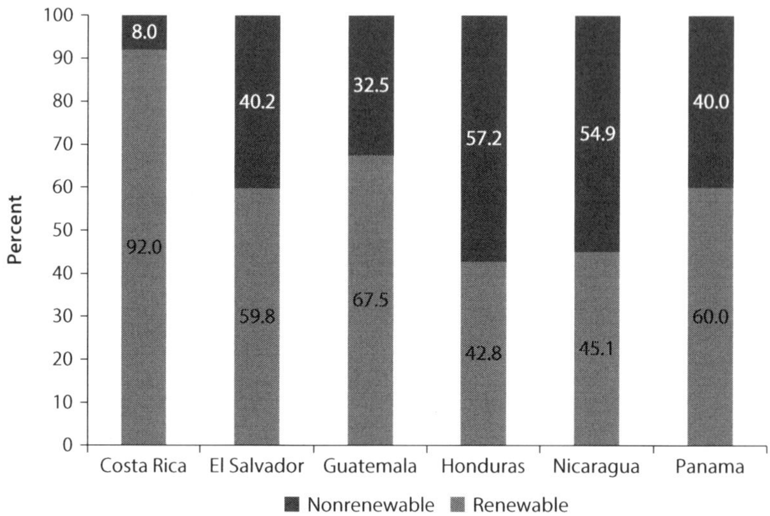

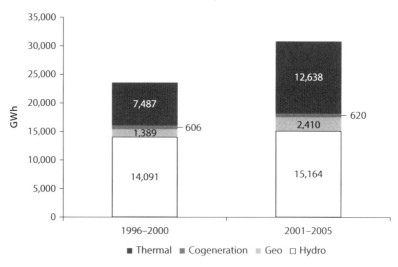

Source: Economic Commission for Latin America and the Caribbean 2001 through 2016.

Figure 2.4 Electricity Generation, Average, 1996–2000 and 2001–05

Source: Economic Commission for Latin America and the Caribbean 2001 through 2016.

especially compared with large hydroelectric power plants. High perceived country risks led private investors to opt for less capital-intensive technologies such as oil-fired plants.[4] Additionally, fuel-based generation provided an alternative to hydroelectric power, which droughts in the region had affected. Finally, there was a lack of obvious alternatives to oil-fired generation in the region, given growing social opposition and awareness of the environmental harms of hydroelectric and, in some cases, geothermal projects; the inherent risk associated with geothermal technology; and the unavailability of natural gas and limited availability of coal in the region.

The shift toward new thermal generation, based on diesel and gas, increased oil imports through the region—except in Costa Rica, which continued to focus on hydroelectric, wind, and geothermal energy. Increased demand for oil imports was due not just to new thermal electricity generation but also to a shift in the overall energy matrix toward oil, driven in part by the transportation sector. Oil imports rose by an average of 7 percent between 2001 and 2013 in every country except Costa Rica, where they fell by 10 percent (figure 2.5).[5] By 2013, oil imports accounted for approximately 75 percent of Panama's primary energy supply. In El Salvador, Honduras, and Nicaragua, imports accounted for between 40 percent and 60 percent of the energy supply, and although Guatemala met less than 30 percent of its energy requirements through imports, this was partly due to its heavy reliance on wood fuel. Despite renewed investment in hydroelectricity, wind, solar, and geothermal power in the late 2010s, most Central American countries remain heavily dependent on oil imports.

Figure 2.5 Energy Imports as a Share of Total Energy Consumption, 1991–2000 and 2001–13

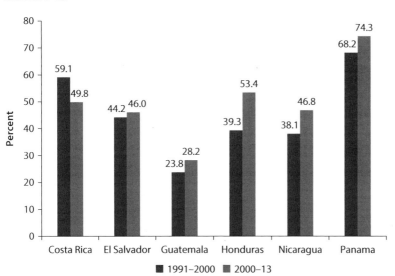

Source: World Bank tabulations using the World Development Indicators (World Bank).
Note: Energy is measured as kilotons of oil equivalent. Energy imports include oil and other inputs for electricity.

Fiscal and Welfare Impacts of Electricity Subsidies in Central America
http://dx.doi.org/10.1596/978-1-4648-1104-3

Figure 2.6 Crude Oil Prices (West Texas Intermediate), 1982–2015

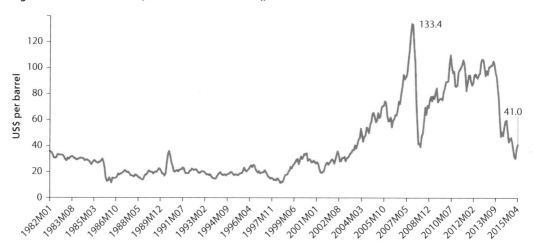

Source: World Bank tabulations using the Global Economic Monitor (World Bank).

Increased reliance on oil imports intensified Central America's exposure to oil price shocks. During the 2000s, oil prices rose sharply and became increasingly volatile. Oil prices rose from US$21 per barrel in 2002 to a peak of US$133 per barrel in July 2008 and then fell to approximately US$40 per barrel in 2008 before rebounding to US$110 per barrel in April 2011 and then falling again to US$30 per barrel in 2016 (figure 2.6).[6] Oil prices are expected to recover over the near term, although they are not projected to reach the same heights observed over the past decade.

Although several countries have attempted to mitigate oil price shocks through long-term contracts with generating companies and, in some cases, through the regional PetroCaribe agreement, these efforts have not been able to shield households fully from the pass-through effect of oil-price fluctuations. As electricity consumption grew and prices rose, household electricity spending not only increased as a share of household consumption but also became significantly more volatile (figure 2.7). This confluence of trends intensified political pressure to reduce and stabilize consumer prices. Across the region, rising electricity access rates expanded the constituency that stood to benefit from residential electricity subsidies, and high and unstable prices created strong incentives for policy action. Relative to total private consumption in each country, electricity spending rose substantially in Costa Rica, El Salvador, Guatemala, and Nicaragua during the 2000s, whereas the share fell in Honduras and Panama because of the large subsidy programs both countries implemented to counter the phenomenon. By 2015, every country in the region had established at least one subsidy mechanism designed to reduce or stabilize residential electricity prices. These have resulted in lower residential electricity prices in Honduras and Panama than in the other countries of Central America, and in prices similar to those of energy exporters such as Ecuador and Chile (figure 2.8).

Figure 2.7 Index of Ratio of Residential Electricity Consumption and Total Private Consumption from National Accounts, 2000–15

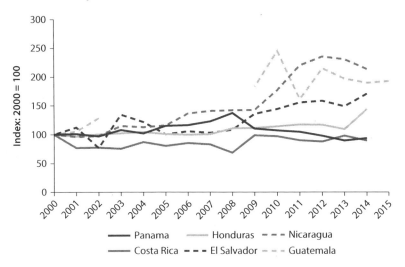

Source: World Bank tabulations based on Economics and Energy Information System—Latin American Organization of Energy (accessed November 2016).

Figure 2.8 Average Price per Unit of Residential Electricity Consumption, Select Countries, 2013

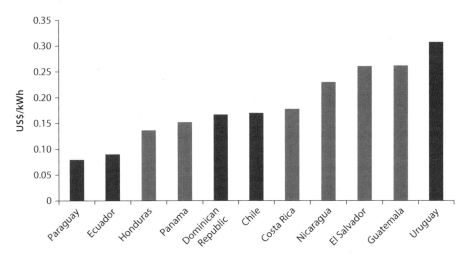

Source: World Bank tabulations based on Economics and Energy Information System—Latin American Organization of Energy (accessed November 2016).

Subsidy Mechanisms in Central America

Governments across Central America established a variety of subsidy regimes in response to oil and energy price volatility. Residential price stability, rather than long-term poverty reduction or socioeconomic equity, was the explicit rationale for the subsidy regimes that Honduras implemented in 1994; El Salvador and Guatemala in 1999, Panama in 2004, and Nicaragua in 2005. As a result, the distribution of benefits is regressive under almost all existing subsidy schemes, although the few exceptions yield important lessons for policy makers. Most regimes combined explicit interventions in the electricity market with indirect or implicit price supports (box 2.1).

All six Central American countries have established at least one targeted electricity subsidy, and, although mechanisms differ, commonalities between them allow for a systematic examination of their fiscal and distributional impact. Targeted subsidy mechanisms apply explicit criteria to define which users are eligible to receive certain subsidies. Although targeted subsidies tend to have higher administrative costs, targeting has important advantages from a policy perspective. By distributing subsidy benefits to specific consumer groups, such as poor households or those located in remote regions, targeted subsidies can advance the government's economic objectives and development priorities.

Box 2.1 Untargeted and Indirect Subsidies

Although the focus of this chapter and, to a significant degree, this study is on explicit, targeted residential subsidy regimes in Central America, these are not the only policy instruments that governments can use to reduce electricity prices below the cost of production. Untargeted subsidies apply to all consumers regardless of consumption level or household characteristics. These can take the form of preferential tax treatment, fiscal transfers to electricity sector firms, or between-sector cross-subsidy schemes, in which the commercial or industrial sector pays above-cost tariffs to finance below-cost rates for residential consumers. Because this type of intervention is generally not recorded in the country's budget, the size and impact of untargeted subsidies are difficult to track and measure.

Pricing mechanisms that underestimate production costs can create implicit untargeted subsidies. When prices are administratively determined, the financial sustainability of electricity utilities depends on the accuracy of pricing mechanisms. By setting prices below the cost of production and then recapitalizing insolvent electricity providers, policy makers can create an informal, ad hoc subsidy mechanism. If pricing mechanisms affect regional electricity providers in different ways, these indirect subsidies can be targeted to specific geographic areas, although they usually remain untargeted at the firm or household level. For example, Panama created two compensation funds, Fondo de Estabilización Tarifaria and Fondo de Compensación Energética, to transfer the forgone revenues arising from the fact that electricity tariffs were not adjusted for changes in generation costs to distributor companies.

box continues next page

Box 2.1 Untargeted and Indirect Subsidies (*continued*)

Some governments indirectly subsidize electricity through preferential tax treatment. For electricity producers, preferential tax treatment may entail lower tax rates or exemptions of capital goods, fuel, and other inputs. Consumers may receive indirect subsidies in the form of lower value-added tax or sales tax rates or exemptions of electricity purchases. In all cases, subsidies based on preferential tax treatment do not involve an explicit transfer of fiscal resources to producers or consumers and are not accounted for in the national budget. Instead, this type of subsidy is financed through forgone tax revenue, which can complicate efforts to analyze its extent and effects. All countries in Central America, with the exception of Guatemala, apply tax relief or tax exemptions at different stages of electricity production. For example, fuels used in electricity generation are exempt from import taxes in Honduras, Panama, and El Salvador. Similarly, the sale of electricity is subject to exemptions and discounts in Costa Rica, Honduras, Panama, and Nicaragua.

Governments can also indirectly subsidize electricity by covering the nontechnical losses of electricity providers. The government may recapitalize electric companies that fail to collect accurate payments or disconnect unmetered connections, effectively subsidizing consumers, who pay less than they owe or nothing at all. The extent of electricity fraud and theft is difficult to measure accurately, because nontechnical losses are often hard to distinguish from technical losses incurred through inadequate maintenance, outdated infrastructure, or inefficient asset management. Moreover, the beneficiaries of fraud and theft are not easily identifiable, individually or as a group. Consequently, gauging the fiscal impact of nontechnical losses is inherently problematic. For example, in Honduras, the state electricity utility, whose debts the state guarantees, absorbs nontechnical losses.

Targeted electricity subsidies are usually allocated according to a process of administrative selection or a self-targeting mechanism. Under administrative selection, a government agency selects specific targeting criteria, such as household income level, demographic composition, or location. Under self-targeting, household behavior determines eligibility.[7] Household electricity consumption is the most common self-targeting criterion for electricity subsidies.

Using consumption patterns as the basis for self-targeting is known as "quantity targeting." Quantity-targeting regimes in Central America take the form of increasing block tariffs (IBTs) and volume-differentiated tariffs (VDTs). Quantity targeting is simpler to implement administratively than means-test targeting such as that typically used in cash-transfer programs, and because poorer households tend to use less electricity than wealthier ones, quantity-targeting mechanisms typically apply lower tariff rates to households with lower levels of electricity consumption. Nevertheless, as shown in chapter 5, correlation between income and electricity consumption is imperfect, resulting in some poor households being excluded from the subsidy regime, whereas some wealthy households are beneficiaries.

Under an IBT system, higher marginal tariffs are applied to higher levels of electricity consumption. All households pay the same low rate for the first "block" of electricity consumption. Higher consumption levels are then charged at

Figure 2.9 Illustration of a Hypothetical Tariff Rate and Electricity Bills under Increasing Block Tariff (IBT) and Volume-Differentiated Tariff (VDT) Systems

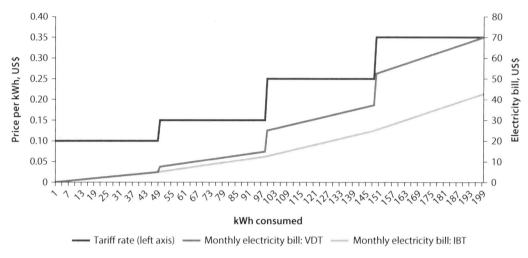

Source: World Bank elaboration.

higher marginal prices. Households whose consumption exceeds the first block pay more for electricity in the second consumption block and so on, for as many consumption blocks as the IBT system defines. For example, in figure 2.9, all households would pay US$0.10 per kWh for the first 50 kWh consumed per month and then US$0.15 per additional kWh consumed until reaching 100 kWh. The difference between the tariff rate for each block and the unit production cost of electricity is known as the depth of the subsidy.

Under a VDT system, each household's overall level of electricity consumption determines the price per kWh. Only households consuming below a certain threshold receive a subsidized price, whereas households whose consumption exceeds that threshold typically pay a cost-reflective tariff. Unlike an IBT system, in which tariff rates are based on *marginal* consumption, VDT tariff rates are based on *total* consumption. As a result, exceeding the VDT threshold leads to a much larger cost increase than moving from one IBT block to another. As can be seen in figure 2.9, under an identical tariff structure, the VDT system prices higher consumption more steeply. In theory this can create an incentive for consumers to "bunch" just below the VDT threshold, although recent research does not find this result, possibly because of imperfect information (Ito 2014). Some VDT systems apply multiple thresholds to smooth the transition between consumption levels.

In principle, IBT and VDT systems can both yield cross-subsidization, resulting in a subsidy system that is partially or wholly independent from central government financing. In Central America, three countries have IBT mechanisms with cross-subsidies and one, Panama, has a cross-subsidy as part of its VDT. Costa Rica's and Nicaragua's IBT systems are almost entirely financially self-sufficient. The above-cost tariffs applied to electricity consumption in the highest blocks nearly cover the cost of subsidized electricity consumption in the lower blocks, and modest transfers from the commercial and industrial sectors finance the difference. By contrast, the IBT system in Honduras and the VDT mechanism in Panama involve very little cross-subsidization and depend heavily on public funding.

VDT and IBT schemes differ in terms of design and impact. Because IBT systems result in a smoother distribution of total cost for electricity consumers, the VDT mechanisms yield a more progressive distribution of subsidies under similar thresholds and tariffs, particularly in cases in which electricity consumption patterns closely reflect household income levels, although a well-designed set of IBT consumption blocks and tariffs can concentrate net subsidies on low-volume consumers as effectively as a VDT scheme, with the added advantage of a smoother transition from subsidized to nonsubsidized consumption blocks.

Country Summaries of Existing Subsidy Mechanisms

All Central American countries use residential electricity subsidy mechanisms based on an IBT system, a VDT system, or a combination of the two. Many Central American subsidy regimes have undergone multiple rounds of reform, as well as ad hoc administrative interventions. Consequently, their current policy and institutional frameworks can be complex, contradictory, or opaque. A summary of the design features and key characteristics of the electricity subsidy schemes currently used in Central America is presented in table 2.1. The direct subsidy mechanisms, the focus of this study, are detailed for each country in the following subsections.

Costa Rica

Revenue from Costa Rica's above-cost tariff for high-volume consumption creates a cross-subsidy that finances low-volume consumption. Costa Rica applies an IBT tariff structure with different rates for residential, commercial, industrial,

Table 2.1 Overview of Direct and Indirect Residential Subsidy Mechanisms, by Country, April 2016

Country	Direct subsidy	Implicit subsidy
Costa Rica (IBT)	First 200 kWh/month subsidized for residential consumers; above-cost tariff for additional kWh	Reduced sales tax rate; sales tax exemption for households consuming less than 250 kWh/month
El Salvador (VDT)	For households consuming less than 99 kWh/month	Import tax exemption for fuel used in electricity generation
Guatemala (VDT)	For households consuming less than 100 kWh/month	Import tax exemption for renewable energy equipment

table continues next page

Table 2.1 Overview of Direct and Indirect Residential Subsidy Mechanisms, by Country, April 2016 *(continued)*

Country	Direct subsidy	Implicit subsidy
Honduras (IBT & direct transfer)	Direct transfer for households consuming less than 75 kWh/month, with geographical targeting; IBT for households with implicit threshold of 840 kWh/month; special tariff for older customers	Sales tax exemption for households consuming less than 750 kWh/month and import tax exemption for fuel used in electricity generation
Nicaragua (VDT & IBT)	VDT for households consuming less than 150 kWh/month; IBT for households with implicit threshold of 150 kWh/month	Reduced sales tax rate and sales tax exemption for households consuming less than 1,000 kWh/month
Panama (VDT & IBT)	VDT for households consuming up 100 kWh/month; VDT (Fondo de Estabilización Tarifaria) for households consuming up to 350 kWh/month; stabilization fund for all consumers in Western region (Fondo Tarifario de Occidente); IBT for retirees; surcharge on households consuming more than 500 kWh/month	-

Source: World Bank elaboration.
Note: IBT = increasing block tariff; VDT = volume-differentiated tariff.

and social sector consumers.[8] The residential IBT system is based on two consumption blocks. Households pay a below-cost tariff for the first 200 kWh and an above-cost tariff for all additional consumption. The residential sector is not fully self-sufficient, and above-cost commercial tariffs cover any shortfall in the cross-subsidy, although the depth of the residential subsidy has been declining over time, and the sector is now approaching financial equilibrium. As of April 2016, the below-cost tariff was between US$0.121 and US$0.156 per kWh, and the above-cost tariff ranged from US$0.156 to US$0.261, with rates varying across the country's eight distribution companies (figure 2.10).[9]

In 2016, 77 percent of residential consumers received a net benefit under Costa Rica's IBT mechanism. The average subsidy was approximately 10–11 percent of the average electricity bill, although this share was 13 percent in households consuming less than 200 kWh per month. The other 23 percent of households paid a net negative subsidy (a tax) equal to 13 percent of their average electricity bill. As noted above, the negative subsidy imposed on high-volume consumers now almost fully offsets the positive subsidy that low-volume consumers receive.

Although most residential consumers receive a positive subsidy, the amount of the subsidy has declined over time. In 2015, the average tariff per kWh that residential consumers paid was only slightly below the average. Commercial consumers paid 14.2 percent more per kWh than residential consumers, and industrial consumers paid 7.2 percent less. The residential tariff increased from 18.6 percent below the average in 2000 to just 2.9 percent below the average in April 2016, and as a result, the residential sector is now close to achieving its own cross-subsidy equilibrium.

Figure 2.10 Electricity Consumption and Average Price per kWh, Costa Rica, April 2016

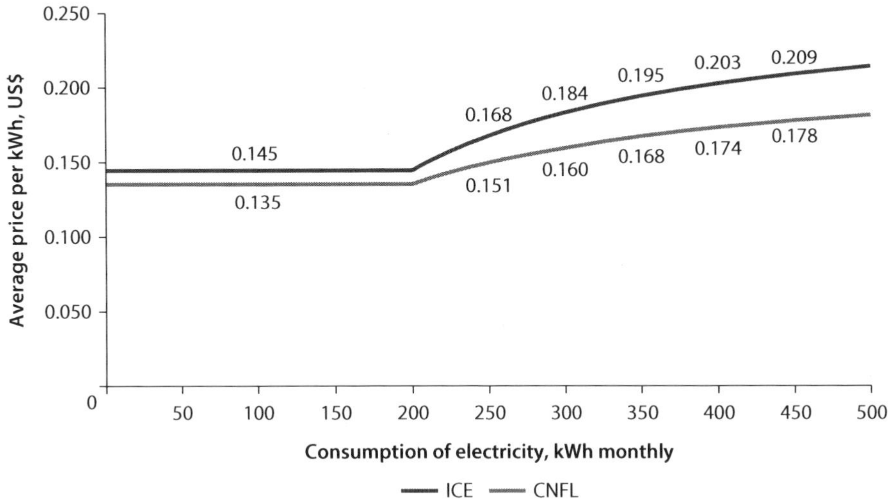

Source: World Bank elaboration based on data from country authorities.
Note: The two lines represent the different rates charged by the Costa Rican Electricity Institution (Instituto Costarricense de Electricidad, ICE) and the National Power and Light Company (Compañía Nacional de Fuerza y Luz, CNFL).

El Salvador

El Salvador operates a single VDT subsidy regime with two consumption thresholds. In 2016, approximately 66 percent of households connected to the grid (60 percent of all households in El Salvador) received the VDT subsidy. The subsidy covered an average of 65 percent of the electricity bill of beneficiary households.[10] The two thresholds are less than 50 kWh per month and 50–99 kWh per month.

A third, temporary, threshold of 200 kWh was introduced in April 2012, when oil prices were rapidly increasing. The mechanism was simple: households consuming 100–200 kWh paid what their bill would have been under the electricity tariffs that prevailed from January to April 2011. That is, the subsidy fully absorbed increases in the cost of electricity production for beneficiaries. This scheme was originally intended to last three months but was in effect until April 2015, when the unsubsidized electricity tariff dropped below the 2011 rate, making the temporary VDT irrelevant.

The depth of the subsidy diminishes when production costs rise. As of April 2016, the cost-reflective tariff ranged from US$0.130 to US$0.186 per kWh, depending on the distribution company. But under the VDT system, households that consumed less than 99 kWh paid an average rate of US$0.071 to US$0.080, indicating a subsidy per kWh of US$0.059 to US$0.086. The average tariff rate rose sharply above the 100 kWh threshold (figure 2.11). Although the unsubsidized rates differ between the distribution companies with the highest and lowest tariffs, overall the subsidized rates are similar.

Fiscal and Welfare Impacts of Electricity Subsidies in Central America
http://dx.doi.org/10.1596/978-1-4648-1104-3

Figure 2.11 Electricity Consumption and Average Price per kWh, El Salvador, April 2016

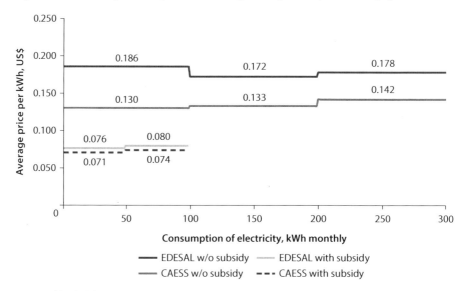

Source: World Bank elaboration based on data from country authorities.
Note: The four lines represent the different rates that the Compañía de Alumbrado Eléctrico de San Salvador (CAESS) and the Empresa Distribuidora Electrica Salvadoreña (EDESAL) charge with and without subsidy.

Guatemala

Guatemala applies a multiple-threshold VDT mechanism. Households consuming less than 100 kWh per month pay a "solidarity tariff" based on three consumption ranges (0–60, 61–88, and 89–100 kWh). The depth of the subsidy varies from 56 percent to 71 percent of the average electricity bill, depending on the distribution company for households consuming less than 60 kWh, from 34 percent to 57 percent for those consuming 61–88 kWh, and from 23 percent to 50 percent for those consuming 89–100 kWh.[11]

The VDT system provides subsidies to approximately 50 percent of the country's households, including 63 percent of those connected to the grid. The original version of the subsidy mechanism established in 1999 benefited households consuming up to 650 kWh, a threshold so high that the subsidy covered 98 percent of all households with a connection to the grid. Since then, the authorities have enacted gradual reforms, resulting in improved targeting. Coverage is also limited to those served by one of the country's three main distribution companies—which, combined, cover 87 percent of households connected to the grid.[12]

In principle, Guatemala also applies a subsidized VDT "social tariff" rate to households consuming between 100 and 300 kWh; this rate is linked to global oil prices, and the recent price slump has effectively nullified the subsidy. As of April 2016, the social tariff rate was greater than the nonsocial tariff rate. As a result, households in the 100–300 kWh range may be paying more per kWh than those that consume more than 300 kWh, because falling global oil prices have transformed the subsidy into an implicit tax (figure 2.12).

Figure 2.12 Electricity Consumption and Average Price per kWh, Guatemala, April 2016

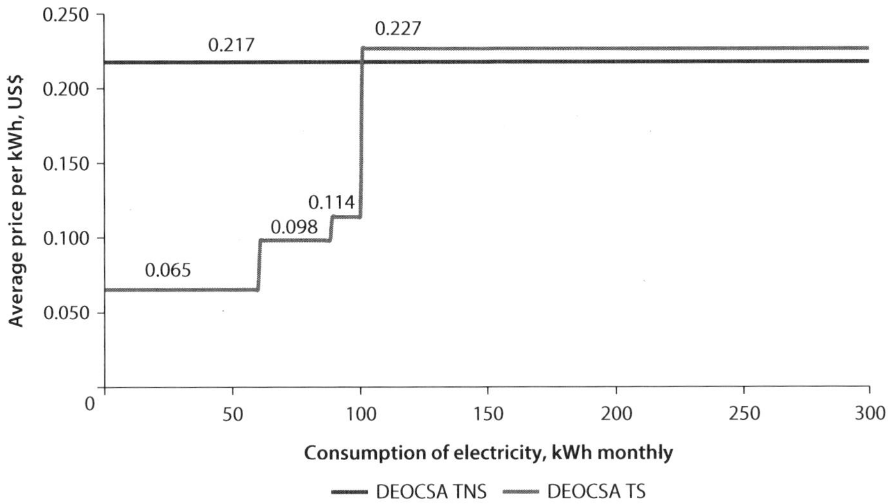

Source: World Bank elaboration based on data from country authorities.
Note: Data are for Distribuidora de Electricidad de Occidente, Sociedad Anónima (DEOCSA) customers only
(Western Distributor). The volume-differentiated tariff subsidy is labeled DEOCSA TS.

Honduras

Honduras operates a targeted cash transfer akin to a VDT mechanism as well as an IBT cross-subsidy.[13] Although the National Electric Energy Company (Empresa Nacional de Energía Eléctrica), the country's sole electricity distributor, is technically responsible for financing electricity subsidies, in practice these costs are passed on to the national budget.

Although Honduran electricity subsidies rely primarily on electricity consumption for targeting, the country's cash transfer to households consuming less than 75 kWh per month also uses geographic targeting to exclude households in high-income neighborhoods. This subsidy, targeted similarly to a VDT, is designed to deliver a cash transfer of 120 Honduran lempiras, or approximately US$5.20.[14] The number of potential beneficiaries was estimated at 278,000 in April 2016. Direct transfers to beneficiary households had not yet begun as of the end of 2016 due to delays in implementation. However, the analysis in this study assumes full implementation.

The Honduran IBT system, as established in 1994, provided subsidies to households that consumed up to 1,450 kWh per month; although targeting has improved over the years, it still subsidizes close to 99 percent of households.[15] As of April 2016, the estimated level of consumption at which total payments aligned with total costs remained relatively high (840 kWh), and hence did not create a substantial cross-subsidy.[16] As illustrated above in figure 2.8, because IBT subsidies are applied to all consumers at the same marginal rate, the total amount billed aligns with electricity costs only at consumption levels greater than the threshold associated with below-cost tariffs.

Until a reform that went into effect in June 2016, Honduras' IBT mechanism had four consumption blocks (0–100, 101–300, 301–500, and ≥500 kWh). The tariff schedule approved in 2009 applied a subsidy equal to 70 percent to the first 100 kWh, and the tariff for 101–300 kWh was 98 percent of the cost of production. Tariffs for consumption between 301 and 500 kWh were cost reflective, whereas the tariff on consumption greater than 500 kWh was 110 percent of the cost of production.[17]

Because of its limited degree of cross-subsidization, budgetary transfers continue to be necessary to cover the cost of the IBT subsidy. The combined subsidy regimes result in households that consume less than 75 kWh paying nothing, with those that consume between 75 and 840 kWh paying a below-cost rate and those that consume more than 840 kWh paying a slightly above-cost rate (figure 2.13). As of April 2016, the cost-reflective tariff rate was US$0.147 per kWh.

Nicaragua

Nicaragua applies both IBT and VDT mechanisms, as well as an implicit subsidy resulting from value-added tax (VAT) exemptions. The country's relatively complex IBT scheme uses seven consumption blocks (0–25, 26–50, 51–100, 101–150, 151–500, 501–1,000, and 1,000+ kWh). Households consuming up to 150 kWh per month receive a net subsidy, and those consuming more than 150 kWh pay a cross-subsidy. In addition, a VDT scheme was created for

Figure 2.13 Electricity Consumption and Average Price per kWh, Honduras, April 2016

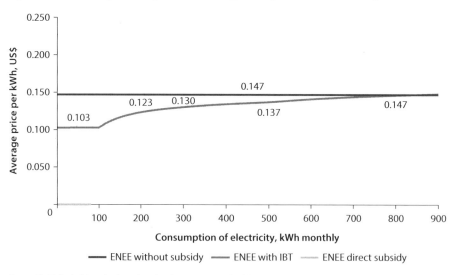

Source: World Bank elaboration based on data from country authorities.
Note: The upper line indicates the cost-reflective tariff, the middle line shows the incremental block tariff scheme, and the lower line corresponds to the direct subsidy. ENEE = Empresa Nacional de Energía Eléctrica.

households consuming less than 150 kWh. Nicaragua also offers VAT exemptions or preferential VAT rates for certain levels of electricity consumption.[18] In 2015, an estimated 85 percent of households that were connected to the grid qualified for the VDT.

The seven-block IBT scheme provides relatively deep subsidies for households consuming less than 100 kWh per month. Although data are limited, households consuming up to 150 kWh appear to receive a net subsidy. Only households consuming more than 150 kWh make a net contribution to the scheme, which is almost certainly insufficient to cover the cost of the subsidy. As a result, it is likely that the commercial sector subsidizes the residential sector, although data constraints make this impossible to confirm.

Nicaragua's VDT scheme, the country's largest electricity subsidy, was introduced in 2005 as a temporary measure to limit the impact of rising oil prices on household consumption. The Energy Stability Law froze electricity tariffs for all households consuming less than 150 kWh. The scheme was reviewed in 2008 and has been extended repeatedly; today, households consuming less than 150 kWh continue to pay almost the same tariff rates as in 2005. The discount per kWh relative to the IBT tariff rates *increases* for higher consumption levels.[19] Because the tariff rate is fixed, the depth of the subsidy increases when production costs rise and decreases when they fall. As of December 2015, the subsidy covered 52.8 percent of the cost. Because of the continued extension of this temporary measure, the average tariff drops substantially for households consuming less than 150 kWh (figure 2.14).

Panama

Panama operates a number of electricity subsidy schemes that were implemented at different times and designed to serve different policy purposes. A VDT subsidy was adopted in 2001 covering all households that consume up to 100 kWh per month. Beneficiaries receive a discount of up to 20 percent on their electricity bill, which can be combined with the retiree discount and the FET fund subsidy. In 2016, approximately 29 percent of households connected to the grid qualified for the VDT. Because 100 kWh per month is low relative to the average household electricity consumption in Panama, a majority of beneficiaries of the VDT live below the poverty line. It is cross-subsidized by a 0.6 percent surcharge on the electricity bill of households consuming more than 500 kWh of electricity per month.

To absorb oil price fluctuations, Panama also uses the Fondo de Estabilización Tarifaria (FET), a stabilization fund that acts like a nontraditional VDT mechanism.[20] When the FET was introduced in 2004, electricity tariffs for all households were based on a reference oil price of US$40 per barrel, and the FET absorbed the difference between the market price and the reference price.[21] As oil prices rose and the fiscal burden of the subsidy became

Figure 2.14 Electricity Consumption and Average Price per kWh, Nicaragua, December 2015

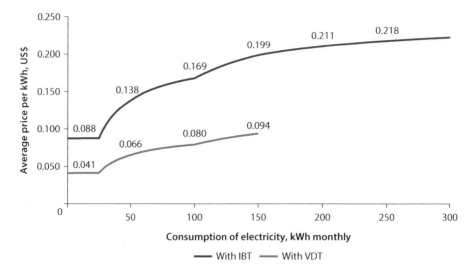

Source: World Bank elaboration based on data from country authorities.

unsustainable, the authorities established an eligibility threshold of 600 kWh; this has been adjusted downward repeatedly.[22] As of April 2016, the beneficiary threshold was 350 kWh per month.[23] The government is again lowering the threshold; by the end of 2016, only households consuming less than 300 kWh were expected to continue receiving benefits under this scheme.

A second fund is dedicated to subsidizing consumers in the country's Western region, where structural electricity production costs are above the national average. The Western Tariff Fund (Fondo Tarifario de Occidente, FTO) benefits all electricity consumers that the Chiriqui Electricity Distribution Company (Empresa de Distribución Eléctrica Chiriqui S.A., EDECHI) serves, including not only residential but also commercial and industrial consumers.[24] In the first half of 2016, the FTO created implicit discounts of 20 percent for consumers in the EDECHI service area consuming up to 300 kWh per month, 25–26 percent for those consuming 301–750 kWh, and 31 percent for those consuming more than 750 kWh (figure 2.15). Combined, the FTO and FET provide subsidies to 68 percent of connected households.

There are also subsidies allocated to agriculture, political parties, and households where the electric service is billed to a person over retirement age. The first two cover few consumers, but roughly one-fifth of households connected to the electricity grid receive the "retiree" discount.[25] These households receive a 25 percent discount on the first 600 kWh of electricity consumption per month. This subsidy scheme has been in place since 1987 and has been updated repeatedly. The average depth of this subsidy is more than five times as large as that of the basic consumption VDT.

Fiscal and Welfare Impacts of Electricity Subsidies in Central America
http://dx.doi.org/10.1596/978-1-4648-1104-3

Figure 2.15 Electricity Consumption and Average Price per kWh, Panama, April 2016

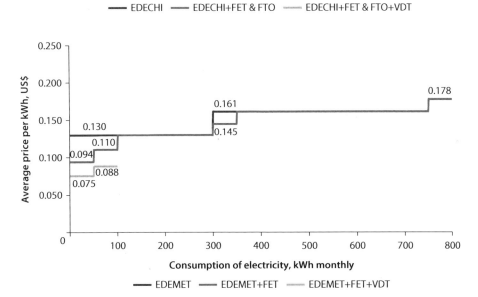

Source: World Bank elaboration based on data from country authorities.
Note: This figure illustrates the tariff structure for Empresa de Distribución Eléctrica Chiriquí S.A. (EDECHI) customers and for customers of one of the country's other two distribution companies, the Metro-West Electricity Distribution Company (Empresa de Distribución Eléctrica Metro-Oeste S.A., EDEMET). The top graph shows the unsubsidized tariff, the tariff with the combined Fondo de Compensación Energética (FET) and Fondo Tarifario de Occidente (FTO) subsidies, and the tariff with the combined FET, FTO and basic consumption VDT scheme subsidies. The bottom graph shows tariffs including the FET and VDT subsidies, but not the FTO, which only applies to EDECHI customers.

Electricity Subsidies in Central America: Key Messages

Whereas periods of high oil prices encouraged governments to create new subsidy regimes, the current climate of low international oil prices has presented an opportunity to reform and streamline these policies. The countries of Central

America have been responding rapidly to the drop in oil prices by adjusting the electricity subsidy designs. El Salvador has eliminated a VDT range that benefited middle-range consumers. Guatemala has virtually eliminated an indirect subsidy and reduced the scope of the VDT regimes. Honduras is reforming its subsidy schemes in an effort to increase the degree of IBT cross-subsidization and reduce the residential sector's reliance on fiscal resources or cross-subsidies from other sectors, based on an agreement reached with the IMF in the context of the country stabilization program. Nicaragua is planning to eliminate its VDT scheme and has focused on improving its IBT mechanism. Panama has been progressively reducing its beneficiary threshold for several years in response to the spike in oil prices combined with a drought in 2014, which strained the government's fiscal resources.

Although price stability has been a driving force in the design of many electricity subsidy programs, subsidy regimes have increasingly targeted low-volume consumers, who are systematically more likely to be poor. All electricity subsidy mechanisms in Central America use eligibility thresholds to target middle- and lower-income households, and Honduras's VDT system also applies a geographic criterion designed to screen out wealthier households. Costa Rica's IBT scheme delivers a relatively small subsidy, but the use of cross-subsidies eliminates the need for budgetary financing and increases its distributional equity. The IBT scheme in Honduras also extends substantial benefits to low-volume consumers, but limited cross-subsidization at the upper end of the consumption range leaves it dependent on cross-subsidization from the industrial and commercial sectors as well as government funding. Nevertheless, as shown in chapters 4 and 5, eligibility thresholds are often high, and leakages to upper-income households are common in nearly every country in the region.

Despite their increasing focus on low-volume consumers, electricity subsidies in Central America continue to benefit large segments of the population, which increases their fiscal cost and reduces the progressivity of their distribution. Nicaragua's VDT subsidy mechanism covers 85 percent of households with electricity service. Panama's VDT covers 29 percent of households connected to the grid, and the stabilization funds FET and FTO cover 66 percent. In Costa Rica, 77 percent of households connected to the grid receive a net benefit from the IBT mechanism. In El Salvador, 66 percent of households connected to the grid benefit from electricity subsidies. In Honduras, the IBT provides net benefits to practically all households (almost 99 percent).[26] Guatemala's VDT scheme also benefits more than half of the population, although current reform plans would cut the beneficiary rate to 57 percent of households connected to the grid.

Structural design, thresholds, and targeting criteria play a major role in determining the fiscal cost and distributional impact of subsidies. Under IBT and VDT systems, the thresholds for different rates play a critical role in determining the distribution of benefits. High thresholds will extend subsidies to a larger share of households at higher income levels, and low thresholds will focus subsidy benefits on low-volume consumers, who are also systematically more likely to have lower income levels. Finally, the use of targeting criteria can more precisely concentrate the distribution of benefits based on household characteristics, including income level, demography, and geographic location.

Annex 2A: The Electricity Sectors of Central America

Costa Rica

The main actor in Costa Rica's electricity sector is the state-owned Costa Rican Institute of Electricity (Instituto Costarricense de Electricidad, ICE).[27] ICE is a vertically integrated company that participates in electricity service generation, transmission, and distribution. The Regulatory Authority for Public Utilities (Autoridad Reguladora de los Servicios Públicos, ARESEP) is responsible for establishing and monitoring compliance with electricity sector regulations, and the Ministry of the Environment and Energy (Ministerio de Ambiente y Energía) is in charge of defining the sector's policies and planning.

Unlike its neighbors in Central America, Costa Rica has not made significant adjustments to its electricity sector in recent years, in part because of ICE's generally satisfactory performance. Costa Rica has the highest rates of electricity access and per capita electricity consumption in Central America, with near-universal coverage. Moreover, the quality and reliability of the country's electricity services are high, and technical and administrative efficiency are strong, according to regional standards, resulting in low rates of electricity loss. ICE has remained financially sustainable, expanding the country's electricity generating capacity, particularly from renewable sources, without resorting to transfers from the central government budget.

Concerns in the early 1990s about ICE's ability to build sufficient generating capacity led the government to amend several laws to allow private companies to participate in the development of renewable energy.[28] Private power plants are required to sell to ICE, which is authorized to purchase up to 30 percent of the country's total installed capacity. As of 2012, 29 private generators accounted for approximately 14 percent of the country's installed generation capacity and 17 percent of the total electricity generated. Four rural electrification

Table 2A.1 Overview of Energy Sector Ownership Structure, April 2016

Country	Generation	Transmission	Distribution	Source of generation (% thermal)[a]
Costa Rica	Largely public (80% public)	Public	Public (90%)	8
El Salvador	Mostly private (25% public)	Public	Private (100%)	40
Guatemala	Mostly private (20% public)	Public and private	Private (94%)	33
Honduras	Mostly private (20% public)	Public	Public (100%)	57
Nicaragua	Largely private (less than 10% public)	Public	Private (100%)	55
Panama	Largely private (less than 10% public)	Public	Private (100%)	40

Source: World Bank elaboration, based on data from country authorities.
a. Five-year average (2011–15).

Fiscal and Welfare Impacts of Electricity Subsidies in Central America
http://dx.doi.org/10.1596/978-1-4648-1104-3

cooperatives and two municipal companies are also authorized to generate electricity.[29] Unlike the private firms, which—in the absence of a wholesale electricity market—sell all of the electricity that they produce to ICE, the cooperatives and municipal companies are authorized to distribute and sell the electricity they generate to users in their concession area. ARESEP establishes the purchase and sale prices for electricity.

The private sector is not involved in electricity transmission. ICE is responsible for the operation, maintenance, and expansion of the National Transmission System, which is connected to the electricity systems in Nicaragua and Panama. Eight public companies distribute electricity. ICE, directly or through its subsidiary, the National Power and Light Company (Compañía Nacional de Fuerza y Luz), covered 77 percent of all subscribers in 2013. The two municipal companies and four rural cooperatives covered the remaining subscribers.

El Salvador

The Executive Commission of the Lempa River (Comisión Ejecutiva Hidroeléctrica del Río Lempa, CEL) was established in 1945, with the mandate to develop the country's hydroelectric potential. With the inauguration of the first hydroelectric power plant in 1954, CEL began building the infrastructure necessary to provide electricity services throughout the country. Additional plants were built in subsequent years; although these were mainly hydroelectric, thermal and geothermal power plants were also built to ensure a diverse energy mix. CEL also developed systems for electricity transmission and distribution. In this way, CEL became the dominant actor in El Salvador's electricity sector as a vertically integrated company.

The structural stabilization and adjustment plan that followed the 1992 peace accords, which ended El Salvador's 12-year civil war, reorganized the energy and electricity sectors. In line with similar reforms enacted in other Latin American countries during that time, the restructuring of El Salvador's electricity sector involved the unbundling of electricity generation, transmission, and distribution services and increased private sector involvement in the electricity sector. The reform process began in 1996 with the enactment of the General Electricity Act, which restricted CEL's mandate by unbundling and restructuring electricity services, as well as creating the General Superintendency of Electricity and Telecommunications to regulate the sector and implement the act. The act also tasked the Ministry of Economy with overseeing the development of electricity sector policies; the National Energy Commission currently fills this role.

In 1998, electricity distribution was privatized; eight private companies currently manage it.[30] In 1999, electricity transmission was assigned to two independent corporations under CEL: the Transactions Unit, which operates the transmission system and manages the contracts market and the wholesale electricity market; and the Transmission Company of El Salvador (Empresa Transmisora de El Salvador), which oversees maintenance of the transmission network. Thermal and geothermal power plants were privatized in 1999 and

2002, respectively. As of 2012, CEL accounted for approximately one-third of the country's installed capacity and electricity generation. In 2015, CEL finalized a buy-back process and acquired the shares of LaGeo (geothermal generation) in the hands of the electricity company (ENEL), nationalizing "de facto" geothermal generation.

Thermal power has driven the expansion of electricity generation in El Salvador, leaving the country exposed to fluctuations in oil prices. As oil prices began to rise in early 2005, the government responded by adjusting the rules for determining spot prices. Because this new pricing approach was not effective in controlling further increases in the spot price, in 2006 the government introduced a subsidy on any increase in generating costs above the reference cost, set at US$91.10 per MWh. To do this, the CEL would pay the difference between actual generating costs and the reference price.

These policies helped mitigate the effect on the average retail tariff, but the subsidy was not sustainable and was partially reversed. In response, the National Energy Commission issued the 2010–14 National Energy Policy, which reinstated the state's role in guiding the expansion of the energy sector and promoting the diversification of the country's energy mix through the development of clean energy sources.

Guatemala

The National Institute of Electrification (Instituto Nacional de Electrificación, INDE) was established in 1959, with a mandate to engage in electricity generation, transmission, and distribution. INDE was also responsible for carrying out certain regulatory functions and determining electricity sector policies. INDE and its distribution affiliate, the Empresa Eléctrica de Guatemala S.A., were the dominant actors in Guatemala's electricity market until the mid-1990s.

By the early 1990s, electricity rates had been insufficient to cover INDE's operational and maintenance costs for years, and INDE faced serious financial constraints. Moreover, there were shortages in generation capacity due to lagging investment, as well as increased electricity demand. At the same time, there was a decrease in hydroelectric generation potential due to a prolonged drought. These developments triggered a major crisis in the electricity sector in the first half of the 1990s, resulting in frequent service interruptions.

In response to the crisis, the government began promoting private sector participation in the electricity sector by entering into power-purchasing agreements based on a noncompetitive direct contracting process. This significantly increased the country's installed capacity; and in 1995, Guatemala and Honduras were the two Central American countries with the highest share of supplied electricity from private generators (32 percent). In the rest of the region, the share of electricity that the private sector supplied was not greater than 6 percent. More significant reforms followed in 1995 and 1996 that further increased private sector participation in the electricity market and restricted INDE's mandate.[31] The Ministry of Energy and Mines assumed responsibility for electricity sector policies and planning from INDE, and the National Electrical Energy Commission

Fiscal and Welfare Impacts of Electricity Subsidies in Central America
http://dx.doi.org/10.1596/978-1-4648-1104-3

was created and tasked with regulating the sector. A private entity—the Wholesale Market Management Company—was also created and tasked with overseeing energy and power-purchasing transactions.

Vertical integration of companies participating in the electricity market was prohibited, even in the case of state-owned companies, and electricity generation, transmission, and distribution were unbundled. As a result, INDE assigned its generation, transmission, and distribution activities to different companies. INDE's Electric Power Generating Company (Empresa de Generación de Energía Eléctrica) was created in 1998. By 2012, it accounted for 20.2 percent of installed capacity and generated 29.3 percent of the electricity sold in the wholesale market, mainly through hydroelectric power plants. Fifty-two private generation plants, which are primarily thermal and to a lesser extent hydroelectric, accounted for the remainder of installed capacity and electricity generation. INDE's Electricity Transport and Control Company (Empresa de Transporte y Control de Energía Eléctrica) was created in 1998 and manages 67.2 percent of the country's electricity transmission networks. Three private transmission companies manage the remaining 32.8 percent of electricity transmission networks,[32] and three private companies and 13 municipal companies manage electricity distribution services in clearly delineated geographical areas.

As in other Central American countries, thermal power plants have driven the overall expansion of installed capacity in Guatemala. When oil prices began rising at the turn of the century, the government sought to moderate the increase in tariffs for residential consumers and to increase investment in renewable energy. The 2003 Incentives Act for Renewable Energy Projects introduced fiscal and customs duty incentives to promote investment in electricity generation projects based on renewable energy sources.

Honduras

The vertically integrated National Electricity Company (Empresa Nacional de Energía Eléctrica, ENEE) has been responsible for electricity provision in Honduras since its inception in 1957. It contributed to the country's growing generating capacity through the construction of several hydroelectric plants and expanded the national electricity transmission system. Anticipating a rapid increase in electricity demand, ENEE launched the El Cajón hydroelectric plant in 1985, which increased installed capacity from 250 to 550 MW.

A combination of factors—including ENEE's significant debt; an ambitious rural electrification program; below-cost electricity rates; and major operational deficiencies, including nontechnical losses currently estimated at 32 percent—led ENEE into an unsustainable financial situation by the early 1990s. At the same time, demand for electricity reached the available generation capacity. This situation was compounded in 1993, when a severe drought reduced the country's hydroelectric generation potential and unleashed a major energy crisis that led to heavy rationing and daily electricity outages between April and December 1994. Although emergency measures were implemented, such as reinstating idle thermal plants, it became evident that more comprehensive reforms were needed, which resulted in the passing of the Electricity Act of 1994.

Because of Honduras's growing dependence on thermal generation and imported oil, the sharp increase in oil prices in the mid-2000s raised electricity production costs. Average retail tariffs failed to keep pace with rising generation costs, and in early 2008, it was estimated that the average residential tariff covered only 80 percent of supply costs. Because of high fuel prices and nontechnical losses, ENEE could not cover its energy purchases from private thermal generators with revenues from electricity sales, and the government had to finance this shortfall and, as a result, began to promote electricity generation using renewable energy sources.[33]

The Electricity Act established reforms similar to those in other Central American countries; called for the creation of a competitive wholesale electricity market; and proposed the vertical breakup of energy generation, transmission, and distribution activities, which were a state monopoly at the time. The act also encouraged competition in different segments of the electricity sector and introduced cost-based price regulations in segments that were natural monopolies.

Ultimately, the reforms were only partially implemented, and ENEE remained the dominant actor in all areas of the electricity market. The separation of energy policy planning and electricity market regulation was never fully implemented, and ENEE retained significant influence over sectoral policies and regulations.[34] It is the only company participating in electricity transmission and distribution. Moreover, ENEE's generating plants, which are primarily hydroelectric, accounted for approximately one-third of installed capacity and total electricity generation in 2012. ENEE is also the sole buyer of the energy that private generators produce. The tariff rate structure was not adjusted to allow for recovery of the company's operational and maintenance costs, and sufficient resources were not generated to offset depreciated capital and invest in the improvement and expansion of electricity service. Although incomplete, the reforms led to increased electricity generation, because greater involvement by the private sector, particularly in thermoelectric plants, significantly increased installed capacity.[35] In 2012, 43 private companies generated 67.5 percent of all electricity, with 55.4 percent of electricity generated in the 12 private thermal power plants.

As a result of the incomplete implementation of the sector reforms and as part of agreements reached with the International Monetary Fund in 2014, Honduras enacted a new Electricity Act in December 2014. Among other changes aimed at resolving the problems with the previous framework, the act provides additional support for unbundling ENEE and reforming the power sector. It mandated the creation of a regulatory body, the National Electricity Commission, and the president nominated the three commissioners, who have been charged with setting the regulatory framework for the restructured sector, including the formulation of cost-reflective tariffs.

Nicaragua

The Nicaraguan Institute of Energy (Instituto Nicaragüense de Energía, INE), a public power company, was created in 1979 under the Sandinista government, and quickly became the sole participant in Nicaragua's energy sector, including the electricity and hydrocarbon markets. Under the 1985 Organic Act on the INE, INE was also charged with establishing national energy sector policies and regulations.

INE managed all aspects of electricity generation, transmission, and distribution until the early 1990s. The economic crisis of the late 1980s, which resulted in high levels of debt and inflation, severely damaged INE's operations. The company was suffering from years of little to no investment, which limited its ability to expand installed capacity and meet service demand.

The government implemented a series of reforms in the 1990s to address the worsening situation in the electricity sector, adopting an approach similar to that of other countries in the region. In 1992, the Organic Act on the INE was amended to allow for private sector participation in the electricity market. As a result, INE gradually transitioned from being a vertically integrated, monopolistic, state-owned energy company to becoming the regulatory body of the national energy sector. In 1994, INE's electricity assets were transferred to the state-owned Nicaraguan Electricity Company (Empresa Nicaragüense de Electricidad, ENEL). The following year, INE's responsibilities were further limited to regulation of the electricity and hydrocarbons sectors, and responsibility for policy design was assigned to the Ministry of Trade and Transportation.

The Electric Industry Act of 1998 replaced the existing legislation, advanced reforms, and fostered further private sector engagement. It called for the creation of the National Energy Commission, which was tasked with developing the sector's strategic policies; consolidation of INE's regulatory role; fully opening electricity generation and distribution to private firms; state ownership of the transmission system; and elimination of participation of vertically integrated companies in the electricity sector. As a result of this fifth provision, several companies were split off from ENEL and privatized.[36] Even so, ENEL owns the country's public generation assets, including geothermal and hydroelectric plants. As in other Central American countries, privatization increased the installed capacity of thermal power plants.

A sharp increase in international oil prices raised production costs in the electricity sector, especially for thermal generation. In response, the Renewable Energy Sources Promotion Act was passed to reduce the country's dependence on hydrocarbons. In addition, the Energy Stability Act of 2005 established subsidies for residential electricity consumption and policies to prevent oil price increases from being fully passed through to generation and distribution companies.

Under the Energy Stability Act of 2005, if West Texas Intermediate prices rose above US$50 per barrel, the country was officially in an energy crisis, and the government could take temporary measures to reduce the effect of high fuel prices on consumers, including freezing electricity tariffs for residential consumers with monthly consumption levels below 150 kWh. Spot prices were calculated not based on marginal costs, but on a weighted average of the variable costs of thermal units plus 10 percent. Moreover, the public undertaking that owned the hydroelectric plants was compelled to enter into contracts with the distribution companies at below-market prices ranging from US$55 to US$65 per MWh. Furthermore, the average share of the generating costs that was passed through to tariffs was significantly less than the real cost (the spot price plus contract market), and private distribution companies—which were already in a difficult financial position because of large electricity losses—were forced to cover the shortfall. In 2008, the government and private investors signed a memorandum of understanding in which they agreed to settle arrears, approve a law penalizing electricity fraud, transfer 16 percent of the shares of distribution companies to the government, and apply cost-reflective tariffs; but few consumers pay cost-reflective tariffs, and power sector losses are typically covered through public fiscal spending.

Panama

In 1961, the Institute of Water Resources and Electrification (Instituto de Recursos Hidráulicos y de Electrificación, IRHE) was created to help develop the infrastructure necessary to meet the country's growing electricity needs. Although IRHE was responsible for overseeing and managing electricity generation, transmission, and distribution services, given the private sector's active participation in the electricity sector, IRHE's role was initially limited. In 1969, IRHE assumed regulatory and policy design responsibilities for the sector, and from 1972 to 1973, IRHE took complete control of the Panamanian electricity market through the nationalization of the Panamanian Power and Light Company (Compañía Panameña de Fuerza y Luz) and the forceful acquisition of all private sector electricity assets.

In the 1990s, Panama—like other countries in the region—implemented institutional reforms that restructured several public companies, including IRHE. At the time, IRHE was facing serious administrative problems, high levels of technical and commercial losses, rising tariffs, and relatively low levels of electricity service coverage. The 1995 Electricity Service Reform Program established the main guidelines for the restructuring program, including the creation of a competitive wholesale market, opening IRHE's transmission and distribution networks to private firms, and the promotion of private generation projects, although the electricity sector was not effectively reformed until the approval of the Framework Act in 1997.

The Framework Act repealed previous electricity laws and regulations and limited the state's participation in the electricity sector to strategic policy design,[37] regulatory oversight,[38] operation of transmission networks, and serving areas that the private sector did not cover. The Framework Act also eliminated vertical integration in electricity companies, leading to the dissolution of IRHE. Privatization reforms allowed for the sale of at least 51 percent of thermal generation plants and distribution companies and up to 49 percent of hydroelectric generation plants. Electricity transmission remained entirely under the control of the state-owned Electricity Transmission Company (Empresa de Transmisión Eléctrica S.A.). As part of the privatization process, IRHE was divided into four electricity generation companies,[39] one transmission company, and three distribution companies.[40]

Additional reforms helped shape Panama's electricity sector. Several amendments to the Framework Act were passed in an attempt to reduce the exposure to oil price volatility that resulted from the sector's increasing reliance on thermal generation. Other reforms included restructuring the Regulatory Board for Public Utilities, which is now known as the National Public Utilities Authority, and creation of the state-owned Electricity Generation Company (Empresa de Generación Eléctrica S.A) in 2006. In 2008, the National Energy Secretariat was created and tasked with designing electricity sector policies.

Notes

1. See annex 2A for an overview of the key players and reforms in each country's electricity sector.

2. Annex 2A provides more detailed information on the institutional arrangements and reforms in the energy sector of each country.

3. In 2015, some of this privatization was reversed in El Salvador through the nationalization of the LaGeo geothermal generator.

4. Global oil prices were low in the late 1990s, at approximately US$20 per barrel (Global Economic Monitor).

5. This reflected not just electricity generation becoming more reliant on oil, but also an increased reliance on oil across the whole energy matrix. Because of data limitations, we cannot separate the imports of inputs destined for electricity generation. Instead, we report energy imports.

6. All oil prices are for West Texas Intermediate Crude Oil.

7. Pricing mechanisms based on household behavior, such as hourly differentiated tariffs, are not considered part of the subsidy mechanisms.

8. Social sector consumers encompass a range of educational, public health, religious, and civil society institutions.

9. Because there are no official estimates of costs, these are estimated from household surveys (see annex 4A).

10. More precisely, the subsidy scheme works as follows. Households consuming less than 99 kWh per month receive a subsidy equal to 89.5 percent of the difference between the cost-reflective tariff and the amount obtained by multiplying the electricity consumption in kWh by a reference or maximum price per kWh. Those reference prices vary according to consumption block: US$0.0635 for monthly consumption of less than 50 kWh and US$0.0671 for monthly consumption between 50 and 99 kWh.

11. Households consuming less than 60 kWh pay US$0.065 per kWh, those consuming between 61 and 88 kWh pay US$0.098, and those consuming between 89 and

100 kWh pay US$0.114. As of late 2016, the government was moving toward phasing out the subsidy for households consuming more than 88 kWh per month, which would limit its beneficiaries to the approximately 57 percent of households connected to the grid.

12. Although other small local distributors are active in Guatemala, only customers of the three major companies are eligible for electricity subsidies. These include the Western Electricity Distributor (Distribuidora de Electricidad de Occidente, Sociedad Anónima), the Eastern Electricity Distributor (Distribuidora de Electricidad de Oriente, Sociedad Anónima) and the Guatemala Electricity Company (Empresa Eléctrica de Guatemala Sociedad Anónima).

13. There is an additional electricity subsidy for older heads of households (equivalent to a 25 percent discount on their electricity bill), but there are no official estimates of the extent to which this subsidy is used. As a result, it is not included in this study.

14. This direct subsidy was introduced in 1994, but its characteristics have changed significantly over time. The subsidy, which was established to protect consumers from rising electricity costs, originally covered the total bill for all households consuming less than 300 kWh per month. In 2001, the system was reformed so that only the first 135 kWh would be subsidized, although the beneficiary threshold remained at 300 kWh. In 2006, the government introduced the Bono 80 program to provide direct cash-transfer electricity subsidies. In 2009, Bono 80 was extended to cover all electricity costs up to 150 kWh. In December 2013, the amount of the direct subsidy was limited to 120 Honduran lempiras, the threshold was lowered to 75 kWh per month, and households in high-income areas were excluded. This direct subsidy law remained in force as of 2016.

15. Honduras's IBT system is the product of an arguably erroneous interpretation of the Framework Law of the Electricity Sub-Sector (Ley Marco del Sub-Sector Eléctrico), because the law's ambiguous wording could be interpreted as an IBT or a VDT scheme. A VDT interpretation of the law would have implied a more progressive distribution of subsidies and considerably lower fiscal cost.

16. This threshold is estimated using the methodology included in annex 4A.

17. A revised IBT that went into effect in June 2016 consolidated these into three consumption blocks (0–50, 50–500, and 501+ kWh). By lowering the threshold for the lowest-volume consumption block and raising tariffs for the higher-volume blocks, it is expected to have increased the system's progressivity and reduced its fiscal cost.

18. Households consuming less than 300 kWh per month are exempt from the VAT on electricity, and those consuming 301 to 1,000 kWh pay a 7 percent VAT, well below the national rate. As a result, almost all residential consumers benefit from preferential tax treatment. In practice, this forgone tax revenue is an implicit budgetary subsidy.

19. We estimated the following discount rate relative to the IBT tariff rate per consumption block: (1) 0–25 kWh per month: 4.4 cordobas per kWh; (2) 26–50 kWh per month: 5.6 cordobas per kWh; (3) 51–100 kWh per month: 6.9 cordobas per kWh; and (4) 101–150 kWh per month: 25.8 cordobas per kWh.

20. Different tariffs are applied to each consumption level, but discounts benefit only households consuming less than a certain threshold.

21. Every six months, Panama reviews its electricity tariffs, estimating the cost-reflective tariff and adjusting electricity prices accordingly. At the same time, they decide the

percentage of discount or subsidy offered by the FET during the next six months and the consumption threshold defining who receives these benefits.

22. By 2014, the threshold had been lowered to 400 kWh, and households consuming between 350 and 400 kWh received 66.6 percent of the full FET-related subsidy. This share was reduced and then eliminated entirely in 2015.

23. Subsidies are provided to Empresa de Distribución Eléctrica Metro-Oeste S.A. customers consuming up to 100 kWh and between 301 and 350 kWh, Elektra Noreste, S.A. customers consuming up to 350 kWh, and Empresa de Distribución Eléctrica Chiriqui S.A. customers consuming up to 200 kWh.

24. The FTO replaced the Energy Compensation Fund (Fondo de Compensación Energética, FACE), which had been created to finance below-cost tariffs for consumption above 400 kWh in the commercial and industrial sectors. In 2014, US$240 million was used to cover FET and FACE, an unsustainable amount given the low levels of tax revenue in Panama. For that reason, in 2015, amid the drop in oil prices, the government replaced FACE with the smaller FTO. This reform decreased subsidy expenditures by US$178 million, which helped reduce the country's fiscal deficit.

25. An electricity subsidy for the agroindustry was introduced in 1986. The value of this subsidy is small, accounting for approximately 0.9 percent of total electricity subsidies in 2012. Approximately 600 consumers benefited from the subsidy in 2012, and the subsidy represented approximately 5 percent of the electricity bill. Another subsidy in place since the mid-1980s permanently reduces electricity tariffs by 50 percent for political parties' headquarters in regional capitals. The fiscal cost of this scheme is low, even if the tariff discount is considerable

26. Honduran electricity subsidies were reformed after April 2016 and are now expected to reach a smaller proportion of households.

27. This annex is based on consultations with World Bank energy specialists and World Bank (2010).

28. Initially, the installation of private power plants with a capacity of up to 20 megawatts was allowed for an extendible concession period of 20 years, provided they did not together surpass 15 percent of the country's total installed capacity. In 1995, the maximum installed capacity of private power plants was increased to 50 megawatts, with concessions of 20 years, after which their assets were to be transferred to ICE.

29. The two municipal companies are Empresa de Servicios Públicos de Heredia and Junta Administrativa del Servicio Eléctrico de Cartago; the four rural cooperatives are Coopeguanacaste, Coopelesca, Coopesantos, and Coopealfaro.

30. These are CAESS, AES-CLESA, Delsur, Deusem, EEO, EDESAL, B&D, and Abruzzo.

31. In early 1995, the Organic Act of INDE redefined the organization's mandate, transferring some of its responsibilities to other entities. In 1996, the government enacted the General Electricity Act (Ley General de Electricidad), establishing the current framework and rules for the sector.

32. Guatemala is the only country in the region to allow private sector participation in transmission services.

33. The government passed several acts to promote renewable energy sources: the Act for the Promotion of Electricity Generation Using Renewable Resources (2007), the Biofuels Act (2008), and the Special Regulatory Act on Public Renewable Energy Projects (2010).

34. The Energy Cabinet (which the Electricity Act created in 1994) and the Secretariat of Natural Resources and the Environment are responsible for formulating electricity sector policies. The National Energy Commission is in charge of regulating the electricity sector.

35. ENEE increased private sector involvement in electricity generation by entering into long-term purchasing power agreements with private generation companies. These agreements ultimately became excessively burdensome financially for the state-owned company.

36. The following companies emerged after ENEL's dissolution: four electric generation companies (Hidrogesa, GEOSA, GECSA, GEMOSA), two distribution companies (DISNORTE, DISSUR), and one transmission company (ENTRESA). The distributors were subsequently sold to a single company, the Spanish group Unión-Fenosa. In 2002, GEOSA and GEMOSA were privatized. Hidrogesa and GECSA were never privatized.

37. The Energy Policy Commission was created as part of the Ministry of Energy Planning and Policy to oversee the sector's strategic policy development.

38. Regulatory oversight was assigned to the Regulatory Board for Public Utilities.

39. Three of these companies focused on hydroelectric generation, and the state remained the majority shareholder.

40. These include Edemet and Edechi, held by the Spanish group Unión-Fenosa, and ENSA, of which the state held a 40 percent share.

Bibliography

Economic Commission for Latin America and the Caribbean (ECLAC, or CEPAL). 2001. *Centroamérica: Estadísticas del Subsector Eléctrico, 2000*. Mexico City: ECLAC.

——. 2002. *Centroamérica: Estadísticas del Subsector Eléctrico, 2001*. Mexico City: ECLAC.

——. 2003. *Centroamérica: Estadísticas del Subsector Eléctrico, 2002*. Mexico City: ECLAC.

——. 2004. *Centroamérica: Estadísticas del Subsector Eléctrico, 2003*. Mexico City: ECLAC.

——. 2005. *Centroamérica: Estadísticas del Subsector Eléctrico, 2004*. Mexico City: ECLAC.

——. 2006. *Centroamérica: Estadísticas del Subsector Eléctrico, 2005*. Mexico City: ECLAC.

——. 2007. *Centroamérica: Estadísticas del Subsector Eléctrico, 2006 – Informe Preliminar*. Mexico City: ECLAC.

——. 2008. *Centroamérica: Estadísticas del Subsector Eléctrico, 2007*. Mexico City: ECLAC.

——. 2009. *Centroamérica: Estadísticas del Subsector Eléctrico, 2008*. Mexico City: ECLAC.

——. 2010. *Centroamérica: Estadísticas del Subsector Eléctrico, 2009*. Mexico City: ECLAC.

——. 2011. *Centroamérica: Estadísticas del Subsector Eléctrico, 2010*. Mexico City: ECLAC.

——. 2012. *Centroamérica: Estadísticas del Subsector Eléctrico, 2011*. Mexico City: ECLAC.

——. 2013. *Centroamérica: Estadísticas del Subsector Eléctrico, 2012*. Mexico City: ECLAC.

——. 2014. *Centroamérica: Estadísticas del Subsector Eléctrico, 2013*. Mexico City: ECLAC.

——. 2015. *Centroamérica: Estadísticas del Subsector Eléctrico, 2014*. Mexico City: ECLAC.

——. 2016. *Estadísticas de Producción de Electricidad de los Países del Sistema de la Integración Centroamericana (SICA) - Datos Preliminares a 2015*. Mexico City: ECLAC.

Ito, K. 2014. "Do Consumers Respond to Marginal or Average Price? Evidence from Nonlinear Electricity Pricing." *American Economic Review* 104 (2): 537–63.

Michalet, C., and O. Bouin. 1991. "Rebalancing the Public and Private Sectors: Developing Country Experience." Development Centre, Organisation for Economic Co-operation and Development, Paris.

World Bank. 2010. *Central American Regional Programmatic Study for the Energy Sector: General Issues and Options—Sector Overview*. Washington, DC: World Bank.

Zhang, Y, C. Kirkpatrick, and D. Parker. 2008. "Electricity Sector Reform in Developing Countries: An Econometric Assessment of the Effects of Privatization, Competition and Regulation." *Journal of Regulatory Economics* 33 (2): 159–78.

CHAPTER 3

The Fiscal Impact of Electricity Subsidies in Central America

Ewa Korczyc, Marco Antonio Hernández Oré, Laura Olivera, and Luis Rizo Patrón

Central American governments collect less fiscal revenue than their peers in Latin America and worldwide, yet nearly all Central American countries spend an important share of their budgets on electricity subsidies. The preferential tax treatment of the electricity sector and the contingent liabilities that public utilities generate compound the fiscal costs of electricity subsidies. Moreover, these costs are rarely justified, because the regressive distribution and structurally procyclical nature of electricity subsidies undermine the efficiency and equity objectives of fiscal policy. In a context of tight fiscal constraints, electricity subsidies come at a high opportunity cost in terms of public investment and social services, and even the most conservative estimates indicate that spending on electricity subsidies significantly exceeds spending on flagship social programs. Reforming electricity subsidy schemes—or eliminating them altogether—would enable Central American governments to rebuild fiscal buffers, reinforce medium-term macroeconomic sustainability, and help accelerate poverty reduction.

Central American Electricity Subsidies in the International Context

This section evaluates the cost of electricity subsidies in Central America and situates them in the international context. The analysis reveals that the average cost of electricity subsidies in Central America exceeds the average for Latin America and the Caribbean (LAC). Although the cost of subsidies declined in 2015 because of low global oil prices, subsidy spending continued to consume a large share of government revenues and contributed to high fiscal deficits across the region. Faced with tight fiscal constraints and an uncertain global outlook, it is important to reevaluate the costs and benefits of electricity subsidy regimes.

Globally, the explicit fiscal cost of energy subsidies reached an estimated average of US$540 billion per year between 2012 and 2014. In LAC, this cost is estimated at more than US$74 billion, 70 percent of which was devoted to fuel subsidies while 30 percent supported the electricity sector. Central American countries spent a combined US$1.25 billion per year on energy subsidies between 2012 and 2014, with the bulk of subsidy spending devoted to supporting the electricity sector.

The cost of electricity subsidies in Central America increased rapidly from 2010 to 2014 as rising oil prices drove up the cost of existing subsidy regimes, intensifying political pressure to create new subsidies to shield households from higher electricity prices.[1] Estimates derived from the International Monetary Fund's (IMF's) global database on energy subsidies suggest that, from 2011 to 2014, as oil prices hit record levels, the cost of electricity subsidies in Central America reached an average of US$1.3 billion, or 1 percent of the region's aggregate GDP (figure 3.1).[2] Although subsidy spending in Central America declined to approximately US$1.1 billion in 2015, following a steep drop in international oil prices and implementation of subsidy reforms, the fiscal cost of energy subsidies remains high, particularly given the low revenue-to-GDP ratios of most Central American countries (figure 3.2). Box 3.1 presents key concepts about electricity subsidies and the data sources used in this study.

The fiscal cost of electricity subsidies in Central America should be examined in the context of the common fiscal characteristics of the six countries in the region. The first common characteristic is the small size of public revenues as a share of GDP. From 2011 to 2015, Central America's average revenue-to-GDP ratio was 18.8 percent, the lowest of any region in the world and a full 10 percentage points below the LAC average and the average for emerging markets and developing countries worldwide.[3] The second common feature is

Figure 3.1 Electricity Subsidies as a Percentage of Gross Domestic Product, 2011–14 Average

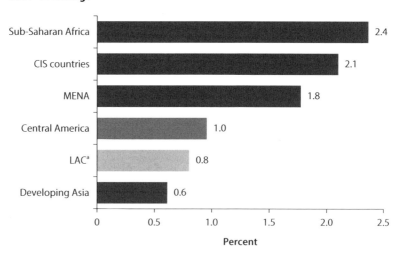

Source: World Bank elaboration based on International Monetary Fund data.
Note: The regional average is a simple average. Country coverage reflects data availability. A list of regional aggregates is provided in annex 3A.
a. Latin America and the Caribbean (LAC) excludes Central American countries.

Figure 3.2 Ratios of Revenue to Gross Domestic Product, 2011–15 Average

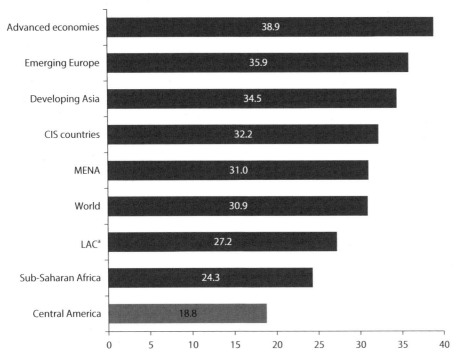

Source: World Bank elaboration based on the International Monetary Fund's World Economic Outlook.
a. Latin America and the Caribbean (LAC) excludes Central American countries.

Box 3.1 Electricity Subsidies: Key Concepts, Definitions, and Data Sources

Policy makers can influence electricity prices using both on-budget and off-budget subsidies. On-budget subsidies are explicit transfers from the government to producers or consumers, which are recorded in the national budget. In many cases, governments establish consumer prices that are below the cost of production and then compensate electricity companies for supplying the power. Sometimes subsidy benefits are directly transferred to households. As discussed in the second section of chapter 4, a government can also provide off-budget subsidies in the form of tax exemptions for electricity companies or tax credits for investment. These subsidies are implicit, because they reflect tax expenditures and are not accounted for as budgetary expenditures.

The most common method of estimating the cost of subsidies is known as the price-gap approach, which compares actual consumer prices with production costs and then multiplies that differential by the volume of electricity consumed to obtain the level of subsidies. Although conceptually straightforward, the price-gap approach faces numerous practical limitations.[a] As a result, subsidy estimates based solely on price-gap measurements may differ from those in budget execution documents.

box continues next page

Fiscal and Welfare Impacts of Electricity Subsidies in Central America
http://dx.doi.org/10.1596/978-1-4648-1104-3

Box 3.1   Electricity Subsidies: Key Concepts, Definitions, and Data Sources *(continued)*

This chapter uses a combination of data sources to estimate the cost of electricity subsidies. International comparisons are based on country-level data from the International Monetary Fund's energy subsidies database, which provides estimates of the cost of electricity subsidies in approximately 90 countries (annex 3A). Furthermore, to facilitate a detailed discussion of the fiscal costs of electricity subsidies in Central America, this chapter presents a new data set that was compiled for the six countries in the region: Costa Rica, El Salvador, Guatemala, Nicaragua, Honduras, Panama. This new data set provides estimates of the cost of residential and nonresidential electricity subsidies, using the price-gap approach, that are based on country-specific assumptions regarding tariff rates and production costs and estimates of the indirect costs of subsidies resulting from the favorable tax treatment of the electricity sector. Taken together, these estimates provide a comprehensive picture of the overall cost of electricity subsidies in Central America.

a. These limitations include measurement challenges in estimating the data necessary to calculate an accurate price gap and effects that the price-gap approach does not capture. Measurement challenges are amplified for goods that are not commonly traded internationally, such as electricity, and in these cases, price-gap calculations generally use the long-run cost of production as a proxy. This is a complex, data-intensive exercise, especially in countries with a variety of energy sources. In addition, subsidies or other distortions in prices for intermediate inputs or factors of production may affect long-run costs. Other measurement considerations include adjustments for domestic tax rates. Price-gap estimates do not capture the full spectrum of electricity subsidies. For example, the price-gap approach captures only the net effect of subsidy policies on electricity prices while distortions in other factor prices are ignored (Koplow 2009).

the large share of taxes in total revenue. Taxes represent an average of approximately 73 percent of total revenue in Central America, well above the rate for any other region, and in Costa Rica and Guatemala, taxes account for more than 90 percent of total revenue. The third common characteristic of Central American countries is the limited scope of their monetary policy. Panama and El Salvador have fully dollarized economies, whereas Costa Rica, Honduras, and Nicaragua use crawling-peg exchange rate mechanisms that constrain their monetary policy latitude, leaving fiscal policy as the primary tool for macroeconomic management. Guatemala operates a managed floating exchange rate mechanism, although it has maintained a relatively stable exchange rate vis-à-vis the U.S. dollar. The overall limited scope of monetary policy requires fiscal buffers to ensure macroeconomic sustainability.

The limited budgetary resources and persistent fiscal deficits that most countries in the region experience underscore the high cost of electricity subsidies. Fiscal imbalances in Central America increased significantly during the global financial crisis (box 3.2). Combined with tight revenue constraints, rising deficits amplified the fiscal pressures that electricity subsidies generate. Although budgetary resources and fiscal costs vary according to country, electricity subsidy spending in Central America represents an average of 4.8 percent of total revenues, 1.4 percentage points more than the LAC average (figure 3.3). Moreover, Central America's electricity subsidies represent an average of 6.6 percent of tax revenues, compared to a LAC average of 4.6 percent. As a result, electricity subsidies have contributed significantly to fiscal deficits.

Box 3.2 The Global Financial Crisis, Fiscal Balances, and Electricity Subsidy Policies in Central America

The 2008–09 global financial crisis highlighted crucial fiscal weaknesses throughout Central America. However, despite their high fiscal costs, the region's electricity subsidy regimes proved difficult to reform. Like many of their peers in Latin America and the Caribbean, most Central American countries have not returned to their precrisis growth rates. Although it is likely that countercyclical fiscal policies attenuated the worst effects of the crisis, they also eroded fiscal buffers, threatening macroeconomic stability and debt sustainability (De la Torre, Ize, and Pienknagura 2015). The aggregate regional fiscal deficit rose from 1.5 percent of GDP in the precrisis period to more than 3 percent from 2009 to 2015, prompting all six Central American countries to pursue major fiscal adjustments (figure B3.2.1). Policy makers strove to cut expenditures while protecting effective poverty-reduction initiatives and growth-focused investments in infrastructure and human capital, but electricity subsidy schemes remained largely intact as political pressure to protect households from macroeconomic shocks mounted. In a postcrisis context marked by high fiscal imbalances, slow growth, and depressed revenues, reforming or eliminating subsidy regimes remains an urgent priority.

Figure B3.2.1 Fiscal Balances and Ratios of Debt to Gross Domestic Product in Central America, 2005–09 and 2010–15

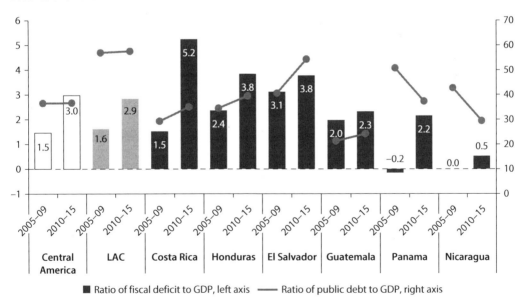

Source: World Bank elaboration based on data from World Economic Outlook.
Note: Fiscal deficit is shown as a positive value. LAC = Latin America and the Caribbean.

Figure 3.3 Electricity Subsidies as a Share of Total Revenues, Tax Revenues, and Fiscal Deficits, 2011–14 Average

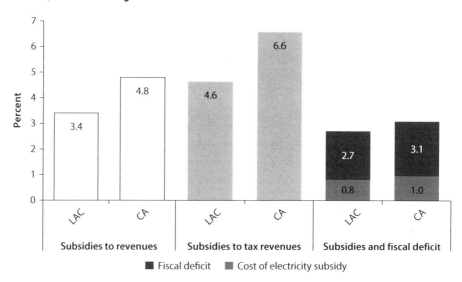

■ Fiscal deficit ■ Cost of electricity subsidy

Source: World Bank elaboration based on data from the International Monetary Fund's Subsidy Database and data from the Organisation for Economic Co-operation and Development and the World Bank.
Note: Fiscal deficit is shown as a positive value. CA = Central America; LAC = Latin America and the Caribbean, excluding Central America.

The cost of electricity subsidies in Central America has especially important implications in the context of tight fiscal constraints. Countries with limited resources must carefully prioritize and continuously improve the efficiency of public spending, yet electricity subsidies are often poorly targeted, generate price distortions, and contribute to negative environmental externalities (see chapter 1). Moreover, the heavy reliance on tax revenues common in Central American countries increases the sensitivity of fiscal policy to economic shocks, and the direct link between subsidies and global energy prices exacerbates the vulnerability of the budget. Finally, Central American countries' limited capacity to use monetary policy increases the importance of using fiscal instruments to respond to exogenous shocks and smooth the business cycle. This can be especially challenging in countries with weak institutions, because the success of electricity pricing mechanisms depends on the degree to which rules and norms are implemented in practice.[4]

Calculating the Cost of Electricity Subsidies in Central America

This section provides estimates of the cost of electricity subsidies for each of the six Central American countries. First, using the price-gap approach, we estimate the average cost of electricity subsidies provided to the residential sector. We also provide estimates for the cost of nonresidential subsidies, which sometimes become cross-subsidies that arise when nonresidential consumers are charged above-cost tariffs that indirectly subsidize residential consumption. Second, we identify the drivers of changes in subsidy costs from 2012 to 2015. Finally, we estimate the total cost of electricity subsidies by supplementing the price-gap estimates of the subsidies with an assessment of tax expenditures. Overall, the analysis reveals that the total fiscal cost of electricity subsidies in Central America is substantial, especially when information on tax expenditures is taken into account. Moreover, the total cost of electricity subsidies can vary significantly across countries and over time.

Methodology

Although the IMF's global database can provide insight into the aggregate cost of electricity subsidies, which is useful for international comparisons, a more detailed, country-specific methodology can deliver more precise estimates at the national level. Global estimates of subsidy levels derived using a price-gap approach are often based on simplified assumptions and may exclude important contextual factors. By contrast, country-specific approaches that use multiple data sources and methodologies can offer a more comprehensive picture of electricity subsidies in each country. For this study, new estimates using the price-gap approach were prepared for each of the six Central American countries, and other indirect costs of subsidizing electricity production and consumption were analyzed to calculate the total cost of subsidies.

This chapter presents country-specific models based on the price-gap approach for Central America that incorporate structural factors and policy decisions that affect electricity supply costs and pricing mechanisms. These include each country's energy mix and market structure, as well as the role of the public and private sectors in electricity generation, transmission, and distribution. For example, in Honduras and Costa Rica, the public sector plays a dominant role in the transmission and distribution of electricity, whereas in the other four Central American countries, electricity generation and distribution have been largely privatized, and the public sector dominates only in transmission. Similarly, the countries differ with respect to their reliance on fossil fuels. Close to 60 percent of Honduras's electricity comes from fossil fuels, whereas in Costa Rica, more than 90 percent of electricity generation comes from renewable energy sources, especially hydroelectric and geothermal power.

Box 3.3 summarizes the methodology used to obtain the cost estimates. A detailed description of the methodology for each country is included in annex 3B.

The Price-Gap Approach in the Six Central American Countries

Residential electricity subsidies in Central America cost an average of 0.6 percent of GDP from 2012 to 2015,[5] although fiscal costs varied significantly across countries.[6] Costa Rica uses a full cross-subsidy within the residential sector, and its net cost to the government was zero on average during this period. Guatemala spent on average 0.3 percent of GDP per year on residential electricity subsidies. El Salvador and Panama each spent on average approximately 0.4 to 0.5 percent of GDP per year. Honduras and Nicaragua spent the most on residential electricity

---

Box 3.3 Methodology for Estimating Electricity Subsidy Costs in Central American Countries

The **price-gap approach** estimates the difference between the average electricity tariff paid by consumers and a reference price of production. As such, price-gap estimates capture the magnitude of the price distortion generated by subsidies. The overall level of subsidies is obtained by multiplying the price gap by total consumption. The formula for determining the level of subsidies using the price-gap methodology is:

$$S_t = (PB_t - PT_t) * UC_t$$

and

$$PB_t = AVG_t + AVT_t + AVD_t$$

where S_t is the cost of the subsidy and PB_t is the reference price, which attempts to measure the true economic cost of production. In the case of electricity, this reflects the average cost of generation (AVG_t), transmission (AVT_t), and distribution (AVD_t).[a] PT_t is the marginal consumer tariff, and UC_t represents the total quantity of electricity sold or electricity consumed. We provide estimates of the level of subsidies using the price-gap approach for the residential and nonresidential sectors.

A positive difference between costs and prices indicates a subsidy, because the tariff is less than the cost of supply, whereas a negative difference indicates an effective tax, because the tariff is greater than the cost of supply.

The price-gap approach also allows us to estimate the cost of cross-subsidies between different groups of consumers. The estimated costs of residential and nonresidential electricity subsidies are presented on a net basis, which means that, in this analysis, we do not show the cross-subsidies within sectors that arise when different groups of customers are subject to different tariffs; instead, we focus on the net estimates for the whole sector.

Indirect subsidy costs in the form of tax expenditures (stemming from tax exemptions) are calculated by comparing the actual revenue from the given tax with the hypothetical revenue that would be obtained using the prevailing tax rate. These calculations are static and do not include price elasticity effects.

Commercial losses are estimated using available reports and studies on the electricity sector in each country.

All data sources are listed in annex 3B.

a. Cost estimates obtained for this study from the regulators are calculated as the efficient cost-recovery price for generation, transmission, and distribution, and as such, they do not take into account inefficiencies arising from technical and nontechnical losses.

---

subsidies, on average 1.1 percent of GDP per year. The results based on the price-gap approach for the six Central American countries are shown in figure 3.4.

In some countries, nonresidential (industrial and commercial) sectors pay above-cost electricity tariffs, thereby cross-subsidizing residential consumption. This can alleviate the total fiscal cost of subsidy schemes, but can limit economic competitiveness.[7] As explained in box 3.3, the nonresidential price gap can be positive (a subsidy) or negative (a cross-subsidy). In El Salvador and Honduras, for example, the price-gap estimates show that the industrial and commercial sectors paid above-cost tariffs. In El Salvador, although the cross-subsidy lowered the fiscal cost of the residential subsidy scheme by more than 60 percent, it also imposed a substantial burden on nonresidential consumers. In Honduras, high industrial tariffs undermine the productivity of the industrial sector by increasing production costs, especially in higher energy intensity activities (see Hernandez Ore, Sousa, and Lopez 2015). This can lead to economic losses and divert investments to neighboring countries with lower industrial electricity prices.

Panama and Nicaragua subsidize the residential and nonresidential sectors, which compounds the total fiscal cost of their electricity subsidy schemes. From 2012 to 2015, the fiscal cost of nonresidential electricity subsidies was 0.3 percent of GDP in Nicaragua and 0.05 percent of GDP in Panama (figure 3.4). Hence, like residential subsidies, nonresidential subsidies involve additional fiscal costs in these two countries.

Electricity Subsidy Spending over Time

The cost of electricity subsidies estimated using the price-gap approach declined between 2012 and 2015 in all six Central American countries, as production costs fell and governments reformed their subsidy schemes. The cost of electricity subsides dropped by an average of more than 0.5 percentage point of GDP from 2012 to 2015 (figure 3.5). As noted above, the price-gap methodology reflects

Figure 3.4 Fiscal Cost of Electricity Subsidies, by Country, as a Percentage of Gross Domestic Product, 2012–15 Average

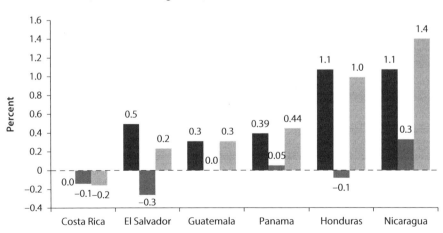

Source: World Bank elaboration based on data from country authorities.
Note: The level of subsidies estimated using the price-gap approach for Honduras was augmented with the cost of direct subsidies to the residential sector in 2014–15. For details, see annex 3B.

Figure 3.5 Cost of Electricity Subsidies Based on Price-Gap Approach in Central America and International Oil Prices, 2011–15

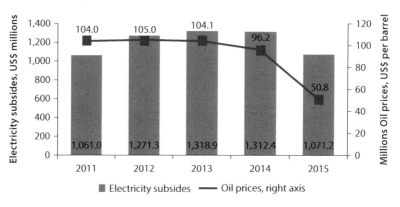

Source: World Bank elaboration based on data obtained from country authorities.

the difference between production costs and consumer prices, multiplied by the volume of electricity consumed. Consequently, the recent decline in the cost of subsidies was a result of a combination of two factors affecting the costs and prices of electricity. First, the rapid decline in the prices of oil during 2014–15 led to a decline in the generation costs of electricity. Second, some governments in the region increased their electricity tariffs, which narrowed the gap between production costs and consumer prices.

Country-specific variables affected the pace and magnitude of the decline in subsidy costs. Falling oil prices had a much bigger impact in countries that rely heavily on fossil-fuel-based thermal generation, such as Honduras, Panama, Nicaragua, and El Salvador (figure 3.6). Similarly, the price-setting mechanisms used in each country influenced the speed of the adjustment. For example, Panama's regulations and price-setting mechanisms tend to reduce the sensitivity of electricity production costs to international oil prices. Whereas Panama revises its electricity cost estimates every two years, Honduras revises its reference fuel prices every two weeks, which intensifies the pass-through effect of oil prices on electricity costs. As a result, the decline in oil prices had a swifter, more pronounced effect in Honduras than in Panama, and a similar trend would be expected if oil prices were to rise. Policy decisions can also influence cost adjustments, especially the design of the price-setting mechanism.

In addition to estimating the total fiscal cost of electricity subsidies, the price-gap approach can distinguish between the effects of policy reforms and changes in production costs.[8] Overall, changes in production costs affected subsidy spending more than policy reforms, as falling oil prices drove the decline in residential subsidy costs over the period. Tariff reforms in Panama and Honduras helped reduce the cost of subsidies, but their effect was relatively modest. Meanwhile, El Salvador lowered its tariff rates in 2015, which would have increased subsidy spending had it not been for the decline in production costs.

Figure 3.6 Cost of Electricity Subsidies Based on Price-Gap Approach, by Country, as a Percentage of Gross Domestic Product, 2012–15

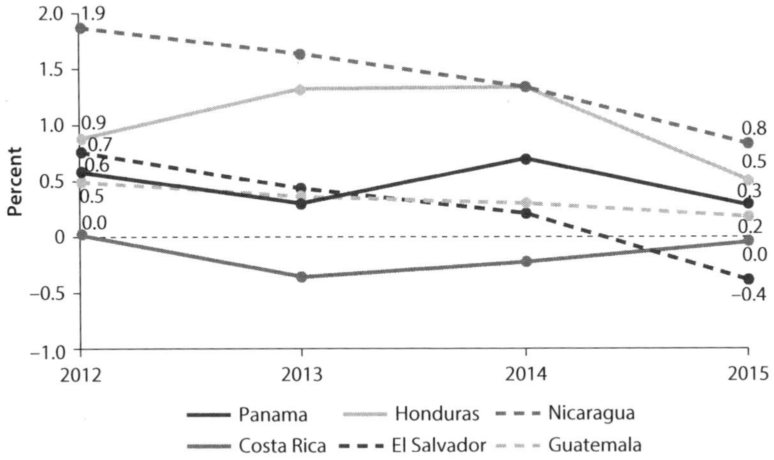

Source: World Bank elaboration based on data obtained from country authorities.
Note: The estimates of electricity subsidies for Honduras using the price-gap method were augmented with the cost of direct subsidies to the residential sector in 2014–15. For details, see annex 3B.

Further details on subsidy dynamics in each country are provided below. The analysis of the drivers of the changes in the level of subsidies estimated using the price-gap approach is presented in figure 3.7.

Costa Rica: Costa Rica's electricity sector does not require budgetary support, because above-cost tariffs on high-volume residential consumers entirely finance subsidies that low-volume residential consumers receive. Moreover, a modest negative price gap in the industrial and commercial sectors indicates that electricity tariffs generate a small amount of fiscal revenue. Prices are set quarterly by the regulator and reflect the costs of electricity provision. Costa Rica's reliance on renewable energy sources insulates it from oil-price volatility, although electricity costs remain vulnerable to weather-related shocks.

El Salvador: Electricity subsidies cost El Salvador an average of 0.2 percent of GDP from 2012 to 2015. This reflects a large degree of cross-subsidization, with above-cost tariffs on high-volume residential consumers and other market segments offsetting more than 60 percent of the cost of residential subsidies. As falling oil prices reduced generation costs, the net subsidy turned negative, yielding a fiscal gain of approximately 0.4 percent of GDP in 2015.

Guatemala: The annual cost of electricity subsidies in Guatemala averaged approximately 0.3 percent of GDP from 2012 to 2015. The subsidies are provided to households that are eligible for the subsidized flat "social tariff." Other consumers are charged according to the standard tariffs that reflect efficient cost structure. Subsidy spending declined gradually, from 0.5 percent of GDP in 2012 to 0.2 percent in 2015, as falling oil prices reduced generation costs, and social tariffs remained constant.

Figure 3.7 Contribution of Changes in Tariffs and Costs of Electricity Provision to Changes in Cost of Residential Subsidies

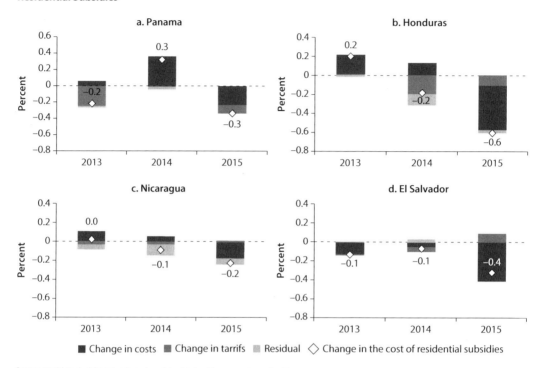

Source: World Bank elaboration based on data obtained from country authorities.
Note: The subsidy estimates derived using the price-gap approach for Honduras were augmented with the cost of direct subsidies to residential sector in 2014–15. For details, see annex 3B. Residual reflects changes in nominal GDP and energy consumption.

Panama: The annual cost of electricity subsidies in Panama averaged 0.4 percent of GDP, with significant annual fluctuations reflecting changes in production costs and in the tariff structure. Subsidy spending fell from 0.6 percent of GDP in 2012 to 0.3 percent in 2013 as the government increased tariffs for high-volume consumers, then rose to a peak of 0.7 percent in 2014 as surging oil prices increased production costs, before falling to 0.3 percent in 2015. The 2013 tariff reform drove the overall decline in subsidy costs that year, whereas the 2014 increase was solely attributable to rising production costs. The 2015 tariff reform was responsible for approximately one-third of the decline in subsidy costs.

Honduras: Honduras spent an average of 1 percent of GDP per year on electricity subsidies. High oil prices pushed subsidy spending to approximately 1.3 percent of GDP in 2013–14, but the subsequent drop in oil prices substantially reduced generation costs. This, combined with reforms of the direct subsidy scheme, reduced the fiscal cost of electricity subsidies to approximately 0.5 percent of GDP in 2015. Pre-2015 increases in the cost of electricity subsidies were attributable to rising oil prices. The sharp drop in subsidy spending in

2015 was due to a combination of tariff reforms (20 percent) and lower production costs (80 percent).

Nicaragua: At 1.4 percent of GDP, the cost of electricity subsidies in Nicaragua was the highest in the region from 2012 to 2015. Tariffs for the residential and nonresidential sectors are largely inflexible vis-à-vis market conditions, which contributes to the relatively high cost of the country's subsidy regime, although rising oil prices in 2013–14 had a relatively minor impact on the overall cost of subsidies, in part because of the country's successful diversification into renewable energy sources, including wind, geothermal, hydropower, and biomass. Fossil fuels declined from 60 percent of the energy mix in 2012 to approximately 48 percent in 2014. Nevertheless, falling oil prices in 2014 reduced subsidy costs in 2015.

Strategies for managing price risk and the use of price-stabilization funds can mitigate some of the impact of changes in electricity production costs on subsidy spending. Risk-sharing mechanisms can attenuate the pass-through effects of oil-price volatility, and price-stabilization funds can help rationalize pricing policies and enable governments to shift toward market-based electricity pricing formulas, although stabilization funds may be susceptible to political pressures.[9] When oil prices drop, the public may expect an instant decrease of the same magnitude in electricity prices, without considering the recapitalization needs of electricity companies or the importance of building reserves against future oil price increases. Moreover, these instruments cannot fully contain a large, protracted increase in production prices, and even a well-capitalized stabilization fund may require further government transfers. An effective strategy for managing price risk should reflect these concerns (Di Bella et al. 2015).

Effective policies over the medium and long terms should focus on addressing volatile energy generation costs, which are the main source of electricity price volatility. Structural reforms to reduce vulnerability to shocks in international oil prices are aimed at reducing oil consumption over the longer term. The most common approaches include energy portfolio diversification from oil-fired power generation, investing in energy efficiency, and increased regional integration with countries with more-diversified supply (Yépez-García and Dana 2012). These instruments provide the potential to reduce exposure to high and volatile oil prices, although making such a structural transition would entail considerable upfront costs to utilities, firms, and households, which would require supportive policies and regulations for renewable energy and energy efficiency.

Indirect Subsidy Costs

All Central American countries except Guatemala subsidize electricity consumption through preferential tax rates. In Costa Rica and Nicaragua, low-volume residential electricity consumption (under 250 kWh in Costa Rica and 300 kWh in Nicaragua) is fully tax exempt, and high-volume consumption is subject to a reduced sales tax rate. Similarly, electricity sales to a large majority of residential

Fiscal and Welfare Impacts of Electricity Subsidies in Central America
http://dx.doi.org/10.1596/978-1-4648-1104-3

consumers in Honduras are tax exempt. In El Salvador and Panama, fuel used to generate electricity is exempt from import duties, and Panama also exempts fuel from domestic sales tax.

Tax exemptions for electricity companies represent a significant indirect fiscal cost that is not captured through the price-gap methodology or official budget documents. The fiscal impact of tax exemptions is not directly comparable across countries, because estimates are based on the prevailing average tax rates in each country. Nonetheless, the estimates provided in this section quantify the cost of tax expenditures that result from tax exemptions, which has especially important implications in countries with tight fiscal envelopes (figure 3.8). Panama's tax expenditures averaged an estimated 0.2 percent of GDP from 2012 to 2015, with sales tax exemptions accounting for close to 80 percent and import tax exemptions making up the rest. In Honduras, tax expenditures averaged approximately 0.43 percent of GDP from 2012 to 2015. El Salvador's tax expenditures were more modest, at approximately 0.1 percent of GDP, because only fuel imports are tax exempt. Similarly, tax expenditures represented approximately 0.1 percent of GDP in Costa Rica and 0.2 percent in Nicaragua from 2012 to 2015 (figure 3.9).

Total Fiscal Impact: Combining Price Gap Estimates and Indirect Costs

Adding the tax expenditures (tax exemptions) to net electricity subsidies, considered to be indirect fiscal costs, yields the total fiscal cost for each country (figure 3.10). In Honduras, the total cost is 1.4 percent of GDP (a cost derived from the price-gap approach of 1 percent of GDP plus 0.4 percent of GDP of tax expenditures). In Panama and Nicaragua, subsidies for residential and nonresidential consumers, combined with relatively large tax exemptions, push the total cost to 0.6 percent and 1.6 percent of GDP, respectively. In El Salvador, a modest price gap in the residential sector and substantial cross-subsidization by

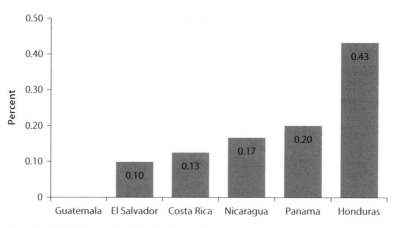

Figure 3.8 Tax Exemptions as a Percentage of Gross Domestic Product, 2012–15 Average

Source: World Bank elaboration based on data obtained from country authorities.

Figure 3.9　Total Tax Revenues and Tax Exemptions as a Percentage of Gross Domestic Product, 2012–15 Average

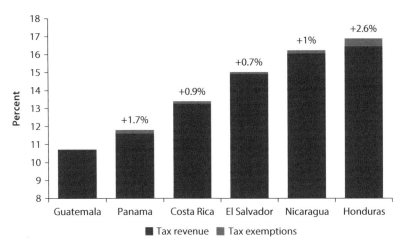

Figure 3.10　Composition of Cost of Electricity Subsidies as a Percentage of Gross Domestic Product, 2012–15 Average

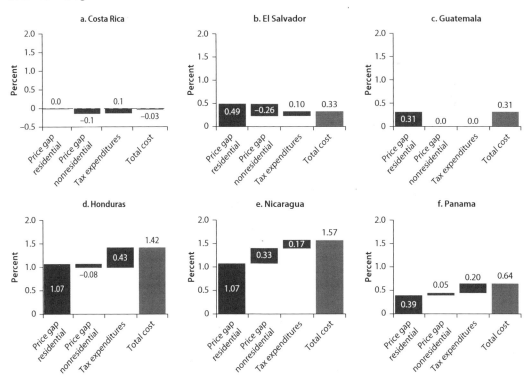

Fiscal and Welfare Impacts of Electricity Subsidies in Central America
http://dx.doi.org/10.1596/978-1-4648-1104-3

industrial and commercial consumers keep the total cost relatively low, at just 0.3 percent of GDP. Guatemala offers no tax exemptions or cross-subsidies, and thus the price-gap estimate is equal to the total cost (0.3 percent of GDP). In addition, the estimates of the fiscal cost of subsidies can be augmented with the estimates of the fiscal impact of nontechnical losses (box 3.4).

Box 3.4 Fiscal Impact of Nontechnical Losses

Not all electricity subsidies are the result of an explicit policy. Unmetered electricity connections, uncollected electric bills, and other forms of electricity theft, fraud, and payment evasion can act as implicit subsidies to certain consumers. Collectively known as "nontechnical losses," electricity theft and nonpayment can threaten the financial sustainability of electricity companies, leading to a vicious cycle in which low revenues erode the administrative capacity of the electricity company, which further weakens its ability to identify unmetered connections and collect arrears. Large nontechnical losses often prompt governments to provide fiscal support to electric utilities, and because the government is effectively covering the bill for illegal connections and nonpaying consumers, this support constitutes an implicit subsidy—one that the price-gap methodology does not record.

From a policy perspective, nontechnical losses are distinct from other electricity subsidies, because they reflect administrative failure rather than a deliberate policy decision. In Honduras, the fiscal cost of nontechnical losses related to illegal connections from 2012 to 2015 averaged approximately 1.4 percent of GDP, equivalent to the amount spent on residential electricity subsidies. According to Beylis and Cuhna (forthcoming), half of all nontechnical losses in Honduras are due to deliberate electricity theft, with more than 100,000 unmetered connections in the country, and unrecoverable arrears account for the other half. Nevertheless, nontechnical losses in Honduras appear to be gradually declining. In El Salvador, nontechnical losses amount to approximately 0.2 percent of GDP. Nontechnical losses in Costa Rica, Guatemala, and Panama are negligible (figure B3.4.1).

Figure B3.4.1 Impact of Nontechnical Losses on Total Electricity Subsidies as a Percentage of Gross Domestic Product, 2012–15 Average

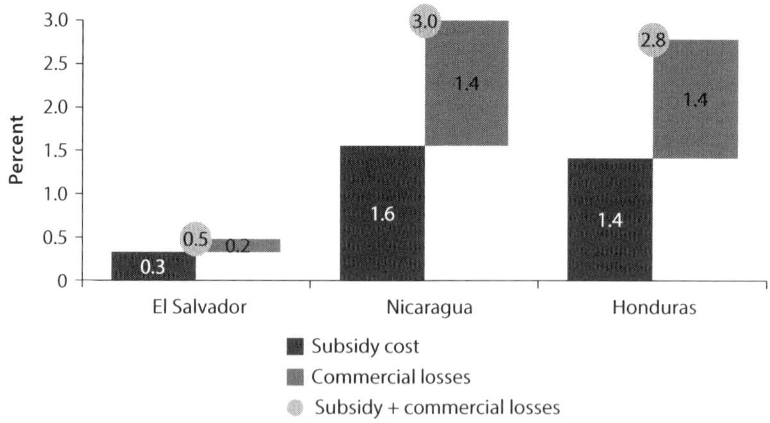

Source: World Bank elaboration based on data obtained from country authorities.

Fiscal Policy Implications of Electricity Subsidies

This section analyzes the role of electricity subsidies in reinforcing macroeconomic stability, shielding households from energy-price volatility, and promoting economic equity by supporting the electricity consumption of poorer households. It also discusses the opportunity costs of spending on electricity subsidies versus alternative policies for achieving the same fiscal objectives.

Electricity Subsidies, Household Consumption, and Macroeconomic Stability

One common objective of residential electricity subsidies is to reinforce macroeconomic stability by shielding household consumption from the impact of energy-price shocks. Unpredictable fluctuations in energy prices stemming from global oil price volatility or exogenous factors (e.g., severe weather conditions in the case of countries that depend on hydropower)[10] can cause electricity generation costs to increase rapidly. Rising electricity prices could significantly constrain household budgets and reduce private consumption, slowing the growth of domestic demand. Residential electricity subsidies can prevent this by stabilizing consumer prices. Under a subsidy regime, the government absorbs some or all of the increase in generating costs, shifting the impact of energy price volatility from household budgets to the government budget. In addition to the explicit cost of price-stabilizing subsidies, the government's obligation to recapitalize utility companies and cover nontechnical losses may be a source of contingent liabilities, compounding the fiscal cost of price stabilization.

The effectiveness of subsidies in stabilizing prices depends on the design and implementation of the pricing mechanism and on the government's fiscal capacity to absorb fluctuations in energy prices.[11] The extent and speed with which changes in generation costs affect the price of supplying electricity to consumers determines the degree of stabilization that a subsidy regime can provide, although the government's budgetary situation may constrain its ability to stabilize prices, because spending on subsidies, especially during periods of persistently high oil prices, can undermine fiscal sustainability. Box 3.5 summarizes Panama's recent experience with its price stabilization fund.

Indirect electricity subsidies do not contribute to the stabilizing role of explicit subsidies, and they may increase fiscal risks and undermine macroeconomic stability. Subsidizing production inputs or eliminating taxes and custom duties on oil products reduces electricity prices but does not smooth price fluctuations.[12] Moreover, the fiscal cost of tax expenditures erodes the government's capacity to manage price fluctuations, intensifying the risk that price stabilization will prove unsustainable.

There is also some evidence pointing to a procyclical nature of electricity subsidies, which may further undermine their contribution to macroeconomic stability. Although data on the cost of electricity subsidies over time are scarce, subsidy spending tends to correlate with fluctuations in oil prices, which often increase during economic booms. In such circumstances, increased spending on electricity subsidies might be structurally procyclical and might worsen the

Box 3.5 Fiscal Implications of Panama's Price Stabilization Fund

In the mid-2000s, Panama, like many of its peers, implemented price-stabilization mechanisms to address the global spike in oil prices. In 2004, the government implemented the Tariff Stabilization Fund (Fondo de Estabilización Tarifaria, FET) to address the address the large and growing cost of electricity generation. The FET targeted households consuming less than 400 kWh, for whom it established a fixed tariff based on a reference oil price of US$40 per barrel. The government compensated electricity companies directly for the difference between the actual price of oil and the reference price. In 2008, as oil prices reached historic levels, the FET was extended beyond its initial 4-year period. In 2011, a second fund was created, the Energy Compensation Fund (Fondo de Compensación Energética, FACE), which targeted industrial and commercial consumers with consumption levels above 400 kWh.

In 2014, the government spent a total of US$240 million (0.6 percent of GDP) on the FET and FACE programs, an unsustainable amount given Panama's low levels of tax revenue. When oil prices eventually declined in 2015, the government replaced FACE with a new fund, the Fund for the Occidental Region (Fondo Tarifario de Occidente, FTO), which targeted consumers in the country's western region, who face higher structural electricity costs. The FTO cut subsidy expenditures by US$178 million (0.4 percent of GDP), which helped reduce the country's fiscal deficit; but the FET, which is much more politically sensitive because it directly affects a large share of voters, remains in place. Although the FET is less costly than the FTO, it remains a large drain on government resources.

vicissitudes of the business cycle. In addition, countries that use energy subsidies tend to consume more energy relative to GDP, and thus rising oil prices generate a greater increase in economy-wide production costs (Matheny 2010). There is substantial evidence that electricity subsidies themselves contribute to energy-intensive and energy-inefficient forms of production, which further increase the cost of subsidies over the long term while amplifying their procyclicality.[13]

It seems that electricity subsidy spending in emerging economies is more procyclical than in advanced economies (figure 3.11). The "subsidy impulse," defined in box 3.6 as the difference in the subsidy expenditure-to-GDP ratios in two consecutive time periods, is positively correlated with real GDP growth rates in emerging economies, indicating that electricity subsidy spending is procyclical. By contrast, in advanced economies, subsidy spending appears to be neutral relative to the business cycle. The differences between emerging and advanced economies are statistically significant. Further research is necessary to investigate the cyclical features of electricity subsidies for different groups of countries.

Electricity Subsidies, Poverty, and Fiscal Equity

Electricity subsidies are often designed to promote poverty reduction and fiscal equity by reducing the cost of electricity for lower-income households. Subsidy regimes across Central America use various targeting mechanisms to ensure that

Figure 3.11 Electricity Subsidies and the Economic Cycle

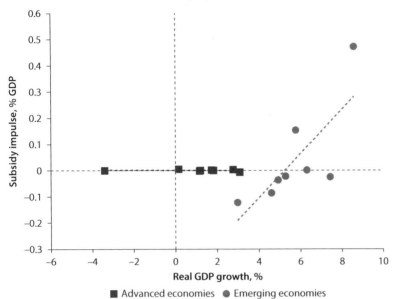

a. Real gross domestic product (GDP) growth rate and electricity
subsidy impulse, 2007–14

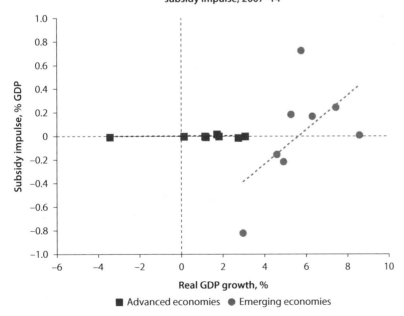

b. Real gross domestic product (GDP) growth rate and fossil fuel
subsidy impulse, 2007–14

Source: World Bank elaboration based on data from country authorities and the International Monetary Fund's Global Subsidy Database.

Box 3.6 Energy Subsidy Impulse

One of the main objectives of fiscal policy is to ensure macroeconomic stability to promote sustained growth and maintain low inflation rates. To achieve this goal, policy makers use countercyclical stabilization policies designed to moderate economic expansions and mitigate recessions. Stabilization policies employ a range of fiscal tools—including taxes, subsidies, and mandatory and discretionary expenditures—to smooth the business cycle.

The fiscal impulse indicator, or the change in the fiscal balance as a percentage of GDP, is a useful instrument to evaluate whether fiscal policy is achieving its countercyclical goals. When this indicator is positive, fiscal policy is deemed expansionary; when it is negative, it is considered contractionary. If this indicator is positive during an economic downturn, the government's fiscal stance is countercyclical. If it is positive when the economy is booming, the government's fiscal stance is procyclical (see figures B3.6.1 and B3.6.2).

Figure B3.6.1 Procyclical Fiscal Policy

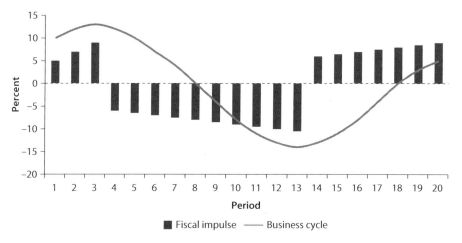

Figure B3.6.2 Countercyclical Fiscal Policy

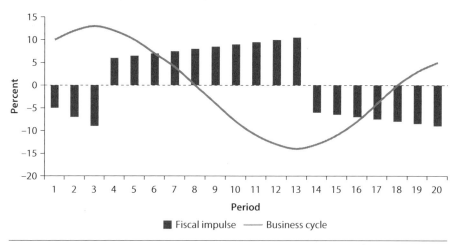

box continues next page

Box 3.6 Energy Subsidy Impulse *(continued)*

To analyze the effect of electricity subsidies on the economic cycle, an equivalent indicator can be constructed. The energy subsidy impulse (ESI) is defined as the difference in the electricity subsidy expenditure-to-GDP ratios in two consecutive periods of time:

$$ESI_{it} = \frac{S_{it}}{GDP_{it}} - \frac{S_{i(t-1)}}{GDP_{i(t-1)}}$$

S_{it} represents the pretax electricity subsidy cost in the $i-th$ country or region during period t, and GDP_{it} represents the nominal GDP in that same country or region during the same time period. When the ESI indicator is positive, electricity subsidies make fiscal policy more expansionary; when it is negative, they make fiscal policy more contractionary.

---

subsidy benefits reach poor households. The most common of these is to charge lower tariff rates to low-volume consumers, because the amount of electricity that households consume is systematically correlated with their income level.

Nevertheless, as noted in chapter 1 and described in more detail in chapter 4 for the specific case of the Central American countries, electricity subsidies are regressive and are an ineffective or even counterproductive means of reducing poverty and promoting fiscal equity. Even when low-volume consumers pay lower tariff rates, wealthier households with higher levels of electricity consumption tend to benefit most from subsidies. Moreover, the fact that a significant share of the poorest households in Central America lack a metered connection to an electricity grid substantially weakens the impact of subsidies on poverty reduction. Globally, the poorest 20 percent of households receive only approximately 8 percent of total subsidies to fossil-fuel consumption (OECD/IEA. 2011. *World Energy Outlook*. IEA Publishing. Licence: www.iea.org/t&c), whereas more than 50 percent of subsidy benefits accrue to the wealthiest 20 percent of households (Arze del Granado, Coady, and Gillingham 2012).

In many cases, electricity subsidies further diminish the already limited impact of fiscal policy on poverty and equity objectives. The Commitment to Equity (CEQ) methodology analyzes the effect of fiscal policy on poverty and inequality by measuring changes in income before and after application of different types of taxes and expenditures (Lustig and Higgins 2013; box 3.7). Across Central America, fiscal policy has a modest—and in some cases, negative—effect on poverty rates and fiscal equity. The net effect of fiscal policy (including direct and indirect taxes, social security contributions, transfers and indirect subsidies) on poverty and extreme poverty rates in Central American countries is generally modest, but in most cases, fiscal policy worsens poverty indicators (figure 3.12). Fiscal policy raises poverty rates in Central America by an average of 2.4 percentage points, compared with just 0.03 percentage point in the rest of Latin America. Similarly, the effect of fiscal policy on inequality, as measured according to the decline in the Gini coefficient, is negligible or modestly negative in most Central

Box 3.7 The Commitment to Equity Methodology

The Commitment to Equity (CEQ) methodology analyzes the effect of fiscal policies on poverty and inequality by measuring changes in income before and after fiscal policies are applied. Household income is measured at five stages: (a) market income, which is the income households receive before taxes and transfers; (b) net income, which is market income minus direct taxes and social security contributions (excluding pensions); (c) disposable income, which is net income plus direct government transfers; (d) postfiscal income, which is disposable income plus indirect subsidies minus indirect taxes; and (e) final income, which is postfiscal income plus the value of free public services such as education and health care minus any applicable user fees.

The CEQ methodology reveals the effect of fiscal policy on poverty rates at each of these five stages, and it measures the distributional effect through changes in the Gini coefficient. By isolating subsidy spending from other poverty-alleviating expenditures, such as transfers and public services, the CEQ methodology can shed light on the effect of electricity subsidies on poverty and equity.

Figure 3.12 (A) Moderate and (B) Extreme Poverty Rates, and (C) the Gini Coefficient before and after Fiscal Policy, Circa 2011–12

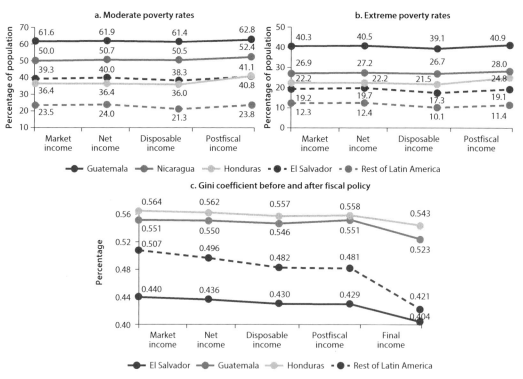

Source: ICEFI 2016.
Note: Moderate and extreme poverty rates are calculated according to poverty lines of US$4 and US$2.5 per day, respectively, in purchasing power parity terms.

American countries, unlike in the rest of Latin America, where fiscal policy tends to reduce inequality. A comparison of the aggregate effect of fiscal policy in El Salvador, Guatemala, Honduras, and Nicaragua with that in regional comparator countries reveals the extent to which fiscal policy in Central America tends to exacerbate poverty. A more detailed discussion of the redistributive aspects of electricity subsidies is presented in chapter 4.

Gauging the Opportunity Cost of Electricity Subsidies

Devoting limited public resources to electricity subsidies entails important policy trade-offs. These trade-offs are particularly acute in Central American countries, given their limited fiscal envelopes and considerable development challenges. When deciding whether to devote scarce resources to electricity subsidies, policy makers must weight the benefits against those of alternative policy options. One common policy goal of electricity subsidy regimes is to shield household consumption from macroeconomic shocks, but the resources devoted to subsidies could instead be used to reduce fiscal imbalances and build reserves for countercyclical stabilization. Another frequent objective of electricity subsidies is to promote fiscal equity and reduce poverty, but subsidies consume revenue that could be used to fund infrastructure investment, health and education services, and social protection programs, or a range of other policies with clear poverty and equity implications.

Limited budgetary resources intensify the importance of public expenditure trade-offs. Central America has the lowest revenue-to-GDP ratio of any region in the world, and the cost of subsidies is high. For example, electricity subsidies consume almost 6 percent of tax revenues in Nicaragua and approximately 4 percent in Honduras (figure 3.13). Electricity subsidies are also costly relative to fiscal deficits, and in Nicaragua, eliminating them would turn a modest fiscal deficit into a substantial surplus (figure 3.14). Reforming electricity subsidies was an important element of Honduras's fiscal consolidation strategy from 2013 to 2015, and even Guatemala and Panama, which spend less on electricity subsidies than their peers, could markedly improve their fiscal position by eliminating electricity subsides.

Comparing subsidy spending with alternative expenditure options capable of generating similar benefits—including cash-transfer programs, greater education spending, and greater investment in research and development—can clarify the opportunity cost of electricity subsidies. Impact evaluations have found that cash-transfer programs (including conditional cash transfers) can significantly reduce poverty while providing incentives for human capital investment and promoting better social development outcomes for poor people. Depending on their design, conditional cash transfers can increase school enrollment rates, reduce child labor, improve child health and nutrition indicators, and bolster household consumption (Rawlings and Rubio 2003). There is also robust evidence that increasing education spending can boost long-term economic growth rates, regardless of what other expenditures are reduced to accommodate it (Acosta-Ormaechea and Morozumi 2013). Finally, public investment research

Figure 3.13 Spending on Electricity Subsidies and Tax Revenues, by Country, as a Percentage of Gross Domestic Product, 2012–15 Average

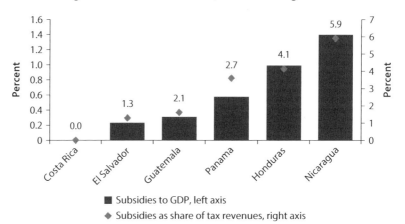

■ Subsidies to GDP, left axis
◆ Subsidies as share of tax revenues, right axis

Source: World Bank elaboration based on data obtained from country authorities and data from the International Monetary Fund's World Economic Outlook Database (October 2016).
Note: Electricity subsidy estimates shown in the figures are derived using the price-gap approach and reflect residential and nonresidential subsidies.

Figure 3.14 Spending on Electricity Subsidies and Fiscal Deficits, by Country, as a Percentage of Gross Domestic Product, 2012–15 Average

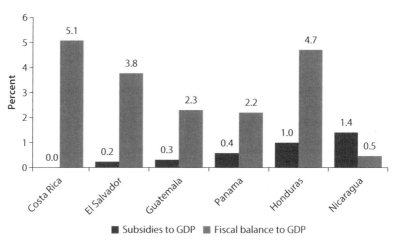

■ Subsidies to GDP   ■ Fiscal balance to GDP

Source: World Bank elaboration based on data obtained from country authorities and data from the International Monetary Fund's World Economic Outlook Database (October 2016).
Note: Electricity subsidy estimates shown in the figures are derived using the price-gap approach and reflect residential and nonresidential subsidies.

and development can accelerate growth by enhancing factor productivity and improving production quality (Coccia 2010).

Spending on electricity subsidies in Central America often equals or even exceeds spending on cash transfers, education, and research and development. For example, Panama spends more on electricity subsidies than it does on its three major cash-transfer programs combined,[14] and El Salvador, Guatemala, and Honduras all spend more on electricity subsidies than they do on social transfers. In Nicaragua, electricity subsidy spending roughly equals the annual budget allocation for secondary and postsecondary education. Public expenditures on research and development in Central America (where data are available) account for a minor share of GDP (figure 3.15). Chapter 6 presents further analysis comparing the effectiveness of spending on electricity subsidies with that of spending on other social programs regarding poverty reduction.

Eliminating electricity subsidies would enable Central American governments to advance important fiscal policy and macroeconomic management objectives. Reducing or eliminating electricity subsidy schemes could help curb fiscal deficits and improve medium-term debt sustainability. For example, simplified simulations show that ending electricity subsidies could reduce Nicaragua's public debt stock by 8.6 percentage points below the baseline projection by 2021 (figure 3.16).[15] If electricity-related tax exemptions were

Figure 3.15 Public Spending on Electricity Subsidies, Cash-Transfer Programs, Education, and Research and Development in Central America as a Percentage of Gross Domestic Product, 2011–13 Average

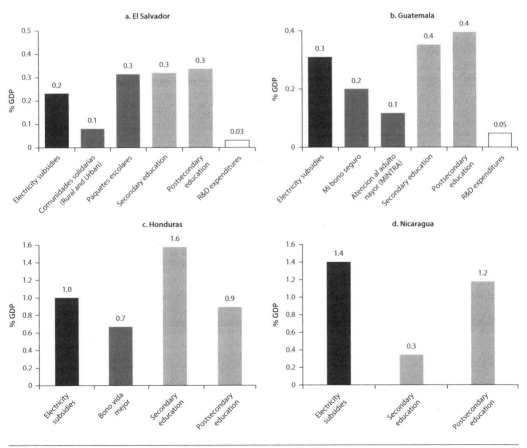

figure continues next page

Figure 3.15 Public Spending on Electricity Subsidies, Cash-Transfer Programs, Education, and Research and Development in Central America as a Percentage of Gross Domestic Product, 2011–13 Average *(continued)*

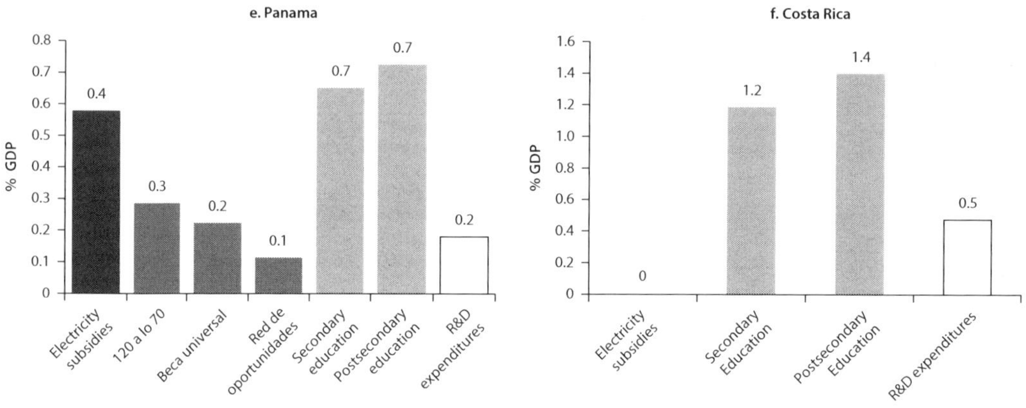

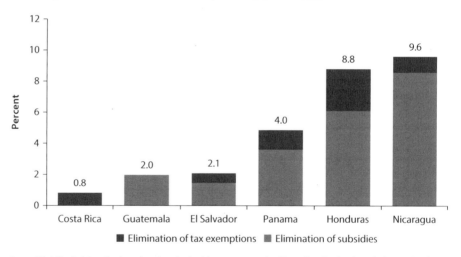

Source: World Bank elaboration based on the World Bank Atlas of Social Protection Indicators of Resilience and Equity database.
Note: Data on spending on research and development refers to 2011 and was derived from the World Bank's World Development Indicators database. Data on spending on subsidies were derived using the price-gap approach and include residential and nonresidential sectors. Labels in this figure reported in Spanish are specific social programs in each country.

Figure 3.16 Projected Reduction in Public Debt–to–Gross Domestic Product Ratios in 2021 If Electricity Subsidies and Related Tax Exemptions Were Eliminated

Source: World Bank elaboration based on data obtained from country authorities and on the data from the International Monetary Fund's World Economic Outlook Database, October 2016.
Note: The subsidy reform scenario assumes no spending on electricity subsidies after 2015. The annual average fiscal cost of electricity subsidies is calculated using the price-gap approach.

also eliminated, Nicaragua's debt-to-GDP ratio would fall by almost 10 percentage points (figure 3.17). In both scenarios, this fiscal adjustment would shift the public debt stock to a downward trajectory. These simulations project similar improvements in medium-term fiscal sustainability in all six Central American countries.

Figure 3.17 Projected Public Debt–to–Gross Domestic Product Ratios under the Baseline and Subsidy Reform Scenarios, 2015 and 2021

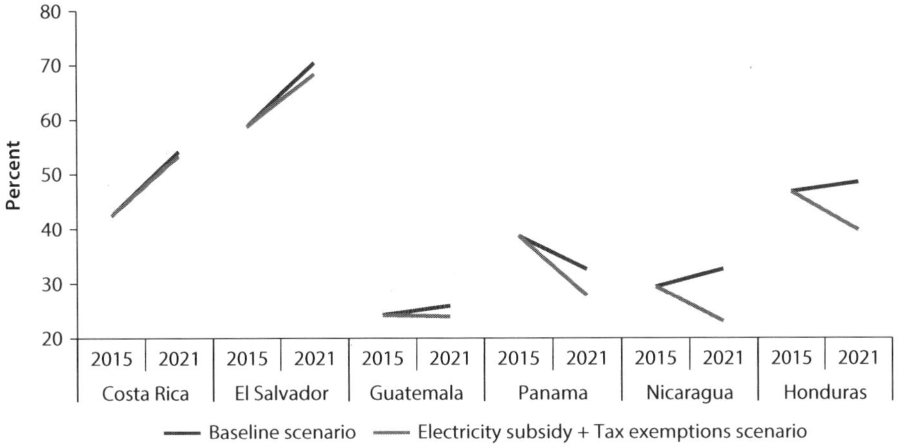

Source: World Bank elaboration based on data obtained from country authorities and on the data from the International Monetary Fund's World Economic Outlook Database, October 2016.
Note: The subsidy reform scenario assumes no spending on electricity subsidies after 2015. The annual average fiscal cost of electricity subsidies is calculated using the price-gap approach.

Conclusion

The impact of electricity subsidies on fiscal policy objectives does not justify the cost they impose on resource-constrained governments in Central America. Subsidy regimes are typically designed to promote poverty reduction and improve fiscal equity or to reinforce macroeconomic stability by shielding households from price shocks, yet electricity subsidies are largely ineffective and even counterproductive regarding both objectives. Electricity subsidies consume a large share of the modest budgets of Central American countries, crowding out spending on other social and economic development policies and straining already weak fiscal balances. Including the implicit costs of electricity-related tax exemptions and the contingent liabilities that public electricity utilities generate reveals the full extent of the fiscal burden that electricity subsidies impose.

In almost all Central American countries, electricity subsidies systematically favor wealthier households while failing to reach a significant share of poor households. Throughout the region, the poorest households are also the most likely to lack access to a metered electricity connection, and therefore are the most likely to derive no benefit from electricity subsidies. In all countries, the contribution of electricity subsidies to poverty reduction is negligible, and most subsidy regimes worsen income inequality. Even in the case of Costa Rica, which has full cross-subsidization within the residential sector combined with a near-total electrification rate, it is likely that the electricity pricing mechanism is less effective than other policy options.

Central American governments could greatly enhance the efficiency and equity impact of fiscal policy by reallocating subsidy spending to programs such as social cash transfers, education, and research and development. Cash transfers can shift resources from wealthier to poorer households with greater accuracy and efficiency than electricity subsidies. Increasing education spending can boost economic growth more effectively, and investment in research and development can have a far greater impact on the structural transformation of Central American economies.

Electricity subsidies are similarly ineffective as a means of reinforcing macro-economic stability. Electricity subsidy spending is structurally procyclical. Although subsidies may protect household budgets from the immediate effects of an increase in electricity costs, they tend to exacerbate the vicissitudes of the business cycle. Moreover, subsidies do not eliminate price volatility but merely shift it from household budgets to the government budget; and with limited fiscal buffers, governments may need to cut subsidies abruptly in the event of a shock, which could significantly affect household budgets. Overall, in countries with large fiscal imbalances and limited revenue capacity, increasing the government budget's exposure to price volatility can have negative implications for fiscal stability and debt sustainability.

Similar to their poverty and equity objectives, alternative policies would better serve the macroeconomic stabilization goals of electricity subsidies. Establishing or adding to existing stabilization funds would increase the government's capacity for countercyclical fiscal policy. If measures to shield households from severe price shocks are warranted, direct cash transfers can accomplish this goal far more efficiently than electricity subsidies—without distorting electricity prices. The following chapters explore these issues in greater detail.

Annex 3A: Regional Aggregates for International Benchmarking of Fiscal Costs of Electricity Subsidies

Electricity Subsidies: The International Monetary Fund (IMF) database includes information on the cost of electricity subsidies for 94 economies for 2011–15. Because there are a limited number of economies in the database representing advanced economies ($n = 2$) and emerging Europe ($n = 1$), the aggregates for these groups are not presented in the study.

Below is the composition of regional economy groupings:

- Central America ($n = 5$): El Salvador, Nicaragua, Honduras, Guatemala, and Panama
- Developing Asia ($n = 9$): Brunei Darussalam, Indonesia, Vietnam, Bangladesh, Malaysia, China, Thailand, India, and Sri Lanka
- Latin America and Caribbean (LAC, excluding Central America), ($n = 22$): Brazil, Ecuador, Paraguay, Dominica, Barbados, Colombia, Bolivia, the Bahamas, Grenada, St. Kitts and Nevis, Antigua and Barbuda, Argentina, República Bolivariana de Venezuela, Trinidad and Tobago, Suriname, Guyana, the Dominican Republic, Belize, Haiti, Mexico, Jamaica, and Peru

- Middle East, North Africa, and Pakistan ($n = 19$): Jordan, Afghanistan, the Arab Republic of Egypt, Kuwait, Oman, the United Arab Emirates, Saudi Arabia, the Islamic Republic of Iran, Djibouti, the Republic of Yemen, Algeria, Mauritania, Qatar, Lebanon, Tunisia, Bahrain, Pakistan, Libya, and Iraq
- Commonwealth of Independent States (CIS economies), ($n = 10$): Armenia, Belarus, Kazakhstan, Ukraine, Turkmenistan, Tajikistan, Azerbaijan, the Russian Federation, Uzbekistan, and the Kyrgyz Republic
- Sub-Saharan Africa ($n = 26$): Kenya, Botswana, Lesotho, Malawi, Ethiopia, Namibia, Mozambique, Tanzania, Madagascar, South Africa, Rwanda, Nigeria, Cameroon, the Democratic Republic of Congo, Zambia, Angola, Senegal, Uganda, Zimbabwe, Côte d'Ivoire, Burkina Faso, Mali, Cape Verde, the Republic of Congo, Republic of Gabon, and Benin

Fiscal Benchmarking: Data for the fiscal benchmarking were derived from the IMF's World Economic Outlook Database, October 2016; the World Bank's World Development Indicators database; the Organisation for Economic Co-operation and Development's Revenue Statistics; and, in rare cases, from individual economy reports of the IMF (Article IV).

The analysis covers 188 economies. Below is the composition of regional economy groupings:

- Advanced Economies ($n = 35$): Australia, Austria, Belgium, Canada, Cyprus, the Czech Republic, Denmark, Estonia, Finland, France, Germany, Greece, Hong Kong SAR, China, Iceland, Ireland, Israel, Italy, Japan, the Republic of Korea, Luxembourg, Malta, the Netherlands, New Zealand, Norway, Portugal, San Marino, Singapore, the Slovak Republic, Slovenia, Spain, Sweden, Switzerland, Taiwan, China, the United Kingdom, and the United States
- Middle East, North Africa, and Pakistan ($n = 21$): Afghanistan, Algeria, Bahrain, Djibouti, the Arab Republic of Egypt, the Islamic Republic of Iran, Iraq, Jordan, Kuwait, Lebanon, Libya, Mauritania, Morocco, Oman, Pakistan, Qatar, Saudi Arabia, Sudan, Tunisia, the United Arab Emirates, and the Republic of Yemen
- Sub-Saharan Africa ($n = 45$): Angola, Benin, Botswana, Burkina Faso, Burundi, Cameroon, Cabo Verde, the Central African Republic, Chad, the Comoros, the Republic of Congo, Cote d'Ivoire, the Democratic Republic of Congo, Equatorial Guinea, Eritrea, Ethiopia, Gabon, the Gambia, Ghana, Guinea, Guinea-Bissau, Kenya, Lesotho, Liberia, Madagascar, Malawi, Mali, Mauritius, Mozambique, Namibia, Niger, Nigeria, Rwanda, São Tomé and Príncipe, Senegal, the Seychelles, Sierra Leone, South Africa, Republic of South Sudan, Swaziland, Tanzania, Togo, Uganda, Zambia, and Zimbabwe
- Commonwealth of Independent States ($n = 12$): Armenia, Azerbaijan, Belarus, Georgia, Kazakhstan, the Kyrgyz Republic, Moldova, the Russian Federation, Tajikistan, Turkmenistan, Ukraine, and Uzbekistan
- Developing Asia ($n = 29$): Bangladesh, Bhutan, Brunei Darussalam, Cambodia, China, Fiji, India, Indonesia, Kiribati, the Lao People's Democratic Republic,

Malaysia, Maldives, the Marshall Islands, the Federated States of Micronesia, Mongolia, Myanmar, Nepal, Palau, Papua New Guinea, the Philippines, Samoa, the Solomon Islands, Sri Lanka, Thailand, Timor-Leste, Tonga, Tuvalu, Vanuatu, and Vietnam

- Emerging Europe ($n = 14$): Albania, Bosnia and Herzegovina, Bulgaria, Croatia, the Former Yugoslav Republic of Macedonia, Hungary, Kosovo, Latvia, Lithuania, Montenegro, Poland, Romania, Serbia, and Turkey
- Latin America and the Caribbean (LAC, excluding Central America) ($n = 26$): Brazil, Ecuador, Paraguay, Dominica, Barbados, Colombia, Bolivia, the Bahamas, Grenada, St. Kitts and Nevis, Antigua and Barbuda, Argentina, República Bolivariana de Venezuela, Trinidad and Tobago, Suriname, Guyana, the Dominican Republic, Belize, Haiti, Mexico, Jamaica, Peru, Chile, St. Lucia, St. Vincent and the Grenadines, and Uruguay
- Central America ($n = 6$): Costa Rica, El Salvador, Guatemala, Honduras, Nicaragua, and Panama

Annex 3B: Methodology for Estimating the Fiscal Cost of Electricity Subsidies in Central American Countries

This annex presents the methodology used to derive the estimates of the total cost of electricity subsidies in the Central American countries: Honduras, Panama, El Salvador, Costa Rica, Nicaragua, and Guatemala. First, we describe the price-gap methodology and present the main assumptions regarding the key variables (final prices and benchmark prices) for all the countries. Second, we present the methodology for compiling forgone revenues related to tax exemptions in the electricity sector.

Price-Gap Approach

As noted in the study, the price-gap approach is defined as the difference between the average electricity tariff that consumers pay and a reference price of production. As such, price-gap estimates capture the magnitude of the price distortion. The overall level of subsidies is obtained by multiplying the price gap by total consumption. The formula for determining the level of subsidies using the price-gap methodology is:

$$S_t = (PB_t - PT_t) * UC_t$$

and

$$PB_t = AVG_t + AVT_t + AVD_t$$

where S_t is the cost of subsidy; PB_t is the reference price, which reflects the average cost of generation (AVG_t), transmission (AVT_t), and distribution (AVD_t); PT_t is the price that the end user pays; and UC_t is total electricity sold or consumed. That difference is considered a subsidy if it is positive (if the tariff is less than the cost of supply) and a cross-subsidy if it is negative (if the tariff is greater than the cost of supply).

The application of the price-gap methodology, although conceptually straightforward, is fairly data intensive and requires multiple country-specific assumptions. The key assumptions regarding end-user prices (PT_t) and reference prices (PB_t) are provided in table 3B.1.

Cost estimates obtained for this study from the regulators were calculated as the efficient cost-recovery price for generation, transmission, and distribution, and as such do not take into account inefficiencies arising from elevated technical and high nontechnical losses.

Data availability guided the level of disaggregation of the price-gap calculations, which reflects publicly available information that energy sector regulators in respective countries provide. Because the levels are not directly comparable across countries (because they reflect specific features of the energy market regulations and sometimes pricing strategies), we also provide aggregated estimates of the cost of subsidies for residential and nonresidential sectors.

The detailed, country-by-country results follow.

Table 3B.1 Key Assumptions Regarding End-User Prices and Reference Prices, by Country

Country	End-user price	Cost of generation	Cost of transmission	Cost of distribution
Honduras	Revenues from electricity sales (adjusted by estimated government transfers in 2012 and 2013) divided by sales of electricity	System average generation cost; total amount billed by all private power generation companies	System average transmission costs	System average distribution costs
	Source: Empresa Nacional de Energía Eléctrica Annual Reports[a]	*Source:* Beylis and Cunha (forthcoming)		
Panama	Data on average tariff applied to customers obtained from regulator[b]	Estimate of average total cost (generation, transmission, distribution) obtained from regulator		
	Source: Autoridad Nacional de los Servicios Públicos			
El Salvador	Own calculations based on "notional" tariffs adjusted for existing legislation governing price formula for final users	Short-term operational marginal cost of electricity: energy price (variable) plus capacity charge	System average transmission costs	Own calculations based on data provided by regulatory entity
	Source: Own elaboration based on SIGET data[c]	*Source:* UT[d]	*Source*: Own elaboration based on SIGET data	
Costa Rica	Revenues from electricity sales divided by sales of electricity	Weighted public and private generators' average sales price	System average transmission costs	System average distribution costs
	Source: Own calculation based on ARESEP data[e]	*Source*: ARESEP	*Source*: ICE	*Source*: ICE

table continues next page

Table 3B.1 Key Assumptions Regarding End-User Prices and Reference Prices, by Country *(continued)*

Country	End-user price	Cost of generation	Cost of transmission	Cost of distribution
Nicaragua	2005 tariffs for households consuming up to 150 kWh month; average applied tariffs for residential customers consuming more than 150 kWh/month and other consumers	System average generation cost estimated by regulator	System average transmission cost estimated by regulator	Average distribution cost according to type of consumer estimated by staff, using methodology established by regulator
	Source: Instituto Nicaragüense de Energía data[f]	*Source*: Ministerio de Energía y Minas; Dirección de Mercado Eléctrico		*Source*: Own calculations
Guatemala	Final prices for beneficiaries of the social tariff; prices for other consumers calculated using information obtained from electricity sales	System average generation cost estimated by regulator	Derived from information on transmission annual costs and total electricity generated	Derived from nonsocial (cost-recovery) tariff and information on unit generation and transmission costs
	Source: Own calculations based on Comisión Nacional de Energía Eléctrica data			

Note: SIGET=Superintendencia General de Electricidad y Telecomunicaciones; ARESEP=Autoridad Reguladora de los Servicios Públicos; ICE= Instituto Costarricense de Electricidad.
a. Annual Reports by ENEE available at: http://www.enee.hn/index.php/planificacionicono;
2012: http://enee.hn/DireccionPlanificacion/index.html;
2013: http://www.enee.hn/planificacion/2014/EstadisticasAnuales2013/index.html;
2014: http://www.enee.hn/planificacion/2015/EstadisticasAnuales2014/index.html;
2015: http://www.enee.hn/planificacion/2017/estadisticas/EstadisticasAnuales2015/index.html.
b. Tabulations available at the website of the Autoridad Nacional de los Servicios Publicos: Estadísticas de Electricidad, http://www.asep.gob.pa/index.php?option=com_content&view=article&id=158&Itemid=154.
c. Data available at https://www.siget.gob.sv/temas/electricidad/documentos/estadisticas/, Boletin de Estadisticas Electricas No.17 año 2015.
d. http://www.ut.com.sv/reportes#.
e. Tabulations available at https://aresep.go.cr/electricidad/estadisticas.
f. Tabulations available at https://aresep.go.cr/electricidad/estadisticas.

Honduras

PT_t (the end-user paid price, i.e., the tariff) was calculated by dividing total revenue from electricity sales by sales of electricity. Revenues were corrected for 2012 and 2013 by the amount of the direct subsidy (the transfer that the government used to make to the electricity company to subsidize consumption of residential users consuming below 150 kWh per month. In 2014 and 2015, the subsidy mechanism changed, and the subsidy was no longer channeled through the electricity bill but instead through a direct transfer of 120 lempiras monthly to eligible households. The price-gap approach no longer captured the cost of this direct subsidy, so it was calculated separately. Hence, we present the cost estimate including the assessment of the direct subsidy in 2014 and 2015 separately. Throughout the study, the cost of the direct subsidy in 2014 and 2015 was integrated into the cost of the residential subsidies using the price-gap approach.

PB_t (the reference price) was obtained as a sum of the average cost of generation, transmission, and distribution for each type of consumer. The costs reflect system average unit costs that the regulator estimated. The average generation unit cost and the average transmission unit cost are fixed for all groups of consumers, and the distribution unit cost is variable. The data used to calculate the unit costs for 2012 and 2013 were derived from the Honduras Latin American and the Caribbean Economist Office Report (Beylis and Cunha, forthcoming). The authors calculated data for 2014 using the available cost structure of the Empresa Nacional de Energía Eléctrica (ENEE), and the data for 2015 were estimated assuming that the adjustment in unit costs of electricity transmission and distribution was proportional to the total cost reduction of ENEE and that the change in the unit cost of generation was proportional to the total cost reduction, excluding transmission, distribution, other expenditures, and depreciation.

UC_t = the electricity sales according to groups of consumers and the data were derived from the ENEE reports.

The results that this approach yielded are shown in table 3B.2.

El Salvador

The authors calculated PT_t (the end-user price paid, tariff) using the published tariff (notional tariff) and adjusting it for the existing legislation, which governs the price-setting formula for the final users. Specifically, for consumers in the first block (<50 kWh per month), the price was calculated as 10.5 percent of the indexed tariff plus 6.35 cents per kWh; for consumers using 50–100 kWh per month,

Table 3B.2 Cost Estimates of Electricity Subsidies, Honduras

	2012	2013	2014	2015	2012	2013	2014	2015
Cost category	PT_t: end-user paid price				PB_t: reference price			
Lempiras/kWh								
Residential	2.2537	2.2372	2.8540	3.0620	4.2118	4.5549	4.7736	3.9042
Commercial	4.6831	4.6632	4.6648	3.9784	4.2118	4.5549	4.7736	3.9042
Industrial	3.9282	3.9937	3.8929	3.4252	3.5117	3.7741	3.9474	3.0585
General high voltage	3.3960	3.3845	3.3607	2.8027	3.4101	3.6608	3.8275	2.9358
Government	5.0618	5.0873	5.0942	4.3407	4.2118	4.5549	4.7736	3.9042
Municipalities	4.7551	4.7878	4.8111	4.1368	4.2118	4.5549	4.7736	3.9042

	2012	2013	2014	2015	2012	2013	2014	2015
Cost category	$PB_t - PT_t$: price-gap structure				S_t: subsidies for electricity			
Lempiras/kWh								
Residential	1.9581	2.3177	1.9196	0.8422	4,221	5,140	4,214	1,907
Commercial	−0.4713	−0.1084	0.1088	−0.0743	−625	−149	152	−111
Industrial	−0.4166	−0.2196	0.0545	−0.3667	−306	−162	43	−292
General high voltage	0.0140	0.2763	0.4668	0.1331	11	232	416	128
Government	−0.8500	−0.5324	−0.3206	−0.4366	−188	−121	−73	−104
Municipalities	−0.5433	−0.2330	−0.0375	−0.2327	−29	−13	−2	−13
Total, lempiras					3,084	4,927	4,749	1,515
Total as % of GDP					0.9	1.3	1.2	0.3
Total including 2014–15 direct transfer					0.9	1.3	1.3	0.5
Residential					1.2	1.4	1.2	0.6
Nonresidential					−0.3	−0.1	0.1	−0.1

Source: World Bank elaboration based on data from country authorities.
Note: Residential cost as a share of GDP includes direct transfer subsidy in 2014–15.

Fiscal and Welfare Impacts of Electricity Subsidies in Central America
http://dx.doi.org/10.1596/978-1-4648-1104-3

the price was calculated as 10.5 percent of the indexed tariff plus 6.71 cents per kWh. The end-user price for consumers using 100–200 kWh per month was capped at the level of the prevailing tariff from 2011. The published tariffs were used for all other segments of users.

PB_t (the reference price) was the sum of the average cost of generation, transmission, and distribution for each type of consumer. The costs reflect system average unit costs that the regulator estimates.

UC_t (electricity that groups of consumers sell) was derived from Superintendencia General de Electricidad y Telecomunicaciones reports.[16]

This methodology yielded the results shown in table 3B.3.

Panama

PT_t (the end-user price paid) was obtained from the Autoridad Nacional de los Servicios Publicos and provided for each type of a tariff scheme[17]:

- Low-voltage, simple tariff
- Low-voltage, maximum-demand tariff
- Low-voltage tariff by hourly blocks
- Medium-voltage, maximum-demand tariff
- Medium-voltage tariff by hourly blocks
- High-voltage, maximum-demand tariff
- High-voltage, tariff by hourly blocks

Table 3B.3 Cost Estimates of Electricity Subsidies, El Salvador

	2012	2013	2014	2015	2012	2013	2014	2015
Cost category	PT_t: end-user paid price				PB_t: reference price			
US$/kWh								
Residential								
1–49 kWh/month	0.0969	0.0966	0.0968	0.0922	0.2987	0.2704	0.2730	0.2124
50–99 kWh/month	0.0964	0.0955	0.0955	0.0911	0.2716	0.2430	0.2350	0.1744
100–199 kWh/month	0.1505	0.1505	0.1505	0.1505	0.2457	0.2308	0.2224	0.1617
200–299 kWh/month	0.2471	0.2519	0.2508	0.2118	0.2558	0.2482	0.2399	0.1794
≥300 kWh/month	0.2492	0.2561	0.2545	0.2143	0.2580	0.2462	0.2379	0.1774
General low voltage	0.2374	0.2406	0.2404	0.1994	0.2410	0.2270	0.2188	0.1581
Public lighting	0.2411	0.2123	0.2185	0.1851	0.2497	0.2331	0.2250	0.1644
Low-voltage consumers (10–50 kW)	0.2864	0.2856	0.2977	0.2422	0.2097	0.1965	0.1883	0.1276
Low-voltage consumers (>50 kW)	0.2742	0.2673	0.3130	0.2547	0.2097	0.1965	0.1883	0.1276
Medium-voltage consumers (10–50 kW)	0.2213	0.2280	0.2308	0.1859	0.2097	0.1965	0.1883	0.1276
Medium-voltage consumers (>50 kW)	0.2035	0.2054	0.2079	0.1669	0.2097	0.1965	0.1883	0.1276
Special services	0.2315	0.2367	0.2534	0.2041	0.2097	0.1965	0.1883	0.1276

table continues next page

Table 3B.3 Cost Estimates of Electricity Subsidies, El Salvador *(continued)*

Cost category	2012	2013	2014	2015	2012	2013	2014	2015
	PB_t-PT_t: price-gap structure				S_t: subsidies for electricity			
US$/kWh								
Residential					168	140	127	48
1–49 kWh/month	0.2019	0.1738	0.1761	0.1203	24	22	18	13
50–99 kWh/month	0.1752	0.1476	0.1394	0.0833	90	79	77	48
100–199 kWh/month	0.0952	0.0803	0.0719	0.0112	49	43	39	6
200–299 kWh/month	0.0087	−0.0037	−0.0109	−0.0324	2	−1	−2	−6
≥300 kWh/month	0.0088	−0.0099	−0.0166	−0.0369	3	−3	−5	−13
General low voltage	0.0036	−0.0136	−0.0216	−0.0412	2	−6	−10	−19
Public lighting	0.0086	0.0208	0.0065	−0.0207	1	3	1	−3
Low-voltage consumers (10–50 kW)	−0.0767	−0.0891	−0.1094	−0.1147	−6	−7	−8	−8
Low-voltage consumers (>50 kW)	−0.0645	−0.0708	−0.1247	−0.1272	0	0	−1	−1
Medium-voltage consumers (10–50 kW)	−0.0116	−0.0315	−0.0425	−0.0583	−4	−10	−15	−22
Medium-voltage consumers (>50 kW)	0.0062	−0.0089	−0.0196	−0.0393	14	−21	−47	−99
Special services	−0.0218	−0.0402	−0.0651	−0.0765	0	0	0	0
Total, US$					175	98	47	−104
Total as % of GDP					0.7	0.4	0.2	−0.4
Residential					0.7	0.6	0.5	0.2
Nonresidential					0.0	−0.2	−0.3	−0.6

Source: World Bank elaboration based on data from country authorities.

For calculation of the residential subsidy, we assumed a total cost of the subsidy for low-voltage schemes (low-voltage, simple tariff; low-voltage, maximum-demand tariff; low-voltage tariff by hourly blocks).

PB_t (reference price) was obtained from the regulator and reflects the average cost of generation, transmission, and distribution for each type of tariff scheme.

UC_t (electricity sales by groups of consumers) was derived from Autoridad Nacional de los Servicios Publicos reports mentioned above.

This methodology yielded the results shown in table 3.B4.

Nicaragua

The authors calculated PT_t (end-user price paid) using the published tariffs for residential users consuming more than 150 kWh/month and other consumers. For households consuming up to 150 kWh month, 2005 tariffs were applied in accordance with the existing legislation. The information was derived from tabulations available at the website of the Instituto Nicaragüense de Energía.

PB_t (reference price) was obtained from the regulator for each group of customers.

Fiscal and Welfare Impacts of Electricity Subsidies in Central America
http://dx.doi.org/10.1596/978-1-4648-1104-3

Table 3B.4 Cost Estimates of Electricity Subsidies, Panama

Cost category	2012	2013	2014	2015	2012	2013	2014	2015
	PT_t: end-user paid price				PB_t: reference price			
US$/kWh								
Low-voltage, simple tariff	0.1425	0.1498	0.1508	0.1726	0.1888	0.1856	0.2197	0.2083
Low-voltage, maximum-demand tariff	0.1975	0.2355	0.2371	0.2255	0.2216	0.2382	0.2650	0.2264
Low-voltage tariff by hourly blocks	0.1743	0.2029	0.1997	0.2199	0.1977	0.2091	0.2190	0.2254
Medium-voltage, maximum-demand tariff	0.1660	0.1971	0.1970	0.2030	0.1888	0.2006	0.2219	0.2030
Medium-voltage tariff by hourly blocks	0.1382	0.1635	0.1694	0.1334	0.1811	0.2029	0.2479	0.1595
High-voltage, maximum-demand tariff	0.1277	0.1467	0.1466	0.1608	0.1488	0.1417	0.1647	0.1608
High-voltage tariff by hourly blocks	0.1008	0.1255	0.1202	0.1282	0.1211	0.1577	0.2119	0.1447

Cost category	2012	2013	2014	2015	2012	2013	2014	2015
	$PB_t - PT_t$: price-gap				S_t: subsidies for electricity			
US$/kWh								
Low-voltage, simple tariff	0.0463	0.0358	0.0689	0.0357	139	112	229	127
Low-voltage, maximum-demand tariff	0.0241	0.0027	0.0279	0.0009	48	6	57	2
Low-voltage tariff by hourly blocks	0.0234	0.0062	0.0193	0.0055	1	0	2	0
Medium-voltage, maximum-demand tariff	0.0228	0.0035	0.0249	0.0000	34	5	38	0
Medium-voltage tariff by hourly blocks	0.0429	0.0394	0.0785	0.0261	3	4	10	4
High-voltage, maximum-demand tariff	0.0211	−0.0050	0.0181	0.0000	3	−1	2	0
High-voltage tariff by hourly blocks	0.0203	0.0322	0.0917	0.0165	0	0	0	0
Total, US$					227	127	338	133
Total as % of GDP					0.6	0.3	0.7	0.3
Residential					0.5	0.3	0.6	0.3
Nonresidential					0.1	0.0	0.1	0.0

Source: World Bank elaboration based on data from country authorities.

UC_t (the electricity sales by groups of consumers) was derived from the website of the Instituto Nicaragüense de Energía.

This methodology yielded the results shown in table 3B.5.

Guatemala

PT_t (the end-user price paid) are equal the Social Tariff. Prices for other consumers were calculated using the information on revenue from electricity sales.

PB_t (the reference price) is equal to the nonsocial tariff, because according to information from the regulator, those consumers not covered by the Social Tariff pay the cost-recovery price.

UC_t (electricity sales by groups of consumers) was derived from the data provided by the Comisión Nacional de Energía Eléctrica.

This methodology yielded the results shown in table 3B.6.

Costa Rica

The authors calculated PT_t (end-user price paid) using data on revenues from electricity sales.

Table 3B.5 Cost Estimates of Electricity Subsidies, Nicaragua

Cost category	2012	2013	2014	2015	2012	2013	2014	2015
	PT_t: end-user paid price				PB_t: reference price			
Cdb/kWh								
Residential	2.3690	2.4618	2.5386	2.4902	5.4032	5.6825	5.8383	5.3256
Commercial	5.2042	5.7675	6.2568	6.1394	6.9922	7.2770	7.4497	6.7187
Industrial	4.7035	5.2126	5.6547	5.5495	5.3491	5.5616	5.6822	5.1479
Public lighting	6.8864	7.9329	8.0968	6.6255	7.7378	7.9326	8.0968	6.6258
Pumping and irrigation	4.6537	5.1574	5.5949	5.5678	4.6809	4.7238	4.9542	4.5545

Cost category	2012	2013	2014	2015	2012	2013	2014	2015
	$PB_t - PT_t$: price-gap				S_t: subsidies for electricity			
Cdb/kWh								
Residential	3.0342	3.2207	3.2997	2.8353	2,843	3,160	3,329	3,010
Commercial	1.7879	1.5095	1.1929	0.5794	1,208	1,077	875	449
Industrial	0.6457	0.3491	0.0274	−0.4017	441	245	20	−310
Public lighting	0.8514	−0.0002	0.0001	0.0003	67	0	0	0
Pumping and irrigation	0.0272	−0.4336	−0.6407	−1.0133	8	−124	−203	−348
Total, Cdb					4,566	4,358	4,021	2,802
Total as % of GDP					1.9	1.6	1.3	0.8
Residential					1.2	1.2	1.1	0.9
Nonresidential					0.7	0.4	0.2	−0.1

Source: World Bank elaboration based on data from country authorities.

Table 3B.6 Cost Estimates of Electricity Subsidies, Guatemala

Cost category	2012	2013	2014	2015	2012	2013	2014	2015
	PT_t: end-user paid price				PB_t: reference price			
Qtz/kWh								
Consumers with social tariff	1.1528	1.2829	1.2918	1.1393	1.9227	1.8431	1.7664	1.4330
Consumers without social tariff	1.9227	1.8431	1.7664	1.4330	1.9227	1.8431	1.7664	1.4330

Cost category	2012	2013	2014	2015	2012	2013	2014	2015
	$PB_t - PT_t$: price-gap				S_t: subsidies for electricity			
Qtz/kWh								
Consumers with social tariff	0.7699	0.5602	0.4746	0.2937	1,866	1,403	1,227	801
Consumers without social tariff	0.0000	0.0000	0.0000	0.0000	0	0	0	0
Total, Qtz					1,866	1,403	1,227	801
Total as % GDP					0.5	0.3	0.3	0.2
Residential					0.5	0.3	0.3	0.2
Nonresidential					0	0	0	0

Source: World Bank elaboration based on data from country authorities.

PB_t (reference price) was calculated using the average weighted generation cost of private and public generation companies that the Autoridad Reguladora de los Servicios Públicos provided; transmission and distribution costs were taken from the tabulations available at the regulator's website.[18]

UC_t (electricity sales by groups of consumers) and the data was derived from Grupo ICE reports.[19]

This methodology yielded the results shown in table 3B.7.

Tax Expenditures

Indirect subsidy costs in the form of tax exemptions were calculated using the tax expenditure method, which entails comparing the actual revenues from the given tax with the hypothetical revenues obtained using the benchmark (prevailing) tax rate.

There are two types of tax relief granted to the electricity sector: input and output relief. They may occur at different stages of electricity production, from generation through transmission to distribution. The most common input relief includes import tax exemption on fuels used for electricity generation and exemptions from the sales tax on domestic fuel purchases.

Output relief is applied to sales of electricity to consumers. In countries with a value-added tax (VAT) or goods and services tax (GST), where VAT/GST payers can claim the input tax, only the value of tax exemptions granted to final users (residential sector) is considered to be forgone revenue. The results are summarized in table 3B.8.

Table 3B.7 Cost Estimates of Electricity Subsidies, Costa Rica

	2012	2013	2014	2015	2012	2013	2014	2015
Cost category	PT_t: end-user paid price				PB_t: reference price			
Cln/kWh								
Residential	73.8288	89.7952	89.5631	84.3567	77.5310	83.5638	85.8265	85.5135
Commercial	87.0130	105.9873	105.4291	96.3461	77.5310	83.5638	85.8265	85.5135
Government	68.7292	81.3111	81.3250	78.3230	77.5310	83.5638	85.8265	85.5135
Municipalities	83.4775	88.6872	68.6034	65.1825	77.5310	83.5638	85.8265	85.5135

	2012	2013	2014	2015	2012	2013	2014	2015
Cost category	$PB_t - PT_t$: price-gap structure				S_t: subsidies for electricity			
Cln/kWh								
Residential	3.7022	−6.2314	−3.7366	1.1568	12,861	−21,662	−13,129	4,172
Commercial	−9.4820	−22.4236	−19.6026	−10.8327	−29,117	−70,634	−63,474	−36,984
Government	8.8018	2.2527	4.5015	7.1905	18,876	4,808	9,487	14,819
Municipalities	−5.9466	−5.1234	17.2231	20.3309	−1,385	−1,221	4,300	5,334
Total, Cln					1,234	−88,709	−62,815	−12,659
Total as % GDP					0.0	−0.4	−0.2	0.0
Residential					0.1	−0.1	0.0	0.0
Nonresidential					0.0	−0.3	−0.2	−0.1

Source: World Bank elaboration based on data from country authorities.

Table 3B.8 Type of Tax Relief Granted to the Electricity Sector, by Country

Country	Input relief		Output relief
	Import exemptions	Sales tax exemptions on intermediate inputs	Sales tax exemption
Honduras	✓		✓
Panama	✓	✓	✓
El Salvador	✓		
Nicaragua			✓
Costa Rica			✓
Guatemala			

Source: World Bank elaboration based on data from country authorities.

Honduras

For Honduras, we calculated the cost of two types of tax exemptions: import exemptions on fuels (heavy fuel oil, HFO, and diesel) used for electricity generation and sales tax exemptions from electricity sales.

To calculate import exemptions, we used the import tariff rate for petroleum according to the World Trade Organization (WTO) and applied it to the volume of HFO and diesel consumption used to generate electricity. The volume of HFO and diesel for 2012 is based on official statistics registered by the Ministry of Finance in Honduras. These were extrapolated to 2013–15 assuming an increase in the volume of fuels proportional to the thermal energy generated from 2013 to 2015 and the share of thermal energy in the Honduran energy generation mix. Average international prices of HFO and diesel that the National Institute of Statistics and Economic Studies reported were used. The average estimated cost of imports exemptions was 0.2 percent of GDP from 2012 to 2015.

To calculate the cost of sales tax exemptions from the sales of electricity, we used the sales tax rate (12 percent in 2012–13 and 15 percent in 2014–15), which was applied to the volume of electricity sold to residential consumers with consumption levels less than 750 kWh. The average estimated value of tax expenditures was 0.2 percent of GDP in 2012–15. Total tax exemptions for Honduras were 0.4 percent of GDP from 2012 to 2015.

Panama

Panama has a national VAT, called the Impuesto a la Transferencia de Bienes Muebles Corporales y la Prestación de Servicios, set at 7 percent. All crude oil and oil products, including fuels used for electricity generation, are exempt from the VAT. Electricity generation, distribution, and transmission are also explicitly exempt, but such exemptions do not constitute tax expenditures because, under the VAT system, they would be subject to input tax credit. In this study, we calculated forgone revenues related to tax exemptions on the imports of fuels (HFO) and tax exemptions on the sale of electricity.

Tax exemptions on sales of fuel: Because data for Panama were unavailable, we used average HFO consumption per kWh from El Salvador and Honduras

Fiscal and Welfare Impacts of Electricity Subsidies in Central America
http://dx.doi.org/10.1596/978-1-4648-1104-3

and applied it to Panama's electricity generation from fuels to obtain total HFO consumption. Then, we applied the average petroleum tariff (reported by the WTO for Panama) to the total consumption of heavy fuels and obtained the estimate of forgone tax revenues. Import exemptions were estimated at 0.04 percent of GDP in 2012–15.

Tax exemptions on sales of electricity were calculated using the standard sales tax rate and applying it to total revenues from sales of electricity (as reported by Autoridad Nacional de los Servicios Publicos) to residential consumers (defined as consumers with low-voltage tariff schemes). The average estimated cost of sales tax exemptions from 2012 to 2015 was approximately 0.16 percent of GDP. The total tax exemptions for Honduras were 0.2 percent of GDP from 2012 to 2015.

El Salvador

Raw materials used for electricity generation are exempt from import duties in El Salvador. The value of HFO was estimated using information on the volume of HFO consumption (derived from the Indicative Plan of Electric Generation for El Salvador, prepared by Consejo Nacional de Energy) and the international price of HFO (reported by the National Institute of Statistics and Economic Studies). The petroleum standard tariff of 6.9 percent (as reported by the WTO) was applied. The fiscal cost of this exemption is negligible, at approximately 0.1 percent of GDP in 2012–15.

Nicaragua

Nicaragua applies a base 15 percent VAT on goods, services, and imported goods. Residential electricity consumption between 300 kWh and 1,000 kWh per month is taxed at a preferential rate of 7 percent. Residential electricity consumption of less than 300 kWh is exempt from VAT, although consumers must pay VAT on their full consumption if they exceed 300 kWh. The estimated cost of tax exemptions is approximately 0.2 percent of GDP.

Costa Rica

Costa Rica has a 13 percent sales tax on all goods and some services. The tax is applied to electricity sales, although a preferential rate of 5 percent is applied to residential electricity customers. In addition, residential consumption of less than 250 kWh per month is fully exempt, although the tax is applied to the total consumption volume if more than 250 kWh is consumed. There is a tax on fuels used in electricity generation are required to pay the sales tax. The estimated cost of tax exemptions is approximately 0.13 percent of GDP.

Guatemala

Guatemala has a 12 percent VAT rate on goods and services consumed within the country, including electricity supply. A VAT is applied to sales of fuels used in electricity generation.

Notes

1. For definitions of subsidy concepts used in this chapter, see box. 3.1

2. Country-level estimates of the cost of energy subsidies were prepared using IMF (2015). The data set is publicly available at http://www.imf.org/external/np/fad /subsidies/data/codata.xlsx.

3. This comparison is based on World Bank classifications.

4. Di Bella et al (2015) ranked countries according to an index that averaged the countries' positions on a number of indicators and surveys of institutional quality and policies. These indicators included the *Institutional Investor*'s 2014 Country Credit survey, the World Bank's 2014 *Doing Business* report, the World Economic Forum's 2014 *Global Competitiveness Report*, the International Budget Partnership's 2012 Open Budget survey, Transparency International's 2014 Corruption Perception Index, and the World Bank's 2013 Worldwide Governance Indicators for the Rule of Law and Government Effectiveness dimensions. Costa Rica and Panama ranked above the regional median in the average measure of institutional quality. Honduras, Guatemala, El Salvador, and Nicaragua all ranked below the regional median.

5. Estimates presented in this chapter follow the price-gap methodology and may not fully capture total fiscal costs. For further information on the price-gap method, see Koplow (2009).

6. Although the price-gap approach allows analysts to determine the size of a subsidy or cross-subsidy at the individual consumer level, the analysis presented in this chapter focuses on the total cost of the subsidy for the residential and nonresidential sectors. All within-sector cross-subsidies are presented on a net basis. Between-sector cross-subsidies arise if the subsidy for the whole sector is negative.

7. The main nonresidential sectors are industry and commerce. Residential, industrial, and commercial electricity connections are separately metered and frequently subject to different tariff rates.

8. As noted above, this exercise assumes that policy makers can affect electricity tariffs only in the short term. In fact, policy decisions can affect the cost of providing electricity through strategic decisions on the composition and functioning of the country's energy market, but these decisions would only be implemented in the medium to long terms. Further details on the data and methodology are included in annex 3B.

9. For example, the experiences of Colombia (for diesel and gasoline) and Peru (for gasoline, diesel, and liquid petroleum gas) offer important lessons on stabilization funds. For more details on these country case studies, see Beylis and Cunha (forthcoming).

10. For example, drought conditions can raise energy prices in countries that rely on hydropower, such as Costa Rica.

11. Electricity tariffs are composed of a fixed rate and a variable rate. The fixed rate covers distribution and transmission costs, and the variable rate is a function of household consumption and generation costs.

12. In most cases, the national budget does not record tax expenditures, and therefore there is no publicly available information on the total size of subsides. Furthermore, the fiscal impact of electricity subsidies can stem from the government's obligation to cover the losses of the utility companies, which are often a contingent liability, especially when these are state-owned enterprises that do not have the same incentives as the private sector to generate profits. This lack of transparency limits the

accountability process, preventing a more active policy debate regarding the real cost of electricity subsidies (for more information, see Clements et al. 2013).

13. Sdralevich et al. (2014) show that energy subsidies in the Middle East and North Africa are procyclical and that oil-exporting countries exhibit greater procyclicality because of the lack of incentives for energy efficiency.

14. These programs target households in extreme poverty (Red de Oportunidades), students (Beca Universal), and older adults (120 a los 65).

15. The simulation results presented here are for illustrative purposes only and should not be considered actual projections at the country level. The analytical framework and underlying assumptions are designed to allow for a cross-country comparison. Data used in this exercise were derived from IMF (2016).

16. Data are available at https://www.siget.gob.sv/temas/electricidad/documentos/estadisticas/, Boletín de Estadisticas Electricas No.17 año 2015.

17. Tabulations are available at the website of the Autoridad Nacional de los Servicios Publicos: Estadísticas de Electricidad, http://www.asep.gob.pa/index.php?option=com_content&view=article&id=158&Itemid=154.

18. Tabulations are available at https://aresep.go.cr/electricidad/estadisticas.

19. Data are available at Información financier, http://www.grupoice.com/.

Bibliography

Acosta-Ormaechea, S., and A. Morozumi. 2013. *Can a Government Enhance Long-Run Growth by Changing the Composition of Public Expenditure?* IMF Working Paper 13/162, International Monetary Fund, Washington, DC.

Arze del Granado, F., D. Coady, and R. Gillingham. 2012. "The Unequal Benefits of Fuel Subsidies: A Review of Evidence for Developing Countries." *World Development* 40 (11): 2234–48.

Beylis, G., and B. Cunha. Forthcoming. *Energy Pricing Policies in Latin America and Caribbean.* Washington, DC: World Bank.

Clements, B., D. Coady, S. Fabrizio, S. Gupta, T. Alleyne, and C. Sdralevich. 2013. *Energy Subsidy Reform: Lessons and Implications.* Washington, DC: International Monetary Fund.

Coccia, M. 2010. *Public and Private Investment in R&D: Complementary Effects and Interaction with Productivity Growth.* ERIEP, Number 1. http://revel.unice.fr/eriep/index.html?id=3085.

de la Torre, A., A. Ize, and S. Pienknagura. 2015. *Latin America Treads a Narrow Path to Growth: LAC Semiannual Report.* Washington, DC: World Bank.

Di Bella, G., L. Norton, J. Ntamatungiro, S. Ogawa, I. Samake, and M. Santoro. 2015. *Energy Subsidies in Latin America and the Caribbean: Stocktaking and Policy Challenges.* Washington, DC: International Monetary Fund. https://www.imf.org/external/pubs/ft/wp/2015/wp1530.pdf.

Hernandez Ore, M. A., L. Sousa, and J. H. Lopez. 2015. *Honduras: Unlocking Economic Potential for Greater Opportunities. Systematic Country Diagnostic.* Washington, DC: World Bank. https://openknowledge.worldbank.org/handle/10986/23119 License: CC BY 3.0 IGO.

ICEFI (Instituto Centroamericano de Estudios Fiscales). 2016. "Honduras: Incidencia de la Política Fiscal en la Desigualdad y Pobreza." Instituto Centroamericano de Estudios Fiscales, Guatemala City.

IEA, OPEC, OECD, and World Bank. 2010/2011. *Analysis of the Scope of Subsidies and Suggestions for the G-20 Initiative Energy.* (Joint Report).

IMF (International Monetary Fund). 2015. "How Large Are Global Energy Subsidies? Country-Level Subsidy Estimates." http://www.imf.org/external/np/fad/subsidies /data/codata.xlsx.

————. 2016. *World Economic Outlook: Subdued Demand: Symptoms and Remedies.* Washington, DC: IMF.

Koplow, D. 2009. *Measuring Energy Subsidies Using the Price-Gap Approach: What Does It Leave Out?* IISD Trade, Investment and Climate Change Series. Winnipeg: International Institute for Sustainable Development. http://www.iisd.org/publications/pub .aspx?pno=1165.

Lustig, N., and S. Higgins. 2013. *Commitment to Equity Assessment (CEQ): Estimating the Incidence of Social Spending, Subsidies and Taxes. Handbook.* CEQ Working Paper 1, Center for Inter-American Policy and Research and Department of Economics, Tulane University and Inter-American Dialogue.

Matheny, A. 2010. "Reducing the Impact of Price Shocks in Energy-Intensive Economies." Discussion Paper 2009-16, Harvard Environmental Economics Program, Cambridge, MA.

Rawlings, L., and M. Rubio. 2003. *Evaluating the Impact of Conditional Cash Transfer Programs: Lessons from Latin America.* Policy Research Working Paper 3119, World Bank, Washington, DC. https://openknowledge.worldbank.org/handle/10986/18119 License: CC BY 3.0 IGO.

Sdralevich, C., R. Sab, Y. Zouhar, and G. Albertin. 2014. *Subsidy Reform in the Middle East and North Africa: Recent Progress and Challenges Ahead.* Washington, DC: International Monetary Fund. https://www.imf.org/external/pubs/ft/dp/2014/1403mcd.pdf.

Yépez-García, R. A., and J. Dana. 2012. *Mitigating Vulnerability to High and Volatile Oil Prices: Power Sector Experience in Latin America and the Caribbean.* Washington, DC: World Bank.

CHAPTER 4

The Distributional Impact of Electricity Subsidies in Central America

Liliana D. Sousa, Marco Antonio Hernández Oré, and
Leopoldo Tornarolli

Electricity subsidies in each of the six Central American countries reduce the burden of electricity costs on low-income households. On average, electricity subsidies save households in the poorest decile approximately 2 percent of household income. Nevertheless, for every US$1 in electricity subsidies that households in the lowest income quintile receive, significantly more than US$1 reaches households in the highest quintile. This "leakage" of benefits to wealthier households reduces the welfare effect of subsidies and thus erodes the efficiency of scarce fiscal resources. Despite significant variations in energy costs and tariffs and important differences in the designs of subsidy regimes, the distribution of electricity subsidies is regressive in every country in the region. Although several Central American countries have recently undertaken reforms designed to improve the targeting of residential electricity subsidies to lower-income consumers, these remain largely poorly targeted and regressive.

One of the policy objectives of residential electricity subsidies is to make electricity more affordable for lower-income households. As noted in the previous chapter, the limited fiscal space in most Central American countries underscores the importance of ensuring that social spending, including spending on subsidy programs, is well designed and effectively targeted. Effective targeting increases the efficiency of social spending by reducing the cost at which a given social goal, such as affordable electricity for households living in poverty, can be achieved.

This chapter examines the distribution of subsidies across households in Central America, analyzes their effect on household budgets, and considers their effect on the efficiency of public spending. Central American countries have adopted a variety of approaches to subsidizing electricity based on household consumption levels. These policies have achieved broadly similar results; although they modestly alleviate the burden of electricity costs on some poor households, they also disproportionately benefit wealthier households. The leakage of public resources to upper-income households reduces the efficiency of public spending.

This chapter measures how electricity subsidies affect the affordability of electricity and evaluates the efficiency of subsidy spending through a benefit-incidence analysis.[1] The section titled "Do Subsidies Make Electricity More Affordable?" evaluates the extent to which subsidy mechanisms reduce electricity costs. The rest of the chapter focuses on the efficiency of subsidy mechanisms and assesses the degree to which subsidies are disproportionately allocated to wealthier households. The analysis presented in the section titled "Are Subsidies Efficiently Targeted?" reveals that subsidies are regressive in absolute terms in all six countries, because in each case, a larger share of subsidy benefits accrues to wealthier households. Because of differences in the designs of subsidy regimes, spending levels, and electrification rates, the distributional effects of subsidies vary substantially, depending on the country, but the regressive distribution of benefits is consistent across the region. Because most countries apply two or more subsidy mechanisms simultaneously, the section below titled "A Closer Look: Incidence Analysis for Each Country" analyzes the overall distributional effect of residential electricity subsidies across the six countries in Central America and the specific effects of different subsidy mechanisms in each country. The final section, titled "Key Messages," summarizes the the chapter's main findings.

Do Subsidies Make Electricity More Affordable?

Globally, nearly 1.5 billion people lack access to electricity; this results in significant economic and social costs for poor households and reduces their ability to escape poverty. A lack of access to electricity increases the labor intensity of common household tasks, which has particularly serious implications for women and girls, who devote more time than men and boys to household labor at the expense of other activities, such as attending school or seeking employment outside the home.[2] A lack of access to electricity also limits production opportunities for microenterprises, reduces the ability to store food, diminishes access to information, and shortens the amount of time that can be spent working or studying. Conversely, greater access to electricity has been found to decrease households' reliance on firewood and other traditional fuels for heat and cooking, which reduces indoor pollution and associated health problems (Heltberg 2004).

In addition to targeting universal electrification, the Sustainable Development Goals emphasize that all households should have access to "affordable, reliable and modern energy services." The affordability and reliability of electricity services are directly related to the pricing mechanisms in effect in a given country. Although subsidy mechanisms can make electricity more affordable, allowing some low-income households to access electricity, these mechanisms also affect the ability of electric companies to recoup their costs. Higher tariff revenues allow electric companies to invest in infrastructure, expand electricity access, and improve service quality.

Electricity subsidies in Central America help make electricity more affordable for low-income households. For the typical Central American household, subsidies reduce average electricity spending from 3.6 percent of household income to 2.6 percent (box 4.1). This creates the equivalent of a 1 percent increase in household income. For households in the poorest decile, electricity costs drop from 6.9 percent to 4.5 percent of household income. However, among subsidy recipients in this group, electricity spending falls from 8.6 percent to 4.6 percent. In other words, for the poorest recipients, electricity subsidies represent the equivalent of a 4 percent increase in household income. Meanwhile, households in the wealthiest decile receive the equivalent of a 0.5 percent increase in income (figure 4.1).[3] Nevertheless, although the subsidy

---

Box 4.1 A Methodological Caveat: No Behavioral Response to Pricing Mechanisms

The analysis presented in this and subsequent chapters implicitly assumes that households will not alter their behavior in response to changes in electricity costs. The estimates for pre- and postsubsidy spending are based on a constant level of electricity consumption by each household. Although this is not a realistic assumption—there is ample evidence that households typically respond to changes in electricity costs by adjusting their consumption patterns—the price elasticity of demand is difficult to reliably estimate. Ito (2014), for example, finds that electricity consumers adjust their demand based on expected average price rather than marginal price and does not find evidence of "bunching" at consumption levels where marginal prices change dramatically. The results suggest that, in response to complex pricing mechanisms and an imperfect assessment of their own consumption, consumers respond to a simplified estimate of pricing mechanisms.

Figure 4.1 Electricity Spending as a Share of Household Income in Central America, by Income Decile, 2016

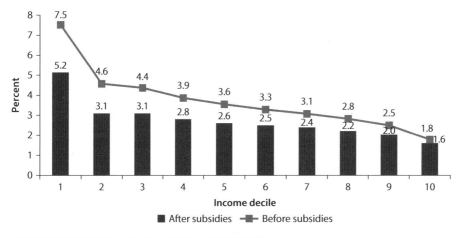

Source: World Bank elaboration using SEDLAC (CEDLAS and World Bank).
Note: Household income estimates are based on 2014 data; subsidy benefits are based on tariffs as of April 2016. See annex 4A for a technical description of the data and simulation methodology. This figure presents unweighted means of presubsidy and postsubsidy electricity spending, by income decile, in each of the six countries. This calculation includes all households, including those without electricity. By definition, these households have electricity costs equal to 0. The importance of electrification rates in explaining the success of subsidy schemes is explored in chapter 5.

Fiscal and Welfare Impacts of Electricity Subsidies in Central America
http://dx.doi.org/10.1596/978-1-4648-1104-3

benefits that accrue to wealthy households are smaller as a share of household income, they are significantly larger in absolute terms than the benefits that poor households receive.

The degree to which electricity subsidies reduce costs for the poorest households in Central America varies significantly, depending on the country. In all countries except Costa Rica, electricity subsidies have a significant effect on overall household electricity spending (table 4.1), although the incidence of subsidies and their effect on electricity spending are not uniform across the region. The average Honduran household in the bottom income quintile spends an average of 8.3 percent of its income on electricity before subsidies and 4.3 percent after subsidies, receiving a net benefit equal to 4 percent of its total household income. In neighboring Guatemala, where electricity spending is lower, subsidies reduce average electricity spending in households in the bottom quintile from 4.3 percent to 2.8 percent, indicating a subsidy benefit of 1.5 percent of household income. Costa Rica's electricity subsidies generate a modest benefit, reducing electricity spending from 6.2 percent to 5.9 percent of household income in households in

Table 4.1 Electricity Costs as a Share of Household Income, by Income Quintile, 2016

Country	Income quintile	Share of household budget spent on electricity (%)		Implicit change in household budget
		Before subsidy	After subsidy	
Costa Rica	1	6.2	5.9	0.2
	2	4.0	3.8	0.1
	3	3.0	2.9	0.1
	4	2.4	2.4	0.0
	5	1.3	1.4	−0.1
	All	3.4	3.3	0.1
El Salvador	1	4.8	2.5	2.3
	2	3.8	2.3	1.4
	3	3.2	2.1	1.0
	4	2.7	2.0	0.7
	5	2.2	1.8	0.3
	All	3.3	2.2	1.2
Guatemala	1	4.3	2.8	1.5
	2	3.0	2.0	1.0
	3	2.6	1.9	0.7
	4	2.4	1.9	0.5
	5	1.7	1.5	0.2
	All	2.8	2.0	0.8
Honduras	1	8.3	4.3	4.0
	2	5.9	4.1	1.8
	3	5.3	4.1	1.2
	4	4.5	3.7	0.8
	5	3.4	3.0	0.4
	All	5.5	3.8	1.7

table continues next page

Table 4.1 Electricity Costs as a Share of Household Income, by Income Quintile, 2016 *(continued)*

Country	Income quintile	Share of household budget spent on electricity (%)		Implicit change in household budget
		Before subsidy	*After subsidy*	
Nicaragua	1	6.1	3.7	2.4
	2	4.4	2.6	1.8
	3	3.7	2.2	1.5
	4	3.3	2.0	1.3
	5	2.4	1.7	0.7
	All	4.0	2.5	1.5
Panama	1	6.6	5.7	1.0
	2	3.8	3.0	0.8
	3	2.8	2.2	0.6
	4	2.4	1.9	0.4
	5	1.8	1.6	0.3
	All	3.5	2.9	0.6

Source: World Bank elaboration using SEDLAC (CEDLAS and World Bank).
Note: Poverty identification and income estimates are based on 2014 data; subsidy benefits are based on tariffs as of April 2016. See annex 4A for a technical description of the data and simulation methodology. This calculation includes all households including those without electricity. By definition, these households have electricity costs equal to 0. The importance of electrification rates in explaining the success of subsidy schemes is explored in chapter 5.

the lowest income quintile. Panama's subsidy regime also has a modest effect on household income. The poorest households in El Salvador spend an average of 2.5 percent of their income on electricity, which is close to the national average.

Electricity subsidies have a positive welfare effect on households living in poverty, although their pro-poor incidence varies, depending on the country. Poverty rates vary significantly across Central America. To better understand the effect of electricity subsidies on poor households across the region, it is important to specifically consider the population living in poverty in each country.[4] The pro-poor incidence of electricity subsidies is greatest in Honduras, where subsidies reduce the electricity spending of poor households from 6.5 percent to 4.1 percent of average household income (figure 4.2). This effect is even larger when only households who receive subsidies are considered. Among these, subsidies result in the equivalent of a 3 percent increase in household income. Even so, poor households in Honduras that receive subsidies spend about 5.5 percent of their income to pay for electricity—a value in line with that spent by poor households in Costa Rica. Nicaragua's subsidy regime delivers benefits to households below the poverty line equal to approximately 2 percent of their household income, representing a boost in household income of 4 percent for subsidy beneficiaries. Although Guatemala's poverty rate is higher than those of Nicaragua and Honduras, its subsidy regime delivers a more modest benefit to poor households, reducing their total electricity spending by 1.1 percent of household income (2 percent for beneficiaries). Nevertheless, in part because of the country's lower

Figure 4.2 Electricity Costs as a Percentage of Household Income of Households Living on Less Than US$4 per Day, 2016

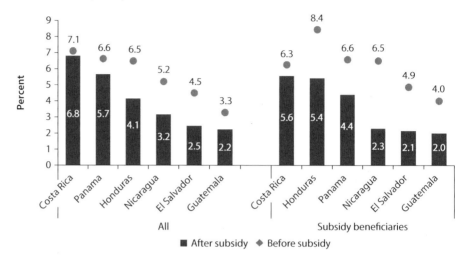

Source: World Bank elaboration using SEDLAC (CEDLAS and World Bank).
Note: Poverty identification and income estimates are based on 2014 data; subsidy benefits are based on tariffs as of April 2016. See annex 4A for a technical description of the data and simulation methodology. The estimates of "All" households are based on all households living in poverty, including those without electricity. The estimates of "Subsidy beneficiaries" are limited to those households living in poverty who received electricity subsidies.

electricity costs, these modest savings yield the region's lowest household electricity burden. Meanwhile, Costa Rica's subsidy regime delivers a modest benefit to the country's small share of poor households. The pro-poor incidence of electricity subsidies reflects not only the design of each country's subsidy regime, but also its electrification rate and the cost of electricity before subsidies, which are discussed further in chapter 5.

Are Subsidies Efficiently Targeted?

In the analysis, targeting efficiency refers to the share of subsidies that reaches low-income households versus the share that "leaks" to high-income households. The analysis measures targeting efficiency by assessing the progressivity or regressivity of the distribution of subsidies across income quintiles or deciles. The methodology for determining the distribution of benefits is described in box 4.2.

Subsidies represent a larger share of household income in poor households, but wealthier households receive a disproportionate share of subsidy benefits. As shown in the previous section, analyzing the distribution of subsidies as a share of household income (or, equivalently, as the share of income spent on electricity before and after receiving subsidies) reveals that the region's subsidies are achieving one of their goals—making energy more affordable for low-income households. However, high-income households receive a disproportionate share of subsidies. Combined, these two results suggest that electricity subsidies

---

Box 4.2 Benefit-Incidence Methodology

The benefit-incidence methodology assesses the distribution of subsidies to households in different income groups. It is frequently used in welfare economics to estimate the distributional effect of subsidy regimes.[a] In interpreting the results of this analysis, two factors should be kept in mind:

(i) Household electricity costs are based on tariff rates that reflect electricity consumption, not household income levels. Poorer households that consume more electricity than their peers may face higher tariff rates, and wealthier households that use less than their peers may face lower rates. However, this analysis calculates only the average effect of the tariff and subsidy structure on consumers in different income groups, which obscures individual variations.

(ii) Assessing the overall progressivity of the subsidy system would require an analysis of the sources of subsidy funding. If a regressively distributed subsidy were funded through a regressive tax, its distribution would be doubly regressive, whereas if it were funded through a progressive tax, it might be less regressive, be neutral, or even be progressive on balance. An analysis of funding sources is possible only in Costa Rica because of its unique system of full cross-subsidization. To maintain comparability, unless otherwise noted, the benefit incidence analyses in this study reflect only the distribution of benefits.

a. For more on welfare economics, see van der Walle (1992), Selden and Wasylenko (1992), Castro-Leal et al. (1999), van der Walle (1998), and Wagstaff (2012). For more on energy subsidies, see Komives et al. (2005, 2006, 2009), Angel-Urdinola and Wodon (2007), and Trimble, Yoshida, and Saqib (2011).

---

are progressive relative to the distribution of income but regressive in absolute terms (box 4.3).

The distribution of subsidies is regressive in absolute terms in all six Central American countries. That is, in each of the six countries of Central America, electricity subsidies accrue largely to higher income households, even as they have a larger relative effect on the household income of the poorest (figure 4.3). The concentration index measures the distribution of an outcome adjusted for income inequality. A positive value means that the outcome—in this case, electricity subsidies—is biased toward higher-income households, and a negative value suggests that the outcome is biased toward poorer households. Electricity subsidies in five of the Central American countries are regressive, based on the concentration index (table 4.2). According to this measure, El Salvador's subsidies are the least regressive, followed closely by Guatemala's; Honduras's and Nicaragua's electricity subsidy mechanisms are more regressive; and Panama's are the most regressive. Because of its perfect cross-subsidy, Costa Rica's concentration index is not calculated.

Fiscal and Welfare Impacts of Electricity Subsidies in Central America
http://dx.doi.org/10.1596/978-1-4648-1104-3

Box 4.3 Measuring the Distribution of Subsidies

Throughout this chapter, the distribution of electricity subsidies is defined in absolute terms; a subsidy is considered progressive (regressive) if a smaller (larger) share of its benefits accrues to higher-income households than lower-income households (figure B4.3.1). However, the distribution of subsidies can also be assessed in relative terms by measuring it against the distribution of per capita household income. Although, in the tax-policy literature, the terms "regressivity" and "progressivity" are almost always used in a relative sense—as a share of income—there is no such agreement in the literature on transfers, social spending, and benefit incidence. In studies of these topics, the concepts of regressivity and progressivity are commonly used in their absolute and relative senses.[a]

Figure B4.3.1 A Graphical Representation of the Definitions of Progressivity and Regressivity

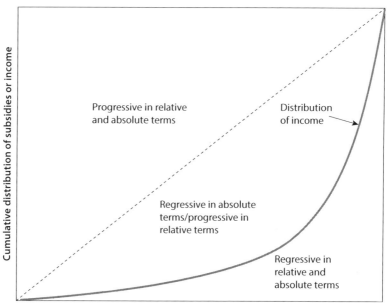

a. For example, O'Donnell et al. (2008) refer to the concepts of weak (relative but not absolute) and strong (relative and absolute) progressivity; Lustig, Pessino, and Scott (2014) define as progressive those transfers that are equalizing and as regressive those that are unequalizing; they then distinguish between relative and absolute; and Wagstaff (2012) uses the term "pro-poor" for transfers that are progressive in absolute terms and "pro-rich" for transfers that are progressive only in relative terms or are regressive.

Figure 4.3 Distribution of Electricity Subsidies and Household per Capita Income, 2016

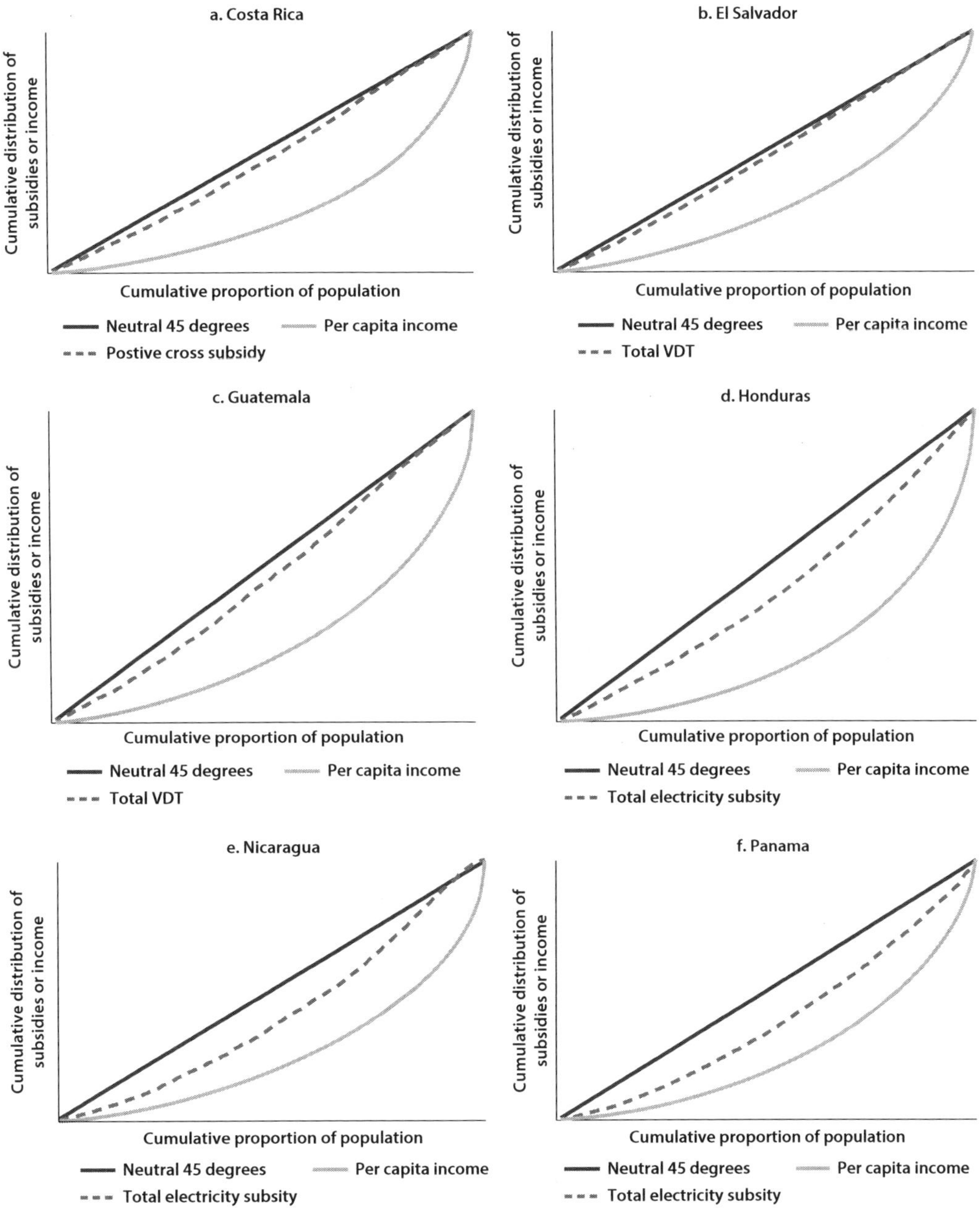

a. Costa Rica

Cumulative distribution of subsidies or income

Cumulative proportion of population

— Neutral 45 degrees   — Per capita income

- - - Postive cross subsidy

b. El Salvador

Cumulative distribution of subsidies or income

Cumulative proportion of population

— Neutral 45 degrees   ⋯⋯ Per capita income

- - - Total VDT

c. Guatemala

Cumulative distribution of subsidies or income

Cumulative proportion of population

— Neutral 45 degrees   — Per capita income

- - - Total VDT

d. Honduras

Cumulative distribution of subsidies or income

Cumulative proportion of population

— Neutral 45 degrees   ⋯⋯ Per capita income

- - - Total electricity subsity

e. Nicaragua

Cumulative distribution of subsidies or income

Cumulative proportion of population

— Neutral 45 degrees   — Per capita income

- - - Total electricity subsity

f. Panama

Cumulative distribution of subsidies or income

Cumulative proportion of population

— Neutral 45 degrees   — Per capita income

- - - Total electricity subsity

Source: World Bank elaboration using SEDLAC (CEDLAS and World Bank).
Note: The dashed line shows the distribution of electricity subsidies and the solid line shows the distribution of income. Because Costa Rica's subsidy mechanism is a perfect cross-subsidy, the distribution of net subsidies is neutral. Instead, the figure shows the distribution of positive subsidies only.

Table 4.2 Gini Coefficient and Concentration Index, 2016

Country	Gini coefficient		Concentration index of subsidies
	Income	*Income + subsidies*	
Costa Rica	0.501	0.500	N.A.
El Salvador	0.418	0.416	0.042
Guatemala	0.487	0.485	0.078
Honduras	0.558	0.555	0.166
Nicaragua	0.487	0.484	0.182
Panama	0.477	0.476	0.227

Source: World Bank elaboration using SEDLAC (CEDLAS and World Bank).
Note: Coefficients and concentration index are calculated using per capita amounts.

Figure 4.4 Percentage of Subsidies That the Bottom and Top 40 Percent Receive, 2016

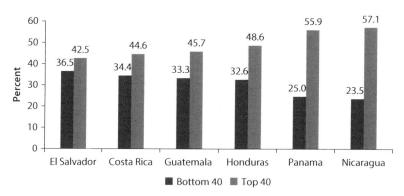

Source: World Bank elaboration using SEDLAC (CEDLAS and World Bank).

Across Central America, for every US$1 in electricity subsidies that households in the lowest income quintile receive, less than 40 cents reaches households in the poorest 40 percent (figure 4.4). In El Salvador, where the distribution of subsidies appears to be the most equal, 36.5 percent of benefits reach households in the bottom 40 percent, and 42.5 percent of benefits go to households in the top 40 percent, followed by Costa Rica, at 34.4 percent and 44.6 percent, respectively. Nicaragua's subsidies are the most regressive; only 23.5 percent of benefits reach households in the first two income quintiles, and 57.1 percent accrue to households in the top 40 percent. Results for Panama are nearly identical, at 55.9 percent for the top 40 and 24.6 percent for the bottom 40.

These shares translate into significant spending differences between quintiles. In El Salvador, US$1.20 in subsidy benefits goes to households in the wealthiest quintile for every US$1 that reaches the poorest quintile. This ratio is slightly higher in Costa Rica (US$1.30), Guatemala (US$1.50), and Honduras (US$1.70), and it is much higher in Panama (US$3.40) and Nicaragua (US$3.50). In Panama, the disparity is even more pronounced at the far ends of the distribution; for every US$1 in subsidies that reaches the poorest 10 percent of the population, US$4.40 is spent on the wealthiest 10 percent (figure 4.5).

Figure 4.5 Distribution of Subsidies, by Income Percentile, 2016

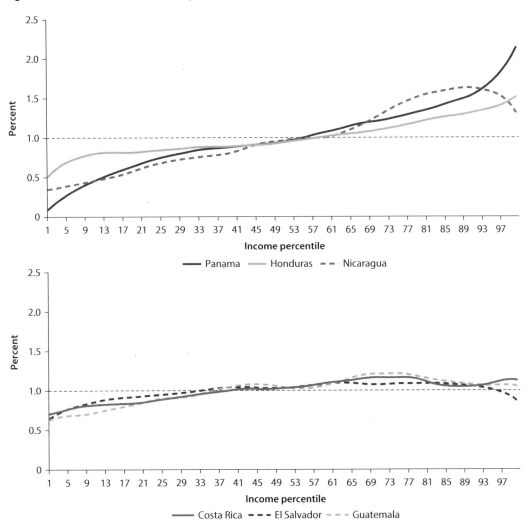

Source: World Bank elaboration using SEDLAC (CEDLAS and World Bank).

Fiscal and Welfare Impacts of Electricity Subsidies in Central America
http://dx.doi.org/10.1596/978-1-4648-1104-3

A Closer Look: Incidence Analysis, by Country

Most Central American countries apply multiple subsidy mechanisms simultaneously. These mechanisms vary in terms of their structure and approach. Although some are well targeted, others are steeply regressive. El Salvador, Honduras, and Panama operate subsidy mechanisms that yield a progressive distribution of benefits (table 4.3); but in each case, other, more regressive mechanisms negate the progressivity of the subsidy mechanism. Although this is true of the distribution of benefits, some countries also impose negative subsidies on high-volume consumers. Costa Rica, Honduras, and Nicaragua apply negative subsidies, although only Costa Rica's system charges enough to fully finance its cross-subsidy mechanism. Each of these negative subsidies is progressive, and a positive value for the concentration index means that higher-income households pay more than lower-income households.

Costa Rica

Costa Rica's subsidy scheme appears to be among the least regressive in the region. Because the benefit-incidence analysis presented in the previous section solely reflects the distribution of benefits and not the distribution of costs, it does not fully capture the distributional effect of the country's cross-subsidy incremental block tariff (IBT) mechanism.[5] Analyzing the distribution of benefits and the distribution of above-cost tariffs required to fund them yields a more complete measure of the overall incidence of Costa Rican electricity subsidies. This measure, referred to as "net IBT," significantly improves the observed progressivity of Costa Rica's electricity subsidies. Costa Rica's cross-subsidy mechanism appears to benefit primarily those in the bottom 60 percent of the income distribution, and it is principally funded through above-cost tariffs on the richest 20 percent (figure 4.6).

Table 4.3 Concentration Index of Electricity Subsidies, by Mechanism and Country, 2016

Costa Rica	IBT Positive[a]	IBT Negative[b]		
	0.064	0.430		
El Salvador	VDT 0–49	VDT 50–99		
	−0.150	0.086		
Guatemala	VDT 0–60	VDT 61–88	VDT 89–100	
	0.015	0.142	0.211	
Honduras	Direct 0–75	IBT Positive[a]	IBT Negative[b]	
	−0.069	0.316	0.818	
Nicaragua	Direct 0–150	IBT Positive[a]	IBT Negative[b]	
	0.247	0.046	0.764	
Panama	FET	Retirees	VDT 0–100	FTO
	0.189	0.303	−0.026	0.219

Source: World Bank elaboration using SEDLAC (CEDLAS and World Bank).
Note: The concentration index is calculated using per capita amounts. VDT = volume-differentiated tariff; IBT = incremental block tariff; FTO = Fondo Tarifario de Occidente; FET = Fondo de Estabilización Tarifaria.
a. Positive subsidies paid as part of the IBT cross-subsidy systems in place.
b. Negative subsidies paid as part of the IBT cross-subsidy systems in place.

Fiscal and Welfare Impacts of Electricity Subsidies in Central America
http://dx.doi.org/10.1596/978-1-4648-1104-3

Figure 4.6 Distribution of Electricity Cross-Subsidies in Costa Rica, by Income Decile, 2016

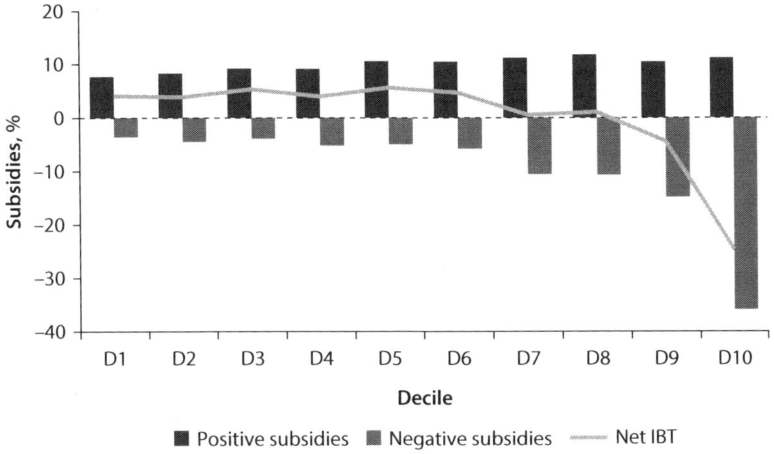

Source: World Bank elaboration using SEDLAC (CEDLAS and World Bank).
Note: See annex 4A for a technical description of the data and simulation methodology.
IBT=income-based tariff.

Two aspects of Costa Rica's subsidy regime should be emphasized. First, when its costs and benefits are assessed, the country's cross-subsidization mechanism appears to be progressive. However, the results of this analysis are not comparable to those of the other five countries, where it is not possible to allocate sources of subsidy funding. Second, although Costa Rica's net IBT is pro-poor, the mechanism distributes a small amount of resources, which limits its impact on the affordability of electricity for lower-income households.

El Salvador

The net distributional impact of El Salvador's volume-differentiated tariff (VDT) subsidy mechanism is regressive, with leakages to higher-income consumers driving its overall regressivity. The distribution of subsidies among consumers in the per-month consumption range of 0–49 kWh is progressive, with the bottom two income deciles receiving approximately 15 percent of subsidies each, compared with 5.2 percent for the top decile (figure 4.7), but the distribution of subsidies in the per-month consumption range of 50–99 kWh is regressive, with the poorest 20 percent of households receiving only 14.2 percent of the benefits. Because the higher consumption range encompasses more households and more electricity consumption, it accounted for an estimated three-quarters of total spending on electricity subsidies in 2016. This illustrates the critical role that consumption thresholds play in determining the progressivity of quantity-targeting subsidy mechanisms.

The removal of a temporary tariff freeze for households consuming between 100 and 200 kWh improved the progressivity of El Salvador's subsidy distribution. In April 2012, rising oil prices increased electricity production costs, prompting

Figure 4.7 Distribution of Electricity Subsidies in El Salvador, by Income Decile in (a) 2014 and (b) 2016, and (c) by Quintile in 2014 and 2016

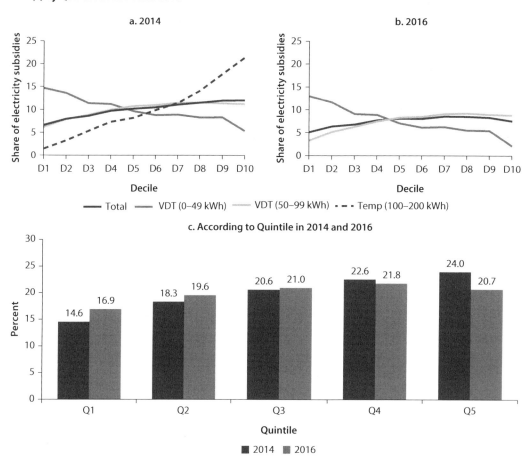

Source: World Bank elaboration using SEDLAC (CEDLAS and World Bank).
Note: See annex 4A for a technical description of the data and simulation methodology. VDT=volume-differentiated tariff.

policy makers to freeze electricity tariffs at their January 2011 level for households consuming between 100 and 200 kWh, effectively creating a temporary subsidy. This tariff freeze mainly benefited wealthier consumers; households in the highest income decile received 21.4 percent of the benefits, and those in the ninth decile received 17.8 percent. Meanwhile, households in the poorest decile received just 1.4 percent of the benefits, and those in the second decile received 2.4 percent. Although only approximately 18 percent of the amount spent on subsidies was allocated through this tariff freeze, it had a notable effect on the overall distribution of subsidies. In 2014, nearly 24 percent of subsidy benefits in El Salvador reached individuals in the top 20 percent of the income distribution, whereas only 14.6 percent accrued to those in the poorest 20 percent. Largely because of the end of the temporary tariff freeze in April 2015, by 2016 the share of subsidies that the top 20 percent received had fallen to 20.7 percent, whereas the share that the poorest 20 percent received had increased to 16.9 percent.

Guatemala

Guatemala's VDT-based subsidy scheme consists of three consumption ranges, each with a regressive distribution of benefits. The two higher consumption ranges account for approximately 46 percent of Guatemala's electricity subsidies. Because these two ranges tend to encompass wealthier households, the distribution of subsidies is highly regressive. The wealthiest 40 percent of the population receives half of the amount spent on subsidies in the middle range (61–88 kWh per month), and 57 percent in the highest range (89–100 kWh). The disparity in the distribution of benefits, depending on the income decile, is especially striking in the highest range, in which the top 10 percent of the distribution receives 15.5 percent of subsidies, and the poorest 10 percent receives 5.4 percent (figure 4.8).

Figure 4.8 Distribution of Electricity Subsidies in Guatemala, by Income Decile in (a) 2014 and (b) 2016, and (c) by Quintile in 2014 and 2016

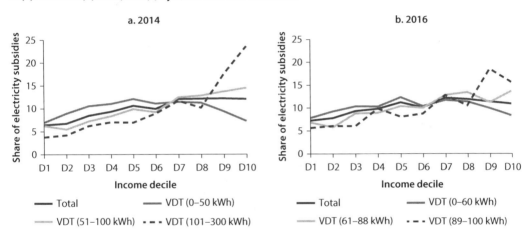

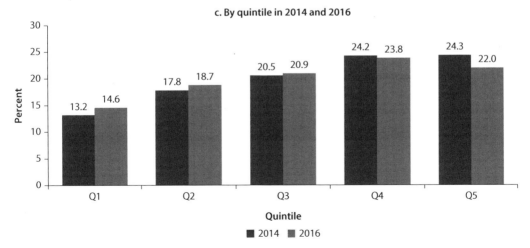

Source: World Bank elaboration using SEDLAC (CEDLAS and the World Bank).
Note: See annex 4A for a technical description of the data and simulation methodology. VDT = volume-differentiated tariff.

Unlike in El Salvador, the distribution of subsidies in Guatemala's lowest consumption range is also regressive. Households in the per-month range of 0–60 kWh receive 54 percent of subsidy benefits. Although this range includes a large share of poor households, 18 percent of benefits reach households in the top two income quintiles, and 17 percent goes to households in the bottom two.

Recent reforms have moderately reduced the regressivity of Guatemala's overall subsidy scheme. In 2014, Guatemala's lowest consumption range was 0–50 kWh, the middle range was 51–100 kWh, and the highest was 101–300 kWh. The distribution of subsidies in the highest range was particularly regressive, with the richest 10 percent of Guatemalan households receiving almost one-quarter of all subsidy benefits—a larger share than what the poorest 40 percent received (21 percent). A new set of thresholds was introduced in 2015, and by 2016, the three ranges had been reduced to cover only households consuming up to 100 kWh per month. As a result, the share of subsidies that the wealthiest 20 percent of households received fell from 24.3 percent in 2014 to 22.0 percent in 2016.

Honduras

Honduras applies an IBT-type cross-subsidy mechanism, which is incorporated into the electricity tariff structure, and a cash-transfer subsidy mechanism, which fully subsidizes households located outside of high-income neighborhoods that consume less than 75 kWh per month.[6] Although Honduras has implemented several reforms designed to improve the distributional impact of each subsidy mechanism and reduce their fiscal cost, they remain regressive overall (figure 4.9). This is due to the regressivity of the IBT cross-subsidy, which accounts for approximately 80 percent of all electricity subsidies.

Honduras's IBT mechanism has an extremely high consumption threshold, which includes almost all residential consumers. Under the IBT system, households that consume up to 840 kWh per month pay an average price per kWh that is less than the unit cost of production.[7] As a result, most Honduran households qualify for benefits under the IBT. Although reforms to the tariff structure in 2014 reduced the IBT threshold from 1,450 to 840 kWh per month and modestly increased the share of subsidies that beneficiaries in the lowest income quintiles received, the share of subsidies that households in the two poorest deciles received grew by less than 1 percentage point each.[8] Meanwhile, the share of subsidies that households in the richest decile received in the IBT scheme fell from 19.1 percent to 16.6 percent.

By contrast, Honduras's direct cash-transfer subsidy is progressive and pro-poor. The cash transfer's low inclusion threshold, combined with the exclusion of households in high-income neighborhoods, results in a progressive distribution of subsidy benefits. The subsidy's focus and distributional impact improved substantially after the most recent round of reforms in 2014,

Figure 4.9 Distribution of Electricity Subsidies in Honduras, by Income Decile in (a) 2014 and (b) 2016, and (c) by Quintile in 2014 and 2016

a. 2014

b. 2016

— Total — Direct (0–150 kWh) — IBT positive

— Total — Direct (0–75 kWh) — IBT positive

c. By quintile in 2014 and 2016

■ 2014 ■ 2016

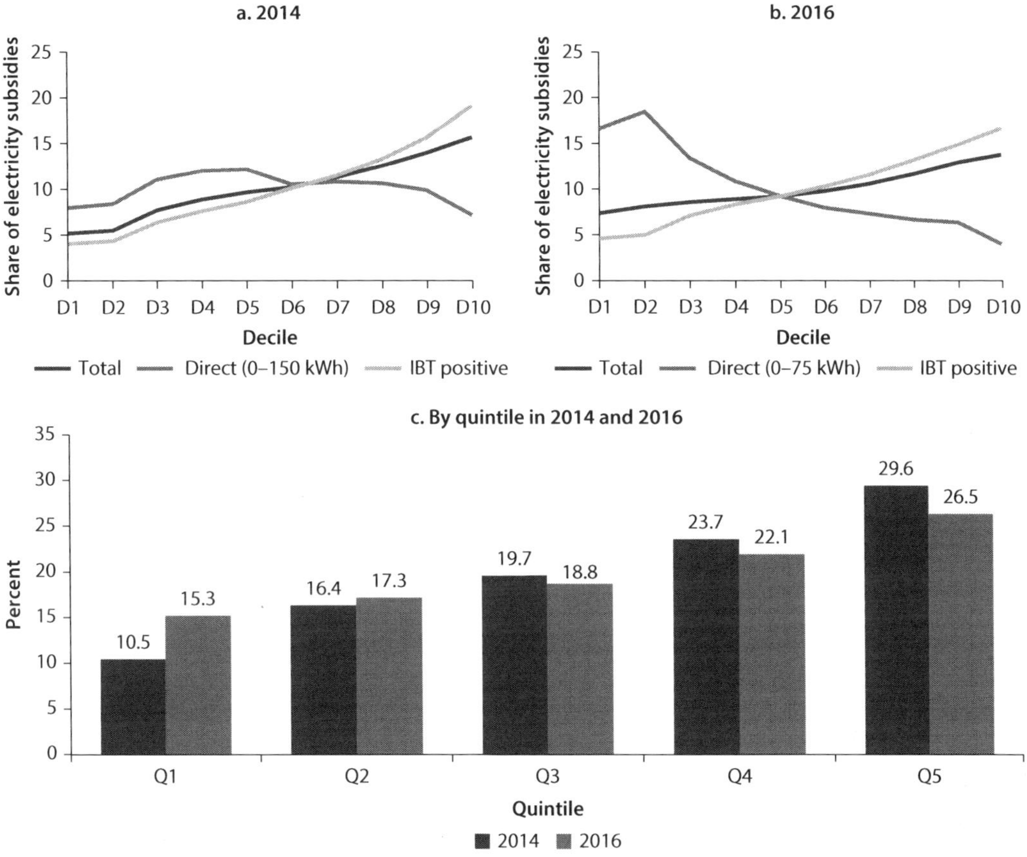

Source: World Bank elaboration using SEDLAC (CEDLAS and World Bank).
Note: See annex 4A for a technical description of the data and simulation methodology. IBT=incremental block tariff.

which lowered the inclusion threshold from 150 to 75 kWh per month and restricted benefits to households located outside of high-income neighborhoods. These reforms increased the share of subsidies that households in the poorest decile received from 7.9 percent to 16.6 percent, whereas the share that households in the second decile received more than doubled—from 8.3 percent to 18.4 percent.[9] Meanwhile, the share of subsidies that households in the four wealthiest deciles received fell from 38.2 percent to 23.9 percent.

Nicaragua

Nicaragua's VDT and IBT mechanisms both result in a regressive distribution of subsidies. The VDT mechanism, which comprises 75 percent of subsidy spending, plays a larger role in determining the overall distribution of subsidies (figure 4.10). Households in each of the top two income deciles receive almost 17 percent of electricity subsidies, whereas benefits for those in the poorest six deciles range from 3.4 percent in households in the bottom

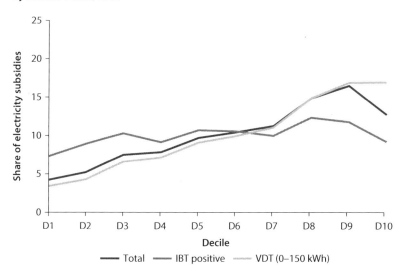

Figure 4.10 Distribution of Electricity Subsidies in Nicaragua, by Income Decile, 2016

Source: World Bank elaboration using SEDLAC (CEDLAS and World Bank).
Note: See annex 4A for a technical description of the data and simulation methodology. IBT=incremental block tariff; VDT=volume-differentiated tariff.

decile to 9.9 percent in those in the sixth decile. Overall, the wealthiest 40 percent of Nicaraguans receive approximately 60 percent of subsidy benefits.

Nicaragua's IBT mechanism is less regressive than the VDT. Households in the four highest income deciles receive 43 percent of IBT subsidy benefits, and households in the four lowest deciles receive 36 percent. The cross-subsidy improves the system's distributional equity, because households in the top two income deciles are net contributors, although the poorest 40 percent of households still receive some IBT benefits. Although VDT subsidy benefits increase with household electricity consumption in the per-month range of 0–150 kWh, the opposite is true for the IBT scheme, in which subsidies decrease and eventually become negative after 150 kWh.

Panama

Panama operates four electricity subsidy mechanisms, and although their characteristics differ, all are regressive. Since 2008, the authorities have implemented a series of reforms that have improved the overall progressivity of the subsidy regime, although the wealthiest 10 percent of households continue to receive almost 18 percent of subsidy benefits, a larger share than the poorest 30 percent (figure 4.11). Consequently, Panama's subsidy regime is the most regressive in Central America.

Panama's largest subsidy is the Fondo de Estabilización Tarifaria (FET). Because of its high inclusion threshold of 350 kWh per month, the FET benefits almost all of the country's households. In 2008, 62 percent of FET subsidy

Figure 4.11 Distribution of Electricity Subsidies in Panama, by Income Decile in (a) 2008 and (b) 2016, and (c) by Quintile in 2008 and 2016

a. 2008

b. 2016

VDT (0–100 kWh) — FET (0–500 kWh) — AGE - - - FTO · · · · Total

c. By quintile in 2008 and 2016

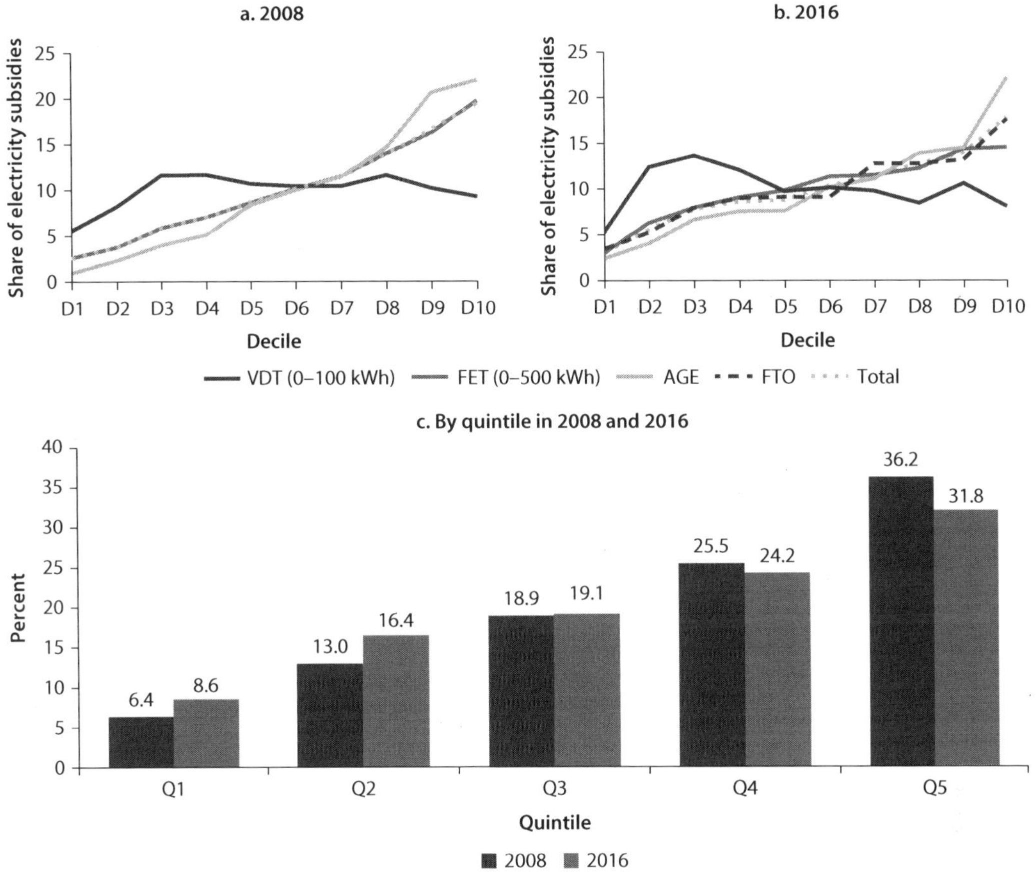

Source: World Bank elaboration using SEDLAC (CEDLAS and World Bank).
Note: See annex 4A for a technical description of the data and simulation methodology. FET= Fondo de Estabilización Tarifaria; VDT=volume-differentiate tariff; FTO=Fondo Tarifario de Occidente; AGE = Retiree discount.

benefits accrued to households in the top four deciles, and only 19 percent reached households in the bottom four. Recent reforms have lowered the inclusion threshold, improving the FET's distributional effect, but in 2016, households in the top four quintiles still received 53 percent of benefits, and households in the bottom four received 26 percent.

Panama's most regressive subsidy mechanisms are the special subsidy targeting retirees and the Fondo Tarifario de Occidente (FTO), which together account for 47 percent of total electricity subsidy spending. Thirty-seven percent of the subsidy for retirees and 31 percent of the FTO accrue to households in the top two income deciles. The subsidy for retirees has a highly regressive distribution of benefits because the subsidy acts as a 25 percent discount on all electricity spending up to 600 kWh per month, and 24.5 percent of Panamanian households with an electric connection qualify for the discount. The FTO is regressive because it lacks an exclusionary threshold and because subsidy levels

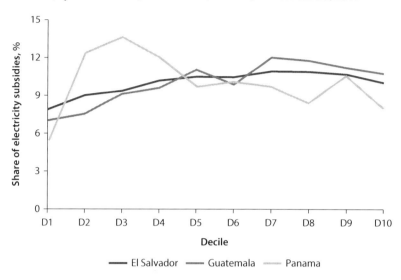

Figure 4.12 Distribution of Volume-Differentiated Tariff Subsidies up to 100 kWh, by Income Decile, in El Salvador, Panama, and Guatemala, 2016

Source: World Bank elaboration using SEDLAC (CEDLAS and World Bank).
Note: See annex 4A for a technical description of the data and simulation methodology.

increase at higher consumption rates, rising to 20 percent for households consuming up to 300 kWh per month and 31 percent for those consuming more than 750 kWh.

The VDT, with its much lower inclusion threshold of 100 kWh per month, is mildly progressive, but it represents just 5.2 percent of subsidy spending. Panama's system applies the same threshold as VDTs in El Salvador and Guatemala, but its distribution is more progressive than El Salvador's, which in turn is more progressive than Guatemala's (figure 4.12). The bottom 40 percent of Panama's population receives 43.4 percent of VDT subsidies, higher than in El Salvador (36.5 percent) and Guatemala (33.3 percent). Though El Salvador and Guatemala's multitiered VDT mechanisms are designed to more heavily subsidize households with lower consumption levels, due to Panama's higher average electricity consumption, the same threshold yields a more progressive distribution.

Key Messages

Across Central America, the distribution of electricity subsidies systematically benefits higher-income households more than poorer households. Costa Rica and El Salvador have the most efficient subsidy systems in the region, but both are still regressive in absolute terms. Honduras's direct cash-transfer subsidy and El Salvador's and Panama's VDT subsidies for low-volume consumers all yield a progressive distribution of benefits; but in each case, other, more regressive subsidy schemes outweigh their effect. Whereas Panama's inclusion thresholds for three of its subsidy mechanisms are set so high that a large share of wealthy households qualifies for subsidies, low inclusion thresholds for schemes in Honduras and El Salvador have successfully produced a progressive distribution of benefits. The Honduran direct cash transfer combines a low threshold with a location-based criterion that enhances its progressivity. Although Costa Rica's subsidy mechanism has a relatively modest effect on the affordability of electricity, it is the only system in the region that is fully self-financed and does not require government transfers.

Some general lessons can be gleamed from this analysis. First, although some ad hoc reforms can improve distributional and fiscal outcomes, reforms should be undertaken considering the entire subsidy system in place and only after setting fiscal and distributional goals. Many subsidy mechanisms in Central America have undergone multiple rounds of reforms but remain poorly targeted. Second, inclusion thresholds should be based on an accurate estimate of the electricity consumption of households in the target group. In some cases, the use of additional inclusion criteria can enhance targeting efficiency. Third, financing subsidy benefits through above-cost tariffs on high-volume consumers (cross-subsidies) can enhance the distributional equity of the subsidy regime and alleviate its budgetary effect—although as shown in Honduras, a poorly designed IBT may increase fiscal pressure rather than reduce it. The following chapter explores in greater detail how the characteristics of various subsidy mechanisms combine with contextual factors to yield a regressive distribution of benefits in each Central American country.

Annex 4A: Methodology for Estimating Electricity Consumption in Central America

This annex explains the methodology used to identify which households benefit from electricity subsidies in each country and to estimate the magnitude of the benefit these households receive. It begins with a general overview and then provides details on the analytical techniques used for each country.

In most cases, household surveys in Central America do not explicitly report whether a household receives electricity subsidies or estimate the value of subsidies received. Instead, some surveys include information on electricity consumption in kWh or electricity spending for the month before the survey. This information can be used as a starting point to identify subsidy beneficiaries and estimate the benefits they receive.

The subsidy benefit is defined as the difference between a household's actual electricity bill and what that bill would be in the absence of subsides.[10] Estimating this difference requires information on household electricity consumption, electricity costs, and the eligibility requirements of each subsidy mechanism. We use a static model, in which household electricity consumption is assumed to remain the same with or without the subsidy.

For Costa Rica and Guatemala, in which the household surveys collected information on electricity consumption, determining the size and distribution of subsidy benefits is relatively straightforward, because most targeting mechanisms are based on the the level of consumption. Applying the rules of the different subsidy mechanisms to the amounts that each household consumes yields an estimate of the amount of subsidy each household receives. In El Salvador, Nicaragua, Panama, and Honduras, the household surveys collected information only on monthly electricity spending, and consumption levels had to be estimated based on the electricity tariffs and subsidy rules that prevailed at the time of the survey. To determine the correct electricity rates for each household, it is necessary to know its location, because most countries have more than one distribution company, and different companies typically charge different rates.

There are several important methodological assumptions and caveats.

- It is assumed that the electricity spending that the household reported for the previous month reflected electricity consumed during that month. In some cases, households may be behind on payments, or the spending reported in the survey may refer to previous consumption or multiple electricity bills. It is not possible to determine this from the survey data.

- Some households that declare positive values for monthly electricity spending are not connected to the public electricity grid and instead access electricity through other sources, such as rooftop solar panels. It is not possible to estimate the electricity consumption of these households or the associated costs.

- Because the amount a household declares that it spends on electricity is usually an approximation reported as a rounded value (e.g., 10, 20, 50, 100), electricity consumption estimates based on these values are also approximations.

- In addition to the cost of electricity per se, a household's total electricity spending may include other expenditures, such as administrative charges, municipal fees for the space that power lines use, taxes to finance public lighting, and sales tax. Although these costs are taken into account whenever possible when estimating household electricity consumption, in some cases there is no information to determine the effect of each of those components on the electricity bill.

- In some countries, there is more than one electricity distribution company, and electricity tariffs differ between them. Although each is usually the sole service provider in its geographic area, the survey data are often insufficient to determine precisely which company sold electricity to which household. In these cases, households and companies are randomly matched according to the share of households each company serves in each given area.

- Tariff structures change over time, and the tariff applied to each household depends on the date it was surveyed. Given that household survey data are usually collected over a period of several months, it is necessary to identify the exact month in which each household was interviewed to accurately determine the tariff structure that prevailed at the time of the interview.

In addition to these general considerations, the specific characteristics of the tariff structures and subsidy schemes used in each country must be taken into account. These challenges are described in detail in the following subsections.

Costa Rica

The estimates for Costa Rica were based on data from the National Survey on Household Income and Expenditure (ENIGH), which was carried out between October 2012 and October 2013.

1. **Matching households and electricity distributors:** There are eight residential electricity distribution companies in Costa Rica. The ENIGH data allowed us to determine which households were clients of four of these, but it was not possible to distinguish the households that were clients of the other four.[11] These households were assigned randomly to a company according to their share of clients as reported by the Autoridad Reguladora de los Servicios Públicos.

2. **Determining the electricity tariffs that applied to each household:** During the period when the ENIGH was conducted, three different tariff schemes were in place for each company: the first was from October 2012 to January 2013; the second, from February 2013 to April 2013; and the third, from May 2013 to October 2013. Based on the month in which the household was interviewed, the information about its electricity supplier, and its consumption of electricity in kWh, it is possible to determine which tariff scheme was applied to each household.

3. **Estimating the electricity consumption of each household:** The ENIGH collected information on the electricity consumption in kWh of each household connected to the electricity grid. A small percentage of households (fewer than 2 percent) did not report their consumption in kWh but instead reported monthly electricity spending. In those cases, electricity consumption in kWh was predicted using a regression analysis based on the electricity spending of the households combined with their per capita income level, where the households were located (urban or rural), and the distribution company that supplies the households with electricity.

4. **Isolating electricity spending and average price per kWh:** Total spending on electricity reported in the ENIGH may include costs other than the price per kWh: households that consume more than 100 kWh are billed an additional 1.75 percent surcharge for the fire department, households that consume more than 250 kWh pay an additional 5 percent in sales tax, and some municipalities impose an additional charge per kWh for public lighting. Information on electricity consumption and tariff rates allows us to isolate electricity spending from these ancillary charges and fees. Once we know electricity spending,

the average price per kWh can be estimated as the ratio between electricity spending and electricity consumption in kWh.

5. **Defining the cost per kWh for each electric company:** To determine the total subsidy that each household receives (or pays), it is necessary to compare the average price per kWh that each household pays with the average cost per kWh that its electricity supplier bears. Assuming that each distribution company faces the same average cost per kWh for all residential customers and that each company balances its revenue and production costs, the average cost per kWh can be obtained by dividing the total sales revenue of each company by the total number of kWh sold.

6. **Assessing the total subsidy benefit that each household received:** Once the average price per kWh that each household pays and the average production cost per kWh are known, it is possible to determine each household's net subsidy benefit. Because Costa Rica uses a cross-subsidy, in some cases, this benefit is negative; that is, some households pay more than the total cost of the electricity they consume.

7. **Extrapolating estimates for 2016:** Electricity subsidy estimates for 2016 were extrapolated based on the following additional assumptions. First, the electricity consumption structure was assumed to have remained unchanged since the 2012–13 ENIGH. (Total electricity consumption of each household is assumed to have remained the same as during the ENIGH.) Second, because Costa Rica had already achieved near-universal electricity access in 2012–13, the electrification rate was assumed to have remained the same as during the ENIGH. Third, the tariff rates in place in April 2016 were applied to the data to extrapolate electricity spending in 2016.

El Salvador
The estimates for El Salvador were based on data from the 2014 Multipurpose Household Survey.

1. **Matching households and electricity distributors:** In 2014, six companies provided electricity to almost all consumers in El Salvador. Although some administrative departments have a single distributor,[12] in most departments, two to four electricity distribution companies operate simultaneously. In these departments, households were randomly assigned to each distribution company according to their share of clients in the department, as reported in the *Bulletin of Electrical Statistics*.

2. **Determining the electricity tariffs applied to each household:** Information was collected through the Multipurpose Household Survey for December 2013 to November 2014. During that period, five tariff regimes were in place: one for December 2013, one from January to March 2014, one from April to June

2014, one from July to September 2014, and one from October to November 2014. Those regimes established tariffs according to consumption range and distribution company. The tariff rate applied to each household was determined using the information from the month when the household was interviewed, its local distribution company, its monthly electricity spending, and the rules of the subsidy mechanism.

3. **Estimating the electricity consumption of each household:** Electricity consumption in kWh was then estimated by combining the information on the electricity spending of the household, the electricity tariff that applies to it, the rules of subsidies, and additional fees. More specifically, in El Salvador, electricity bills include a fixed commercial charge, variable charges (per kWh) for energy and distribution, a municipal fee for power lines, and a VAT.

4. **Resolving inconsistencies in reported electricity spending:** Because of the nature of El Salvador's VDT system, there is a discontinuity in electricity bills when a household passes the 99 kWh threshold, but a small fraction of surveyed households reported paying an amount not consistent with the range of "possible" values. These values were edited using a regression analysis based on household characteristics—such as the number of household members, the month in which they were interviewed, where they were located, the distribution company that supplied them with electricity, and their use of various electrical appliances.

5. **Assessing the total subsidy benefit that each household receives:** The total amount of electricity subsidy each household received can be determined based on its electricity consumption in kWh, its electricity provider, the month when it was surveyed, and the rules of operation of the different electricity subsidies.

6. **Extrapolating estimates for 2016:** El Salvador's 2016 electricity subsidies are estimated based on the following additional assumptions. First, it is assumed that the structure of electricity consumption remained the same as during the Multipurpose Household Survey 2014. Second, because no updated information was available to simulate its expansion, it is assumed that the electrification rate remained constant. Finally, the April 2016 tariff rates and electricity subsidy mechanisms were applied.

Guatemala

The estimates for Guatemala were based on data from the 2014 National Survey of Living Conditions (ENCOVI). Because the ENCOVI explicitly reported electricity consumption in kWh for each household, electricity tariffs before subsidies were published online, and the operating rules of the subsidies were clear, fewer assumptions were necessary to identify subsidy beneficiaries and estimate the total amount of subsidy benefits.

1. **Matching households and electricity distributors:** There are three major electricity distribution companies in Guatemala. As in other countries, in administrative departments with more than one electricity provider, households were randomly assigned to distribution companies according to each company's share of clients in that department, as recorded in the Electrical Statistics Report of the Energy Subsector.

2. **Determining the electricity tariffs applied to each household:** Two different tariff schemes were in place while the ENCOVI 2014 was conducted: the first was in force between August 2014 and October 2014, and the second between November 2014 and December 2014. The applicable tariffs for each household were determined based on its electricity consumption in kWh, the date it was surveyed, and its local electricity supplier.

3. **Estimating the electricity consumption of each household:** The ENCOVI 2014 explicitly reported electricity consumption in kWh for all households that reported having paid for electricity in the month before the interview.

4. **Estimating the total subsidy benefit that each household received:** The total electricity subsidy per household can be estimated by multiplying the household's electricity consumption by the difference between the nonsubsidized and subsidized tariffs. For households that consume between 101 and 300 kWh, electricity subsidies applied only to the first 100 kWh consumed.

5. **Extrapolating estimates for 2016:** Estimates for 2016 were based on the following additional assumptions. First, the structure of electricity consumption was assumed to have remained the same as during the 2014 ENCOVI. Second, the electrification rate was assumed to have remained constant between 2014 and 2016. Finally, the tariff rates and electric subsidy mechanisms in place in 2016 were applied to the data.

Honduras

The estimates for Honduras were based on data from the 2007 Permanent Multipurpose Household Survey (EPHPM). To update this information, additional steps are taken to adjust for the increase in electrification rates between 2007 and 2014.

1. **Matching households and electricity distributors:** In Honduras, there is only one distribution company: the Empresa Nacional de Energía Electrica. This company applies a uniform tariff structure to all households consuming electricity.

2. **Determining the electricity tariffs applied to each household:** The 2007 EPHPM was implemented in May, and all households faced the same IBT tariff structure based on four consumption ranges: 0–100 kWh, 101–300 kWh, 301–500 kWh,

and 501 kWh and above. Consumption ranges were identified using this tariff structure and the electricity spending that each household reported.

3. **Estimating electricity consumption of each household:** Once a household's consumption range was determined, its electricity consumption in kWh could be estimated based on its monthly electricity spending, the tariff structure, and the subsidy rules. The electricity bill for a Honduran household in 2007 included a meter rental fee, a public lighting tax, and an adjustment for fuel price variations, in addition to the variable charge for electricity consumption. Consumption of electricity in kWh, the only unknown variable, could be estimated using the values of the other components of the electricity bill.

4. **Simulating changes in the electrification rate:** Between 2007 and 2014, the latest year for which data were available, Honduras's residential electrification rate rose from approximately 60 percent to 85 percent to 90 percent. This increase was particularly sharp for the lower-income deciles. To take this into account, a simulation of the expansion of the electrification rate was performed. EPHPM data from 2014 was used to estimate electrification rate by income decile. Then the probability of gaining access to electricity was estimated for each unconnected household, using the following independent variables: per capita income of the household, region and area (urban/rural) of residence, a homeownership dummy variable, and variables for housing quality. Households without access to electricity in 2007 were ranked according to their probability of gaining access by 2014. Households with the highest probability were assumed to have electricity in 2014 until the electrification rate for each income decile was achieved. Finally, ordinary least squares regression was used to predict the electricity consumption of these households.

5. **Assessing the total subsidy benefit that each household received:** The total subsidy benefit per household was estimated by applying the prevailing tariff scheme in 2014 to the electricity consumption structure obtained above. Like Costa Rica, Honduras uses a cross-subsidy, and in some cases the subsidy benefit is negative.[13] In addition, the country's direct-transfer subsidy provides free electricity to households that consume up to 75 kWh per month.

6. **Extrapolating estimates for 2016:** Estimates for 2016 were extrapolated based on the following additional assumptions. First, the electricity consumption structure for 2016 was assumed to remain unchanged from the 2014 simulation using the 2007 EPHPM data. Second, the electrification rate was assumed to remain the same between 2014 and 2016, because there was no information on changes during the period. The electricity tariffs and subsidy mechanisms in force in April 2016 were applied to the data, which reflect an increase in the first two consumption ranges since 2014.[14]

Nicaragua

Estimates for Nicaragua were based on data from the 2014 Living Standards Measurement Survey.

1. **Matching households and electricity distributors:** There are two major electricity distribution companies in Nicaragua, but both use the same tariff structure, so there was no need to match households and electricity distributors.

2. **Determining the electricity tariffs applied to each household:** The tariff scheme in force during the time of the survey was structured as an IBT mechanism with seven consumption ranges (0–25, 26–50, 51–100, 101–150, 151–300, 301–500, and >500 kWh. In addition, the use of the 2005 tariff structure for consumption up to 150 kWh effectively created a VDT subsidy, the value of which was calculated as the difference between the electric bill for households consuming up to 150 kWh under the 2005 and 2014 tariff structures.

3. **Estimating the electricity consumption of each household:** The Living Standards Measurement Survey did not directly collect information on household electricity consumption, but it could be estimated based on households' reported monthly electricity spending. The value of the electric bill at the limits of the consumption ranges could be calculated based on the tariff structures for 2005 and 2014, because households that consumed up to 150 kWh were billed using the 2005 tariff structure. Households were then assigned to the appropriate consumption range based on their monthly electricity spending. Electricity consumption was determined by removing ancillary charges, such as the public lighting fee and VAT, from electricity spending.

4. **Resolving inconsistencies in reported electricity spending:** As in El Salvador, household electricity bills in Nicaragua experience a discontinuity (tariff change) between 150 and 151 kWh. Nevertheless, a nontrivial percentage of Nicaraguan households reported electricity expenditures around these values. Hence, the reported values were edited based on household characteristics using the same technique as for El Salvador.

5. **Assessing the total subsidy benefit that each household received:** As in Honduras and Costa Rica, Nicaragua's tariff scheme incorporates a cross-subsidy, and thus the subsidy benefit for some households was negative. The average cost of electricity production per kWh was estimated based on producer data, and the cross-subsidy was defined as the difference between a household's actual electric bill and what it would have been under a cost-reflective tariff.

6. **Extrapolating estimates for 2016:** Electricity subsidies for April 2016 were extrapolated based on the following additional assumptions. First, the electricity

consumption structure was assumed to remain unchanged from 2014. Second, the electrification rate was assumed to remain the same between 2014 and 2016, because there was no information on its evolution during that period. The tariff structure in effect in April 2016 was applied to the 2014 data.

Panama

Estimates for Panama were based on data from the 2015 Multiple Purpose Survey (EPM).

1. **Matching households and electricity distributors:** Panama has three major electricity distributors. In the 2015 EPM, households were asked whether one of these companies served them but were not asked which one. Except in Panama Province, electricity distributors can be matched with households based on location. Households in Panama Province are randomly allocated according to each distributor's share of customers.

2. **Determining the electricity tariffs applied to each household:** Given that the 2015 EPM was carried out during March, the tariff scheme in effect was the one of the first semester of 2015.

3. **Estimating the electricity consumption of each household:** The EPM recorded only information on household electricity spending. Thus, electricity consumption in kWh had to be estimated from electricity spending. This was determined by identifying the distributor and applying the tariff structure and subsidy rules in place at the time of the survey. For households that did not report electricity spending, the consumption of electricity in kWh was predicted using ordinary least squares regression based on the estimated relationship between electricity consumption and other characteristics of households with electricity information, such as per capita income, number of household members, household location, relevant distribution company, and use of electrical appliances. The coefficients from this regression were then used to predict the electric consumption of households with unreported values.

4. **Assessing the total subsidy benefit that each household received:** Determining the amount of subsidy benefit that a given household in Panama received required information on electricity consumption, electricity spending, prevailing subsidy rules, and whether the head of household was elderly. All electricity subsidies in Panama are applied as a percentage discount on the total electricity bill.

5. **Extrapolating estimates for 2016:** Estimates of electricity subsidies in 2016 were based on the following additional assumptions. First, it was assumed that the electricity consumption for 2015 based on the EPM

remained accurate in 2016. Second, electrification rates were assumed to have remained unchanged between 2015 and 2016. The tariff structures and subsidy mechanisms in effect in April 2016 were then applied to the data.

Notes

1. See annex 4A for a technical description of the data and simulation methodology.
2. Dinkelman (2011) and Grogan and Sadanand (2012) find that greater rural electrification in South Africa and Nicaragua is associated with higher female employment levels.
3. See chapter 5 for more detail on usage by income group.
4. For benchmarking purposes, poverty estimates are based on the international poverty line of US$4 per day in purchasing power parity terms, not on official poverty lines, which vary from country to country. Costa Rica's poverty rate was the lowest in the region (12 percent) in 2014, followed by Panama's (17 percent), El Salvador's (31 percent), Nicaragua's (36 percent), Honduras's (58 percent), and Guatemala's (60 percent).
5. An important difference between subsidies in Costa Rica and the other five countries is the source of funding; whereas in Costa Rica, it is possible to measure how much each household contributes to subsides (through the cross-subsidy), this is not possible in the other countries, where subsidies are financed through public resources from tax collection and other sources. Because of this limitation, the benefit-incidence analysis above was limited to the distribution of positive subsidies.
6. The IBT was reformed in June 2016. The new mechanism is not included in this study. The direct cash transfer program was not fully implemented in 2016. The results in this study are based on full implementation.
7. Because the IBT is a cross-subsidy, the progressivity of the distribution is based on the net benefits that households in each decile receive, but because few households are net payers, the net distribution of costs and benefits is not significantly different from the distribution of benefits.
8. This threshold is the minimum value of electricity consumption at which the tariff equals the cost of production.
9. For the purposes of this analysis, the reforms are being simulated as if fully implemented. However, they had not been implemented as of the first quarter of 2017.
10. As indicated by Komives et al. (2005), this methodology is appropriate when the information regarding the average cost per kWh of electricity for residential consumption is not available or is not precise.
11. In particular, it is not possible to separate the households that were clients of ESPH or JASEC or those that were clients of COOPESANTOS or COOPEALFARORUIZ.
12. AES-CLESA is the distributor in Ahuachapán and Sonsonate, DELSUR in La Paz, CAESS in Cabañas, and EEO in Morazán and La Unión.
13. Consumption between 0 and 100 kWh was billed at 45 percent of the cost-reflective rate, 101 to 300 kWh was billed at 80 percent, 301 to 500 kWh was billed at 100 percent, and greater than 500 kWh was billed at 110 percent.
14. This means 70 percent for consumption between 0 and 100 kWh and 98 percent for those between 101 and 300 kWh.

Bibliography

Angel-Urdinola, D., and Q. Wodon. 2007. "Do Utility Subsidies Reach the Poor? Framework and Evidence for Cape Verde, São Tomé, and Rwanda." *Economics Bulletin* 9 (4): 1–7.

Castro-Leal, F., J. Dayton, L. Demery, and K. Mehra. 1999. "Public Social Spending in Africa: Do the Poor Benefit?" *World Bank Research Observer* 14 (1): 49–72.

Dinkelman, T. 2011. "The Effects of Rural Electrification on Employment: New Evidence from South Africa." *American Economic Review* 101 (7): 3078–108.

Grogan, L., and A. Sadanand. 2012. "Electrification and Labour Supply in Poor Households: Evidence from Nicaragua." *World Development* 43: 252–65.

Heltberg, R. 2004. "Fuel Switching: Evidence from Eight Developing Countries." *Energy Economics* 6 (5): 869–87.

Ito, K. 2014. "Do Consumers Respond to Marginal or Average Price? Evidence from Nonlinear Electricity Pricing." *American Economic Review* 104 (2): 537–63.

Komives, K., V. Foster, J. Halpern, Q. Wodon, and R. Abdullah. 2005. *Water, Electricity, and the Poor: Who Benefits from Utility Subsidies?* Washington, DC: World Bank.

Komives, K., J. Halpern, V. Foster, and Q. Wodon. 2006. "The Distributional Incidence of Residential Water and Electricity Subsidies." Policy Research Working Paper 3878, World Bank, Washington, DC.

Komives, K., T. Johnson, J. Halpern, J. Aburo, and J. Scott. 2009. "Residential Electricity Subsidies in Mexico: Exploring Options for Reform and for Enhancing the Impact on the Poor." Working Paper 160, World Bank, Washington, DC.

Lustig, N., C. Pessino, and J. Scott. 2014. "The Impact of Taxes and Social Spending on Inequality and Poverty in Argentina, Bolivia, Brazil, Mexico, Peru, and Uruguay: Introduction to the Special Issue." *Public Finance Review* 42 (3): 287–303.

O'Donnell, O., E. van Doorslaer, A. Wagstaff, and M. Lindelow. 2008. *Analyzing Health Equity Using Household Survey Data: A Guide to Techniques and Their Implementation.* Washington, DC: World Bank.

Selden, T., and M. Wasylenko. 1992. "Benefit Incidence Analysis in Developing Countries." Policy Research Working Paper 1015, World Bank, Washington, DC.

Trimble C., N. Yoshida, and M. Saqib. 2011. "Rethinking Electricity Tariffs and Subsidies in Pakistan." Washington, DC: World Bank.

Van de Walle, D. 1992. "The Distribution of the Benefits from Social Services in Indonesia, 1978–87." Policy Research Working Paper 871, World Bank, Washington, DC.

———. 1998. "Assessing the Welfare Impacts of Public Spending." *World Development* 26 (3): 365–79.

Wagstaff, A. 2012. "Benefit-Incidence Analysis: Are Government Health Expenditures More Pro-Rich Than We Think?" *Health Economics* 21 (4): 351–66.

CHAPTER 5

Determinants of Electricity Subsidy Performance in Central America

Liliana D. Sousa, Marco Antonio Hernández Oré, and
Leopoldo Tornarolli

The efficiency of a given subsidy policy depends on two key questions: Who receives subsidies? and How much do they receive? Using a target group of the poorest 40 percent, the targeting performance indicator shows that, in all cases, the target group receives a smaller share of subsidies than the wealthiest 60 percent. El Salvador's performance is the highest in the region: households in the bottom 40 percent receive 92 percent of what they would have received under a neutral distribution. An important finding of this chapter is that one factor is primarily responsible for the regressivity of Central America's electricity subsidy schemes: higher-income households consume more subsidized electricity. The results of the analysis in this chapter suggest that it is not so much who receives subsidies, but rather how much electricity is subsidized, that drives the regressivity of subsidy systems in Central America.

Electricity subsidy mechanisms that depend on quantity-based targeting rely on a fundamental assumption that lower-income households have lower demand for electricity. To the extent that this assumption holds, electricity pricing mechanisms are able to deliver public resources to poorer electricity consumers, but electricity consumption is an imperfect and often noisy predictor of household need (box 5.1). This results in errors of inclusion, with households that are not in the target group receiving subsidies, and errors of exclusion, with households that are in the target group not receiving subsidies. Minimizing errors of inclusion without increasing errors of exclusion increases the efficiency of subsidy mechanisms. This chapter examines the various factors that determine the extent to which errors of inclusion and exclusion are made in the subsidy mechanisms of Central America.

The fundamental determinants of the efficiency of targeting of electricity subsidies are the underlying country characteristics and the design of the subsidy mechanism (figure 5.1). As described in chapter 2, subsidy mechanisms vary in their design, including whether they are based on a volume-differentiated tariff

Box 5.1 Policy Design with Imperfect Information: Targeting Based on Quantity

At the root of the regressive outcomes detailed in the previous chapter is a fundamental challenge facing policy makers: electricity consumption is an imperfect proxy for household income. To the extent that electricity subsidies are designed to provide more affordable energy for lower-income households, using electricity consumption as an indicator of economic need is an imperfect tool (Coady, Grosh, and Hoddinott 2004). This is illustrated in figure B5.1.1, which plots the distribution of electricity consumption (mean, 25th and 75th percentiles), by household per capita income decile.

Figure B5.1.1 Electricity Consumption per Month, by Income Decile, 2016

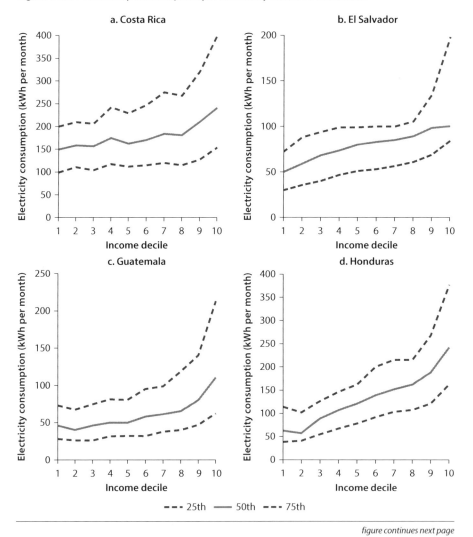

Box 5.1 Policy Design with Imperfect Information: Targeting Based on Quantity *(continued)*

Figure B5.1.1 Electricity Consumption per Month, by Income Decile, 2016 *(continued)*

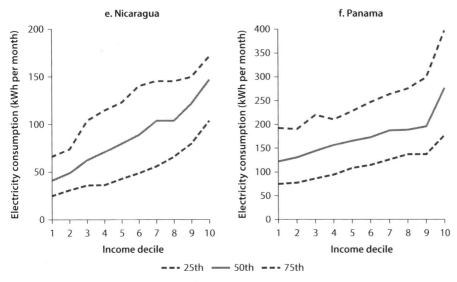

Source: World Bank elaboration using SEDLAC (CEDLAS and World Bank).
Note: The solid line is the median amount of electricity consumed by each income decile, and the dotted lines represent the 25th and 75th percentiles.

The considerable overlap in electricity consumption between the bottom and top deciles underscores the limitations of targeting subsidies based solely on energy consumption. For example, suppose the target group was the poorest 40 percent of the population; 75 percent of households in the fourth decile consumed 81 kWh per month in Guatemala— the same amount as those in the median of the ninth decile. Therefore, setting the threshold at this level would exclude 25 percent of those in the fourth decile and include at least half of those in the fifth through ninth deciles. However, the difference in electricity consumption between income deciles differs between countries, meaning that, in some countries, it is easier to target subsidies to the poorest segment of the population than in others. In Central America, this is the case for Panama and Honduras.

(VDT) or incremental block tariff (IBT) scheme, as well as in their "depth" (i.e., the amount subsidized) and their different thresholds. The extent to which these mechanisms can yield a progressive subsidy-targeting strategy depends on the characteristics of the country, especially the energy mix, access to electricity across income groups, and the relationship between household income and household electricity demand.[1]

The combination of country characteristics and subsidy mechanisms gives rise to four factors that together determine the efficiency of subsidies. These four factors address two basic questions that get at the heart of what drives differences in access to subsidies between the target group and other

Figure 5.1 Framework for Understanding the Distribution of Electricity Subsidies

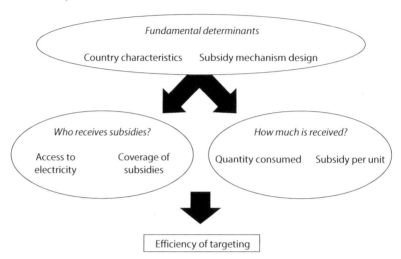

groups: *Who receives subsidies* and *How much do they receive?* Electrification rates and the coverage rate of the subsidies, as defined according to consumption thresholds and limitations on subsidy access (e.g., in Guatemala, not all electricity providers participate in the subsidy scheme), determine who receives subsidies. The depth of the subsidy—which depends on the per-unit subsidy received and the amount of subsidized energy consumed, which depend on consumption thresholds—determines the amount of subsidies received.

The chapter is structured as follows. The first section, "Measuring the Efficiency of the Distribution of Electricity Subsidies," identifies the indicators used to quantify the targeting performance of subsidy mechanisms in Central America and the four components driving this performance. The section titled "Targeting Performance in Central America" compares the results of the analysis across the six countries in 2016. The sections titled "Drivers of Progressivity: Coverage Ratio and Average Per-Unit Subsidy" and "Drivers of Regressivity: Access Ratio and Consumption Ratio" analyze the components associated with progressivity and regressivity, respectively. The final section, "How Do Individual Mechanisms in Each Country Perform?" offers a country-level analysis, focusing on how reforms have affected the factors that determine targeting efficiency in these components.

Measuring the Efficiency of the Distribution of Electricity Subsidies

Building on the framework presented in figure 5.1, the efficiency of a given subsidy policy depends on two questions: Who receives subsidies? and How much do they receive? The distribution of subsidies can be explained through five factors that affect "*beneficiary* targeting performance" and "*benefit* targeting performance" (e.g., Angel-Urdinola and Wodon 2007; Komives et al. 2005; Komives et al. 2007). To provide quantifiable answers to these questions, previous analyses have selected a target group of beneficiaries and compared the subsidies they receive with those that the overall population receives. This measures each mechanism's success at reaching its target beneficiary group and the efficiency with which it does so.

The first question, which determines the extensive margin of coverage of a given subsidy scheme, is decomposed into two factors. In simple terms, there are two key reasons that households may be excluded from receiving electricity subsidies: they are not connected to the electricity grid, and are therefore outside the scope of the subsidies;[2] or they do not receive subsidies because of the targeting design of the subsidy scheme. These two factors determine errors of inclusion and exclusion (box 5.2). Errors of exclusion reflect households in the target group that do not receive subsidies.

The second question determines the extensive margin, or the extent to which the distribution of subsidies is regressive because of how subsidies are allocated between recipients. The amount allocated to each household is, in general terms, *price * quantity*: the average subsidy per kWh consumed multiplied by the quantity of subsidized electricity consumed. That is, a household that consumes $x+1$ kWh of subsidized electricity receives more in subsidies than one that consumes x kWh. At the same time, having a subsidy mechanism with different subsidy rates results in consumers receiving different average subsidy amounts.

The level of regressivity arising from each of these factors can be measured using four ratios. As in the literature (e.g., Komives et al. 2007), each ratio

---

Box 5.2 Errors of Inclusion and Exclusion

How are errors of inclusion and exclusion determined? The first step is to define the target group for the policy. Figure B5.2.1 shows the results, using two target-group criteria: the poorest 40 percent of the population, and the poor (the population living on less than US$4 per day). Nevertheless, although using these target groups yields important insights, they are based on international measures designed primarily for comparative purposes, and hence are unlikely to be the same groups that policy makers are targeting.

Given the high coverage rates of electricity subsidies in Central America, errors of inclusion dominate errors of exclusion for the poorest 40 percent. Errors of inclusion vary from one-third of the population in El Salvador and Guatemala to more than half of Hondurans. That is, between one-third and one-half of the population of the top 60 percent of the income distribution are subsidy recipients in each country. Errors of exclusion, the share of the population that is in the target group but does not receive subsidies, varies from a low of 7 percent in Costa Rica to a high of 19 percent in Guatemala and 20 percent in Nicaragua. Low electrification rates are the main reason for Nicaragua's errors of exclusion. Guatemala's outcomes are due

box continues next page

Box 5.2 Errors of Inclusion and Exclusion *(continued)*

Figure B5.2.1 Errors of Inclusion and Exclusion, by Target Group

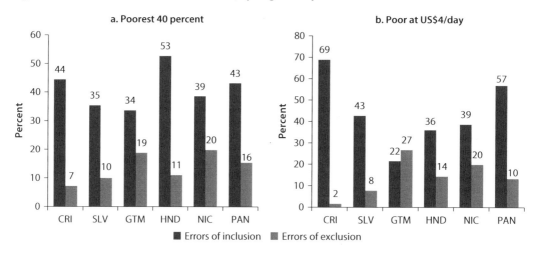

Source: World Bank elaboration using SEDLAC (CEDLAS and World Bank).

to both lower electrification rates and geographical differences in the access to subsidized electricity, because some electric companies do not take part in the country's subsidy scheme.

Significant differences in poverty rates in the six Central American countries suggest that the proportion of the population that should be targeted by electricity subsidies varies significantly across the region. If policy makers targeted households living on less than US$4 per day instead of the poorest 40 percent, errors of inclusion would be lower for Guatemala and Honduras, the two countries with poverty rates in excess of 40 percent, and higher for the three countries with poverty rates below 40 percent. In Honduras, for example, errors of inclusion would fall from 53 percent to 36 percent. In Panama and Costa Rica, the countries with the lowest poverty rates, errors of inclusion would represent the majority of subsidy recipients.

compares the outcomes for individuals in a target group—for example, those with income in the bottom 40 percent of the distribution—with all individuals in the population.

1. *Access ratio* is the share of the target population that is connected to the power grid compared to the share of the total population that is connected. This captures the effect of the differential access to electricity in the distribution of electricity subsidies, an effect that is independent of the design of the subsidy mechanism. Typically, this ratio is less than 1 because lower-income households have lower access to electricity. These lower rates of access undermine the progressivity of potential subsidy mechanisms.

2. *Coverage ratio* is the share of the target population that receives subsidized electricity compared to the share of the overall population receiving subsidized electricity, with both shares limited to those with access to the electricity grid. This is determined according to the subsidy scheme's targeting mechanism. This ratio should be greater than 1 if the electricity subsidy mechanism is targeted to lower-income households.

3. *Consumption ratio* is the average amount of subsidized electricity (measured in kWh) that individuals in the target population consume relative to the consumption of all recipients of electricity subsidies. This indicator is typically less than 1. Even within the consumption ranges that subsidies cover, electricity consumption tends to rise with income. In other words, subsidy beneficiaries with lower incomes tend to consume less electricity than the average beneficiary population. This is a key determinant of how much they receive in subsidies.

4. *Per-unit subsidy* measures the depth of subsidies: the average electricity subsidy per kWh consumed in the target group in relation to the average subsidy received by all beneficiaries. Like the coverage ratio, this factor is directly related to the design of the subsidy scheme and captures the effect of differential subsidy rates across different consumption thresholds. If the design leads to a progressive distribution of per-unit subsidy spending, this ratio is greater than 1, indicating that households in the target group receive a greater average subsidy than other beneficiaries.

The product of these four ratios yields the targeting performance indicator (TPI) (see annex 5A for its mathematical derivation).[3] The TPI is designed to quantify the efficiency with which subsidy mechanisms in the six countries succeed in subsidizing a particular target group. This indicator is calculated as the proportion of subsidies that households in a given target group receive—for example, the poorest 40 percent—divided by the percentage of the population that those households represent. It measures the extent to which the distribution of subsidy benefits between a target group and the overall population deviates from a neutral distribution (Komives et al. 2005). Also of importance is that it can be decomposed into the four ratios above, allowing analysis to identify the relative importance of each in determining the efficiency of subsidy mechanisms.

Targeting Performance in Central America

The TPI was estimated for four target groups: the poorest 40 percent of the population, the poorest 30 percent, the poorest 20 percent, and the poorest 10 percent. When the indicator is 1, the target population receives a share of subsidies equal to its share of the total population—a neutral distribution. TPI values greater than 1 indicate that the target population receives a greater share of subsidies than its share of the population. Because the target populations are all lower-income households, TPI values greater than 1 indicate a progressive distribution. Conversely, TPI values less than 1 indicate a regressive distribution, because the target population receives a share of subsidies that is smaller than its population share.

The TPI shows that the subsidy mechanisms in place in each of the six countries deliver a disproportionately small share of benefits to lower-income households (table 5.1). In all cases, the poorest 40 percent receive a smaller share of subsidies than the wealthiest 60 percent. El Salvador's TPI for the bottom 40 percent is the highest in the region, at 0.91. In other words, households in the bottom 40 percent receive 36.4 percent of subsidies, or 91 percent of what they would receive under a neutral distribution. Panama's TPI for households in the bottom 10 percent is the lowest in the region, at 0.3, indicating that the poorest 10 percent of households receive only 3 percent of subsidies (or 30 percent of what they would have received under a neutral distribution).

The targeting performance can be decomposed into its four components. The decomposition exercise shows that for all six countries two dimensions are progressive and two drive the overall regressivity of the subsidy mechanisms. Table 5.2 presents the results of the TPI decomposition for two target groups: the poorest 20 percent and the poorest 40 percent.[4] The coverage ratio and per-unit subsidy components are always progressive. The target group is slightly more likely to receive subsidies than the average consumer (coverage ratio), and the average subsidy received per kWh consumed of subsidized electricity is higher for lower-income households (the per-unit subsidy effect). As noted above, the selected tariff thresholds and subsidy depths of different consumption ranges directly determine these two components of subsidy mechanisms.

In every country, the key driver of regressivity is the consumption ratio. Put simply, the main reason that electricity subsidies are regressive is that wealthier households consume more subsidized electricity than lower-income households. In Honduras, the worst performer on this factor, subsidy recipients in the poorest 20 percent, consume only 42 percent as much subsidized electricity as the average subsidized consumer. Guatemala and Costa Rica are the best performers on this factor, with a ratio of only 0.68; those in the bottom two income deciles consume 68 percent of what average consumers use.

Although, like the coverage ratio and per-unit subsidy, the subsidy mechanism's design largely determines the consumption ratio, the access ratio cannot be addressed through changes in the electricity subsidy mechanism per se.

Table 5.1 Targeting Performance Indicator for Four Target Groups, 2016

Target group	Costa Rica	El Salvador	Guatemala	Honduras	Nicaragua	Panama
Poorest 10%	0.77	0.79	0.70	0.73	0.40	0.30
Poorest 20%	0.80	0.85	0.73	0.77	0.45	0.43
Poorest 30%	0.84	0.88	0.79	0.79	0.54	0.54
Poorest 40%	0.86	0.91	0.83	0.81	0.59	0.62

Source: World Bank elaboration using SEDLAC (CEDLAS and World Bank).

Table 5.2 Targeting Performance and Decomposition for Poorest 20 Percent and Poorest 40 Percent, 2016

	Costa Rica	El Salvador	Guatemala	Honduras	Nicaragua	Panama
Poorest 20%						
Access ratio	0.98	0.93	0.80	0.79	0.74	0.62
Coverage ratio	1.14	1.32	1.12	1.02	1.04	1.13
Consumption ratio	0.68	0.65	0.68	0.42	0.55	0.53
Per-unit subsidy	1.06	1.07	1.19	2.29	1.06	1.17
TPI	**0.80**	**0.85**	**0.73**	**0.77**	**0.45**	**0.44**
Poorest 40%						
Access ratio	0.99	0.96	0.87	0.87	0.83	0.82
Coverage ratio	1.12	1.24	1.14	1.01	1.04	1.09
Consumption ratio	0.76	0.73	0.74	0.54	0.66	0.63
Per-unit subsidy	1.03	1.04	1.14	1.73	1.02	1.11
TPI	**0.86**	**0.91**	**0.83**	**0.81**	**0.59**	**0.63**

Source: World Bank elaboration using SEDLAC (CEDLAS and World Bank).
Note: TPI= Targeting performance indicator.

Although urban electrification rates approach universal coverage in the six countries, rural electrification rates lag in some countries. Because the rural population is typically more likely to be lower income, the urban–rural divide in electrification rates implies that lower-income households are also less likely to have electricity. *Relative* electrification rates contribute to the magnitude of this factor as well. For example, Nicaragua has the lowest electrification rate for those in the poorest decile (54 percent), but no income decile surpasses 94 percent, whereas Panama has the largest disparity in electrification rates between those in the poorest decile (43 percent) and those in the top 60 percent of the distribution (97 percent above the 40th percentile). As a result, Panama's access ratio indicators for the poorest 20 percent are lower than those of Nicaragua (Nicaragua, 0.74; Panama, 0.62). This suggests that increasing the targeting efficiency of these mechanisms requires increasing connection rates for poor households.

Figure 5.2 shows the contribution of each of the four components to the final TPI score.[5] The per-unit subsidy and coverage ratio vary in importance across the six countries, with the per-unit subsidy being extremely important in Honduras and the coverage ratio dominating in Costa Rica and El Salvador. The access ratio is a secondary factor in explaining regressivity, accounting for 25–35 percent of the TPI in the poorest 20 percent in Guatemala, Nicaragua, and Panama. As noted above, the consumption ratio is the greatest driver of regressivity, accounting for between 43 percent of the value of the TPI in Guatemala and 65 percent in Costa Rica.[6] In Honduras the consumption ratio is nearly netted out by the effect of the per unit subsidy (44 percent and 42 percent, respectively).[7] Figure 5.2 suggests that adjusting subsidy policies to limit the amount of subsidized electricity that higher-income households consume would largely address the regressivity of the subsidy system.

Figure 5.2 Contributions to Targeting Performance Indicator, 2016

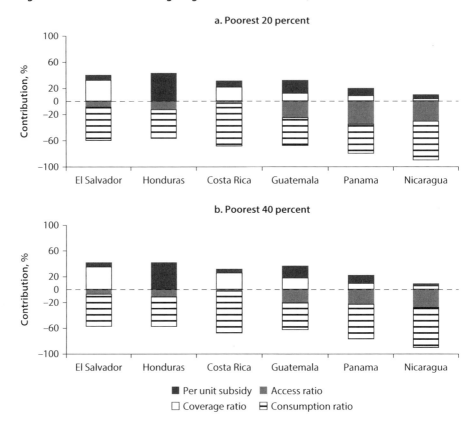

Source: World Bank elaboration using SEDLAC (CEDLAS and World Bank).

Drivers of Progressivity: Coverage Ratio and Average Per-Unit Subsidy

The coverage ratio captures subsidy coverage at the extensive margin. It measures the extent to which subsidies are successfully targeted to poorer households after taking into account inequitable access to electricity. The average per-unit subsidy indicator captures coverage at the intensive margin. It measures whether poorer recipient households receive a larger subsidy per unit of subsidized electricity than wealthier recipient households. Significantly, the subsidy mechanisms' design directly determines both of these dimensions, in particular through the inclusion threshold and differences in subsidy depth across consumption levels.

In Guatemala, Panama, and Nicaragua, these two drivers have nearly identical effects on the TPI and contribute equally to increasing the overall progressivity of their subsidy mechanisms (figure 5.3), but in Costa Rica and particularly in El Salvador, the coverage ratio is the primary driver of progressivity. Although Honduras's coverage ratio is the least progressive because almost all electricity customers receive subsidies, the relative size of recipients' per-unit subsidies is significantly more progressive in Honduras than in any of the other countries.

Figure 5.3 Progressive Drivers of Targeting Performance Indicators (TPIs) for the Poorest 40 Percent, 2016

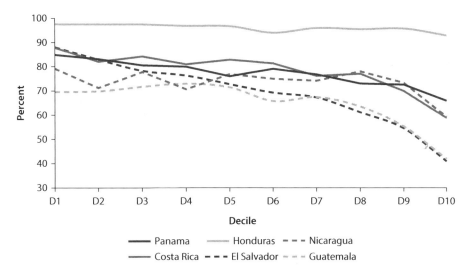

Source: World Bank elaboration using SEDLAC (CEDLAS and World Bank).

Figure 5.4 Coverage Ratio: Share of Households with Electricity That Received Subsidies, 2016

Coverage ratios reveal large errors of inclusion and some errors of exclusion in all six countries. Honduras's targeting is the least effective; subsidies are delivered to more than 90 percent of households in each income decile. This nearly flat coverage ratio has the effect of minimizing errors of exclusion, because nearly all poor households that have electricity receive subsidies, while at the same time guaranteeing large errors of inclusion, because more than 90 percent of top 10 percent of households also receive subsidies (figure 5.4). The downward-sloping curve in figure 5.4 reflects El Salvador's relatively

Fiscal and Welfare Impacts of Electricity Subsidies in Central America
http://dx.doi.org/10.1596/978-1-4648-1104-3

successful targeting mechanism. Nearly 90 percent of the poorest decile receives subsidies, with coverage ratios falling for subsequent deciles and reaching less than 40 percent for those in the top decile.

In terms of successful targeting, the other countries fall between the two extreme cases of El Salvador and Honduras. Guatemala's progressive targeting and low coverage ratios for the poorest households (subsidies cover approximately 70 percent of households with electricity in the low-income deciles) result in larger errors of exclusion than for El Salvador and Honduras and smaller errors of inclusion than for El Salvador. Costa Rica, Panama, and Nicaragua, which provide subsidies to a majority of those in each decile, have smaller errors of inclusion than Honduras but have larger errors of inclusion than El Salvador and Guatemala. Subsidies in these three countries cover 60 percent of the top decile.

Although the coverage ratio is low in Honduras, the average level of subsidy per kWh that Honduran households receive reduces the regressivity of the country's subsidy system. The average per-unit subsidy has the most progressive effect in Honduras, where it reaches a ratio of 2.29 for the bottom 20 percent and 1.73 for the bottom 40 percent. These high ratios are largely due to the country's direct subsidy mechanism, which results in Honduras's subsidy amounts varying the most between income groups. Of those who receive electricity subsidies, the poorest decile receives, on average, a subsidy of more than US$0.11 per kWh, substantially higher than the US$0.03 that the wealthiest 10 percent receives. Costa Rica provides the same average subsidy of US$0.02 per kWh consumed to subsidy recipients in all income deciles.[8] Figure 5.5 also highlights differences in subsidy levels per unit of subsidized electricity, with Guatemala, Nicaragua, and El Salvador surpassing other countries' per-unit subsidies in purchasing power parity terms.

Figure 5.5 Average Subsidy per kWh of Subsidized Electricity, 2016

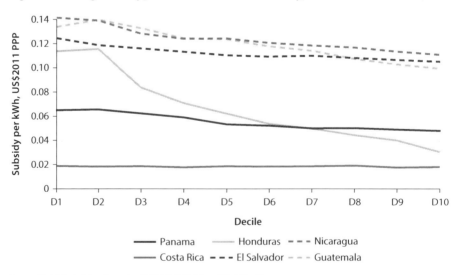

Source: World Bank elaboration using SEDLAC (CEDLAS and World Bank).
Note: PPP = purchasing power parity.

Drivers of Regressivity: Access Ratio and Consumption Ratio

The two key drivers of the regressivity of subsidy mechanisms in Central America are the consumption ratio of subsidized electricity and, to a lesser extent, access ratios. Although subsidy mechanism design does not directly determine access ratios, inclusion thresholds determine consumption ratios.

The high rates of consumption of subsidized electricity by higher-income households is the single biggest driver of regressivity in the region's subsidy mechanisms (figure 5.6). Even though higher-income households are less likely to receive subsidies and tend to receive a lower subsidy amount per unit consumed, the fact that they consume more subsidized electricity drives the regressivity of electricity subsidies in Central America.

National electrification rates vary from a low of 43 percent in the poorest 10 percent in Panama to near-universal access in the wealthiest deciles in the other five countries (figure 5.7). In El Salvador and Costa Rica, the access ratio is only marginally regressive; electrification rates are only 4 percent and 1 percent lower, respectively, for the poorest 40 percent than for the overall population. In the remaining four countries, lower electrification rates in the bottom income deciles contribute to the regressivity of subsidy mechanisms. The effect is largest in Panama and Nicaragua.

Lower-income households tend to consume less electricity; as a result, if thresholds are not set carefully, higher-income households can receive a significant share of subsidies by consuming more subsidized electricity. The consumption of subsidized electricity is particularly regressive in Honduras, resulting in a consumption ratio of 0.54 for the poorest 40 percent. This means

Figure 5.6 Negative Drivers of Targeting Performance Indicators (TPIs), 2016

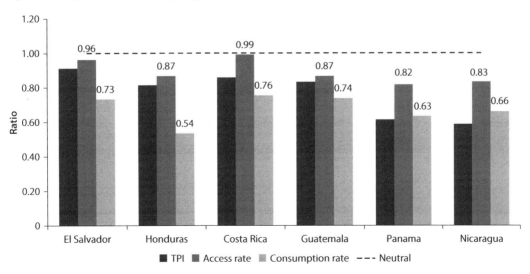

Source: World Bank elaboration using SEDLAC (CEDLAS and World Bank).

Fiscal and Welfare Impacts of Electricity Subsidies in Central America
http://dx.doi.org/10.1596/978-1-4648-1104-3

Figure 5.7 Electrification Rate: Share of Households with Electricity, 2016

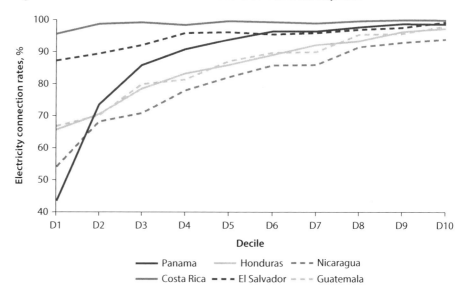

Figure 5.8 Electricity Consumption, kWh, 2016

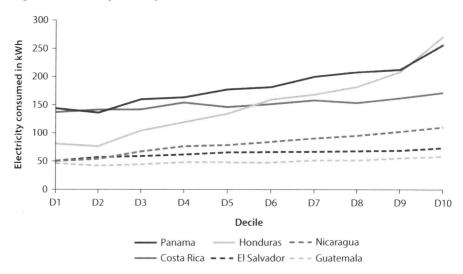

Source: World Bank elaboration using SEDLAC (CEDLAS and the World Bank).

that the poorest 40 percent consume 54 percent as much subsidized electricity as the average household that receives subsidies. Figure 5.8 illustrates the regressivity of consumption ratios; whereas the poorest two deciles combined consume approximately 81 kWh per month of subsidized electricity, the eighth decile consumes 182 kWh, and the wealthiest 10 percent consume 272 kWh. In Guatemala, El Salvador, and Costa Rica, the consumption ratios of the poorest 40 percent are closer to the average (0.72–0.74). In Guatemala, the country with the most compact consumption ratio distribution, the difference in consumption between the first and tenth deciles is approximately 12 kWh per month, a fraction of the difference in Honduras and Panama (190.8 and 113.3 kWh, respectively).

How Do Individual Mechanisms in Each Country Perform?

Costa Rica

In Costa Rica, most households receive a discount on their electricity bill, including almost 60 percent of the wealthiest 10 percent. This is a result of the country's IBT system, which provides a 13 percent discount for consumers under the threshold of 200 kWh per month and a smaller discount for those consuming 310 kWh or less. As a result, only 25 percent of Costa Ricans do not receive a discount.

Like the other electricity subsidy mechanisms in Central America, Costa Rica's results in a regressive distribution of subsidies, due mainly to greater consumption of subsidized electricity by wealthier households (annex 5B). Because of Costa Rica's cross-subsidy, this gives an incomplete picture of the system's distributional effects. Costa Rica's IBT system has a threshold of 200 kWh, with households that consume less than this receiving a 13 percent discount on their electric bill. The residential sector's cross-subsidy is nearly self-funding; this means that consumers who pay above-cost electricity prices "overpay" approximately as much as the system's net beneficiaries "underpay." This system results in three types of consumers: those who consume up to 200 kWh, who receive a 13 percent discount; those who consume more than 230–320 (depending on the electricity company), who pay a "cross-subsidy tax" on their bill; and those who consume between 200 and 230 or 320 kWh, who consume subsidized and unsubsidized electricity and hence receive a discount that averages to less than 13 percent per kWh consumed.

A majority of households in the poorest 80 percent in Costa Rica consumed only subsidized electricity, along with almost half of those in the wealthiest 20 percent. Figure 5.9 shows the distribution of electricity consumers according to the amount consumed per month. This shows that 25 percent of households in the poorest 10 percent consumed 99 kWh or less (or about half the threshold). The 25th percentile of consumption in the richest decile was 153 kWh, approximately 54 kWh per month more subsidized electricity than the poorest decile. This differential is indicative of why the TPI shows Costa Rica as having a regressive distribution of subsidies; of those who are subsidized, the wealthiest consume more subsidized electricity than the poorest,[9] but this misses the distribution of net payers. All households above the net payers line pay an average tariff that is above cost, and those between the subsidy threshold and net payers line pay an average tariff that is below cost but higher than the fully subsidized tariff.

A majority of consumers in each decile are net beneficiaries of the electricity subsidy mechanism. Figure 5.10 plots the factors related to the extensive margin of subsidies—electrification rates and subsidy coverage rates. Net beneficiaries are those who receive more in subsidies than they pay into cross-subsidies, whereas

Figure 5.9 Distribution of Electricity Customers, by Monthly Electricity Consumption, Costa Rica, 2016

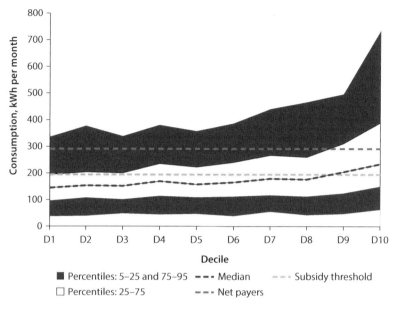

Source: World Bank calculations using SEDLAC (CEDLAS and World Bank).

Figure 5.10 Electrification and Subsidy Coverage Rates, Costa Rica, 2016

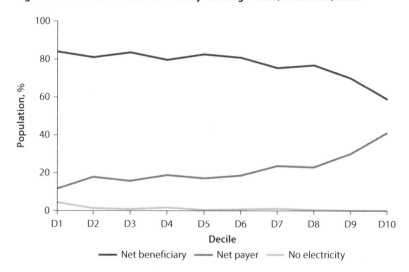

Source: World Bank calculations using SEDLAC (CEDLAS and World Bank).

net payers are those who, on average, pay an average rate that reflects cost or is higher. Net beneficiaries account for approximately 80 percent of each of the poorest eight income deciles. At 59 percent, they remain a majority, even among the wealthiest 10 percent. Overall, only 23.3 percent of households in Costa Rica are net payers, including 16 percent of households living on less than US$4 per day.

El Salvador

El Salvador boasts one of only three subsidy mechanisms in Central America that are progressive: subsidies to households consuming less than 50 kWh per month. Even so, the overall distribution of subsidies is biased toward higher-income households, driven by consumers of its second consumption block of 50–99 kWh per month. As with its neighbors, greater consumption of subsidized electricity by high-income beneficiaries explains this regressivity. The greater depth of subsidies for the lower consumption block somewhat mitigates this.

El Salvador's distribution of electricity subsidies is the most efficient in Central America. Even so, wealthier households accrue a disproportionate share of subsidies. The coverage ratio shows that households with electricity in the poorest 40 percent are more likely to receive subsidies. Its other driver of progressivity, the subsidy per kWh, is in line with most of its neighbors, showing a small bias toward lower-income households. At the same time, El Salvador's drivers of regressivity—access ratio and consumption ratio—reflect the country's relatively equitable access to electricity and a relatively low consumption threshold for subsidies. El Salvador's threshold of 99 kWh per month for subsidized electricity is technically the lowest in the region, just below Guatemala's 100 kWh. This limits the extent to which errors of inclusion can exacerbate the distribution of subsidies.

El Salvador's relative success in targeting and reducing errors of inclusion is due to its multiple-threshold VDT mechanism, with slightly higher subsidies for those who consume 49 kWh or less. Although, overall, El Salvador's subsidy mechanism generates a regressive distribution of electricity subsidies, its lower threshold is progressive. With a TPI of 1.48 for the poorest 10 percent of the population, the subsidy mechanism covering electricity consumption of less than 50 kWh awards 48 percent more subsidies to the poorest decile than to the average household (table 5.3). Along with Honduras's direct subsidy and, to a lesser extent, Panama's VDT, this is Central America's most progressive subsidy mechanism (table 4.3, chapter 4). Effective targeting—that is, households in the lowest income deciles are significantly more likely to consume 49 kWh or less per month, and hence are more likely to receive this subsidy—drives this success. This is reflected in figure 5.1: the amount of subsidized electricity that the median household in the poorest decile consumes is only 51 kWh, suggesting that many of the poorest households fall within the lowest tariff block.

On the other hand, El Salvador's subsidies for households consuming between 50 and 99 kWh per month is regressive, although less so than the subsidy systems in Nicaragua, Honduras, and Panama, and the same as Guatemala's. The overall result of the two consumption blocks is a subsidy mechanism that targets more efficiently than other mechanisms in Central America. Figures 5.11 and 5.12 show the reasons for this relative success: The share of households not receiving any subsidies increases from 23 percent in the lowest decile (more than half of which do not have electricity) to 59 percent in the highest decile, reflecting the exclusion of high-income households due to a

Table 5.3 Targeting Performance Indicator (TPI), by Mechanism, for Four Target Groups, El Salvador, 2016

Target group	Poorest 10%		Poorest 20%		Poorest 30%		Poorest 40%	
Mechanism	0–49 kWh	50–99 kWh	0–49 kWh	50–99 kWh	0–49 kWh	50–99 kWh	0–49 kWh	50–99 kWh
Access ratio	0.92	0.92	0.93	0.93	0.94	0.94	0.96	0.96
Coverage ratio	2.33	0.98	2.05	1.03	1.82	1.06	1.65	1.08
Consumption ratio	0.67	0.66	0.73	0.72	0.76	0.75	0.79	0.78
Subsidy per kWh	1.03	1.05	1.02	1.03	1.02	1.03	1.01	1.03
TPI	1.48	0.63	1.42	0.71	1.33	0.77	1.28	0.83

Source: World Bank calculations using SEDLAC (CEDLAS and World Bank).

Figure 5.11 Electrification and Subsidy Coverage Rates, by Income Decile, El Salvador, 2016

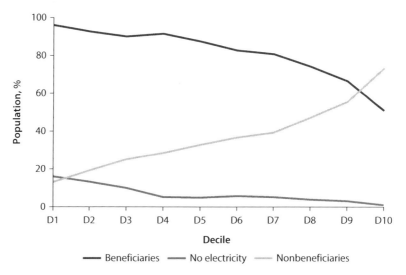

Source: World Bank calculations using SEDLAC (CEDLAS and the World Bank).

successful consumption threshold. At the same time, the average amount of subsidy received per unit is US$0.01 more for the poorest than the wealthiest recipients, reflecting the two-pronged subsidy mechanism's greater depth for consumers in the lower threshold.

The efficient targeting of subsidies in El Salvador means that some poor households do not receive subsidies. As shown in figure 5.11, 10 percent of Salvadorans in the poorest decile do not qualify for subsidies even though they are connected to the grid. Overall, errors of exclusion in El Salvador compare favorably with those of its neighbors, with only 8 percent of households living on less than US$4 per day being excluded. As seen in figure 4.2 in chapter 4, the average Salvadoran household living on less than US$4 per day receives the equivalent of a 2 percent income boost through electricity subsidies, bringing its electricity costs down to 2.5 percent of its household budget, the second lowest in Central America.

Figure 5.12 Subsidy per kWh and Consumption of Subsidized Electricity, by Income Decile, El Salvador, 2016

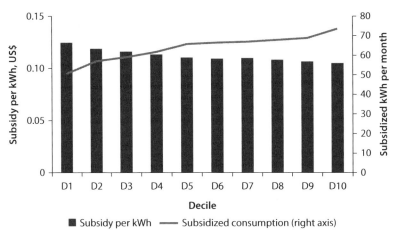

Source: World Bank calculations using SEDLAC (CEDLAS and the World Bank).

Guatemala

Although Guatemala's VDT mechanism is similar to El Salvador's, because of important differences in the countries' characteristics, the resulting efficiency of targeting is different. Guatemala's low electrification rates and incomplete geographical coverage of subsidy mechanisms undermine the country's ability to efficiently provide subsidies for low-income households.

Though it is one of the more efficiently targeted subsidy systems in the region, none of Guatemala's three subsidy thresholds yields a progressive distribution of subsidies. Like El Salvador, Guatemala has a multithreshold VDT mechanism that pays higher subsidies for lower consumption thresholds. Its subsidy mechanism has three levels, with the threshold for its lowest consumption group at 60 kWh (11 kWh higher than El Salvador's lowest threshold) and the highest at 100 kWh (just 1 kWh higher than El Salvador's). Despite the similarities in design, the TPI results indicate significant differences in efficiency of spending between the two countries' mechanisms.

The TPI decomposition given in table 5.2 shows that Guatemala's per-unit subsidy is more progressive than El Salvador's, and its consumption ratio is comparable. The per-unit subsidy ratio in Guatemala for the bottom 40 percent is 1.14, compared with 1.04 for El Salvador, but El Salvador's coverage ratio is more progressive (1.24 vs. 1.14), and its access ratio is less regressive (0.96 vs 0.87). Combined, these factors result in El Salvador's superior targeting performance.

Guatemala's weaker efficiency in spending relative to El Salvador is driven primarily by the two factors that determine the extensive margins of the subsidies: the access and coverage ratios. What drives the differences between the two countries is Guatemala's low electrification rates, which exclude many of the poorest, and its higher coverage rate of households in the top 60 percent.

Guatemala has relatively low electrification rates: electrification rates do not surpass 90 percent for each decile in the bottom 80 percent of the population (figure 5.13). This lack of connection to the electric grid automatically disqualifies one-quarter of the bottom 40 percent, including one-third of the poorest 10 percent, from receiving electricity subsidies.

Guatemala's lowest consumption threshold provides the most efficient targeting of the three thresholds; even so, it awards households in the poorest 40 percent only 92 percent of what a neutral distribution would (table 5.4). Although this lower threshold is more likely to include members of the poorest 40 percent than other groups (as its coverage ratio of 1.27 reflects),

Figure 5.13 Electrification and Subsidy Coverage Rates, by Income Decile, Guatemala, 2016

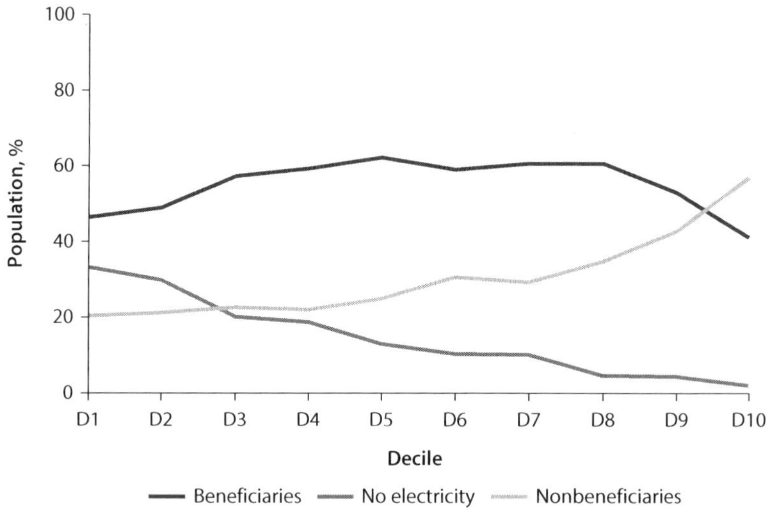

Source: World Bank calculations using SEDLAC (CEDLAS and the World Bank).

Table 5.4 Targeting Performance Indicator (TPI), by Mechanism, for Four Target Groups, Guatemala, 2016

Target group	Poorest 10%			Poorest 20%			Poorest 30%			Poorest 40%		
Mechanism	0–60 kWh	61–88 kWh	89–100 kWh	0–60 kWh	61–88 kWh	89–100 kWh	0–60 kWh	61–88 kWh	89–100 kWh	0–60 kWh	61–88 kWh	89–100 kWh
Access ratio	0.79	0.79	0.79	0.80	0.80	0.80	0.84	0.84	0.84	0.87	0.87	0.87
Coverage ratio	1.24	0.96	0.78	1.29	0.85	0.73	1.29	0.89	0.68	1.27	0.93	0.83
Consumption ratio	0.70	0.77	0.75	0.72	0.77	0.75	0.75	0.81	0.77	0.77	0.82	0.78
Per-unit subsidy	1.12	1.13	1.17	1.12	1.17	1.27	1.11	1.14	1.29	1.09	1.12	1.19
TPI	0.76	0.66	0.54	0.83	0.61	0.56	0.89	0.69	0.57	0.92	0.74	0.67

Source: World Bank calculations, using SEDLAC (CEDLAS and World Bank).

higher-income households qualifying for this subsidy consume more electricity than poorer households. The other two consumption blocks are less likely to include households from the poorest 40 percent.[10] For example, only 35 percent of beneficiaries of the consumption block of 89–100 kWh per month are members of the poorest 40 percent.

Subsidy coverage of households with electricity connections is low for poorer households (figure 5.14). Only two-thirds of the poorest 10 percent that have electricity received electricity subsidies, indicating that 20 percent of Guatemala's poorest decile is excluded from subsidies, even though they are connected to the grid. As shown in figure 5.1, this is not simply because low-income households consume more than 100 kWh per month. The median household in the poorest five deciles consumes 50 kWh or less, and 75 percent consume less than 81 kWh per month. Rather, this is because not all electricity providers offer subsidies, leaving out the poor in some regions.

Guatemala's VDT, with three consumption blocks and no subsidies for consumption over 100 kWh per month, is relatively successful. The different depth of subsidies for the three consumption blocks means that, per unit consumed, poorer households receive a higher subsidy. But the country's relatively low levels of electrification and incomplete geographic coverage of subsidies mean that many of Guatemala's poorest households are automatically excluded from subsides, reducing the effectiveness of targeting through mechanism design. As a result, a full 27 percent of households living on less than US$4 per day do not receive subsidies, the region's highest level of errors of exclusion. The comparison of Guatemala and El Salvador reinforces the importance of country characteristics, such as electrification rates, for the efficiency of even well-designed subsidy mechanisms.

Figure 5.14 Subsidy per kWh and Consumption of Subsidized Electricity, by Income Decile, Guatemala, 2016

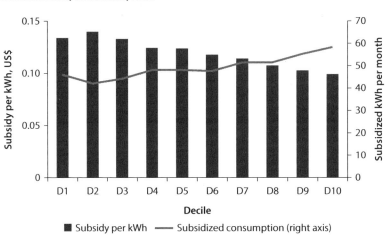

Source: World Bank calculations using SEDLAC (CEDLAS and World Bank)

Honduras

Honduras's two subsidy schemes diverge dramatically in targeting performance. Whereas its direct subsidy is among the best in Central America, its cross-subsidy is among the worst. The two factors underlying the poor targeting of the cross-subsidy are its near-universal coverage and the high amount of subsidized electricity that high-income households consume. Recent reforms are expected to have addressed some of the shortcomings of the cross-subsidy.

Honduras's direct subsidy is progressive and achieves the region's highest targeting performance. Households consuming less than 75 kWh per month receive a direct transfer. In terms of targeting performance, this subsidy achieves a TPI of 1.66 for the poorest 10 percent and 1.48 for the poorest 40 percent, meaning that these target groups receive 66 and 48 percent, respectively, more in direct subsidies than other households (table 5.5).

Although the direct subsidy is a highly successful component of Honduras's subsidy system, the country's other mechanism—its cross-subsidy—overshadows it. As described in chapters 2 and 4, this cross-subsidy is extremely poorly targeted because of its high implied inclusion threshold, which exceeds 800 kWh. This is reflected in its low targeting performance, which is driven by one of the most regressive consumption ratios in the region. For the poorest 10 percent, the consumption ratio, which is measured as the ratio of subsidized electricity that the poorest 10 percent consume relative to the average, is 0.42. That is, the poorest 10 percent consume only 42 percent as much subsidized electricity as the average household does under this mechanism.

There is near-universal coverage of electricity subsidies in households connected to the grid, as figure 5.15 illustrates. Because of low electrification rates among poor households, driven in large part by the lagging electrification of rural areas, the only deciles without near-universal subsidy coverage are those living in poverty. One-third of households in the poorest decile do not have electricity, and electrification rates surpass 90 percent beginning only with the seventh income decile. On the other hand, in the wealthiest decile, only 7 percent of connected households do not receive the cross-subsidy.

Near-universal coverage is combined with high electricity consumption ratios and a high coverage threshold (figure 5.15). Households in the wealthiest

Table 5.5 Targeting Performance Indicator (TPI), by Mechanism, for Four Target Groups, Honduras, 2016

Target group	Poorest 10%		Poorest 20%		Poorest 30%		Poorest 40%	
Mechanism	Direct	Cross	Direct	Cross	Direct	Cross	Direct	Cross
Access ratio	0.76	0.76	0.79	0.79	0.83	0.83	0.87	0.87
Coverage ratio	2.65	1.02	2.67	1.02	2.24	1.02	1.93	1.01
Consumption ratio	0.83	0.42	0.84	0.42	0.86	0.48	0.88	0.54
Per-unit subsidy	1.00	2.24	1.00	2.29	1.00	1.97	1.00	1.73
TPI	1.66	0.73	1.75	0.77	1.61	0.79	1.48	0.81

Source: World Bank calculations using SEDLAC (CEDLAS and World Bank).

Figure 5.15 Electrification and Subsidy Coverage Rates, by Income Decile, Honduras, 2016

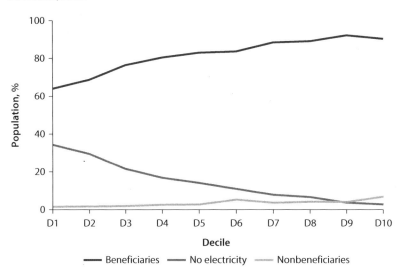

Source: World Bank calculations using SEDLAC (CEDLAS and World Bank).

10 percent consume, on average, 270 kWh per month of subsidized electricity, whereas households with electricity in the poorest 10 percent consume only 80 kWh per month, on average. Although this is significantly lower than in higher-income households, it is much higher than consumption ratios in El Salvador and Guatemala.[11] Households in the wealthiest 40 percent in Honduras consume electricity at rates similar to those in Costa Rica, a country with near-universal electrification and a per capita GDP that is three times as high, and Panama, a country with per capita GDP that is more than four times as high.[12]

One area in which Honduras's subsidies are well designed is their depth; in both schemes, poorer households receive more per unit consumed than wealthier households (figure 5.16). Although the direct subsidy can provide benefits of up to 100 percent of the electricity bill for households that consume less than 75 kWh per month, the cross-subsidy also delivers a per-unit subsidy that is almost four times as high to the poorest 10 percent as to the overall population.[13] Households in the poorest two income deciles receive an average per subsidy of US$0.11 to US$0.12 per kWh consumed. Beneficiaries in the wealthiest income decile receive only US$0.03 per kWh consumed, although their higher consumption means that they receive a far higher share of total subsidies.

These results suggest that improving the targeting of Honduras's electricity subsidies is fairly straightforward: reduce the inclusion threshold. Honduras's two subsidy schemes represent the best and worst outcomes of targeting in Central America. A decrease in the implicit inclusion threshold of the IBT cross-subsidy would greatly improve targeting performance. Its reduction can

Figure 5.16 Subsidy per kWh and Consumption of Subsidized Electricity, by Income Decile, Honduras, 2016

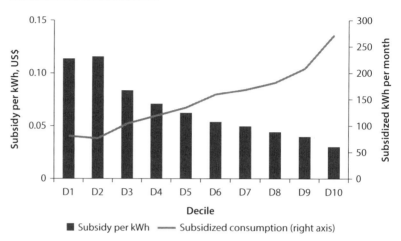

Source: World Bank calculations using SEDLAC (CEDLAS and World Bank).

be achieved in two ways: reducing the thresholds at which electricity is discounted, or decreasing (increasing) the discount (subsidy tax) for each block of consumption. The country's high demand for electricity places extra demand on a power grid that is financially strapped and heavily dependent on thermally generated electricity. Improving the cross-subsidy mechanism so that high-volume consumers face costs that are greater than cost recovery would help provide incentives for energy efficiency, simultaneously improving the fiscal situation of the power sector and decreasing the strain on the grid. It is expected that reforms implemented in June 2016 and not reflected in these results will achieve some of these potential gains.

Nicaragua

Both of Nicaragua's subsidy schemes are inefficiently targeted, partially because of the country's low electrification rates among poor households. However, the bigger reason for Nicaragua's poor targeting efficiency is thresholds that are high relative to the consumption of low-income households, leading to significant coverage rates for higher-income households. In addition, Nicaragua's VDT is one of only two subsidy mechanisms in the region that provide deeper discounts for higher consumption levels. Because higher-income households consume more electricity, these deeper discounts disproportionally go to wealthier consumers.

Both of Nicaragua's subsidy schemes are inefficiently targeted. Nicaragua has a VDT system arising from a temporary tariff freeze first introduced in 2005 and an IBT cross-subsidy system wherein households consuming less than 150 kWh pay below cost-reflective tariffs and households above 150 kWh are net payers.[14] Both of these schemes result in biased distribution of subsidies to upper-income households, as measured by the TPI. For example, the VDT's subsidies for the bottom 40 percent are just half of what is spent on the average beneficiary (TPI 0.53), whereas the IBT's is 89 percent (TPI 0.89) (table 5.6). The IBT yields a less-regressive distribution because it results in deeper per-unit discounts for poorer households as a result of its multiple consumption blocks and gradually decreasing average discount for higher-volume consumers.

Nicaragua's subsidy system is regressive partially because of low rates of electrification among its poorest households. Like Guatemala and Honduras, Nicaragua has a large rural population with high poverty rates and low electrification rates. Overall, one in five Nicaraguans is not connected to the electric grid. This includes almost half of the population in the poorest decile and 30 percent of those in the second decile (figure 5.17). Electrification rates for the wealthiest 30 percent are approximately 93 percent.

The key drivers of regressivity are the factors that determine coverage and consumption ratios, both of which are determined by the subsidy mechanism design. The VDT and IBT are slightly more likely to be allocated to lower-income households that have electricity than upper-income households, but errors of inclusion remain high; 56 percent of households in the wealthiest decile receive subsidies. Additionally, unlike most schemes in Central America, the average per-unit subsidy received through the VDT is higher for high-income households than those in the poorest 40 percent because higher consumption blocks within the VDT receive deeper discounts relative to the IBT tariff; of the mechanisms included in this study, only the FET in Panama has a similarly increasing discount.[15]

The high inclusion thresholds for both schemes result in large subsidies to higher-income households. As shown in figure 5.1, Nicaraguan households do not consume as much electricity as those of some neighboring countries. The median household in the poorest decile consumes 41 kWh per month, and the median household in the top decile consumes 147 kWh. The VDT's and IBT's inclusion thresholds are 150 kWh per month. This mismatch between consumption ratios and thresholds suggests weak quantity targeting. The poorest decile consumes on average only 50 kWh per month of subsidized electricity, and the wealthiest consumes 111 kWh (figure 5.18).

Table 5.6 Targeting Performance Indicator (TPI), by Mechanism, for Four Target Groups, Nicaragua, 2016

Target group	Poorest 10%		Poorest 20%		Poorest 30%		Poorest 40%	
Mechanism	VDT	IBT	VDT	IBT	VDT	IBT	VDT	IBT
Access ratio	0.65	0.65	0.74	0.74	0.80	0.80	0.83	0.83
Coverage ratio	1.11	1.11	1.04	1.04	1.05	1.05	1.04	1.04
Consumption ratio	0.51	0.51	0.55	0.55	0.61	0.61	0.66	0.66
Per-unit subsidy	0.92	1.98	0.91	1.92	0.92	1.71	0.93	1.55
TPI	0.34	0.73	0.38	0.81	0.48	0.88	0.53	0.89

Source: World Bank calculations using SEDLAC (CEDLAS and World Bank).

Fiscal and Welfare Impacts of Electricity Subsidies in Central America
http://dx.doi.org/10.1596/978-1-4648-1104-3

Figure 5.17 Electrification and Subsidy Coverage Rates, by Income Decile, Nicaragua, 2016

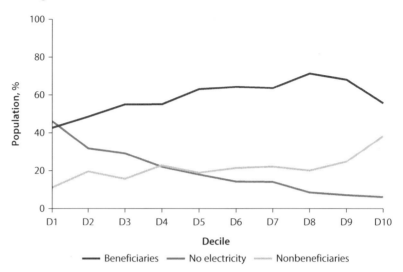

Source: World Bank calculations using SEDLAC (CEDLAS and World Bank).

Figure 5.18 Subsidy per kWh and Consumption of Subsidized Electricity, by Income Decile, Nicaragua, 2016

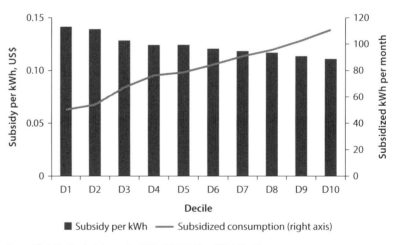

Source: World Bank calculations using SEDLAC (CEDLAS and World Bank).

Panama

Only one of the four electricity subsidy schemes in Panama comes close to targeting the poorest 40 percent at similar rates as the rest of the population; the other three yield significant subsidies to wealthier households. This is particularly the case for the retiree discount and the Western Region Tariff discount. Panama also has the greatest difference in electrification rates between the poorest deciles and the rest of the population, leading to a larger bias related to lack of access than in other countries.

Of Panama's four subsidy schemes in effect as of April 2016, only the VDT subsidy approaches targeting efficiency (table 5.7). The worst performer is retiree benefits: the TPI is 0.24—the poorest decile receives 24 percent of the subsidies received by the average beneficiary. The Fondo de Estabilización Tarifaria (FET) and Fondo Tarifario de Occidente (FTO) are only marginally better at 31 and 35 percent, respectively. The VDT also results in lower benefits for the poorest 10 percent and 20 percent than the average beneficiary but improves if we consider the poorest 40 percent instead. For them, the VDT results in a targeting performance value of 1.09, meaning that the poorest 40 percent receive approximately 9 percent more in VDT subsidies than the average beneficiary. Panama's VDT is one of only three subsidy schemes in Central America with a targeting performance value greater than 1.

The FTO and the retiree discount are regressive across the four factors of TPI; The coverage ratio indicates that beneficiaries of these mechanisms are underrepresented in the bottom 40 percent of the population. The lack of thresholds for the FTO also results in higher subsidies for higher electricity consumption; the FTO subsidizes the highest block of consumption at higher rates than lower blocks.

Of the six Central America countries, Panama has the largest difference in electrification rates between the poorer deciles and the rest of the population. Over half of the poorest 10 percent and a quarter of the second decile are not connected to the power grid, although 96 percent of the top 60 percent of households are connected. The effect of this difference can be seen in the access ratios reported in table 5.7—the access ratio of 0.41 for the poorest 10 percent is the lowest in the region.

Table 5.7 Targeting Performance Indicator (TPI), by Mechanism, for Four Target Groups, Panama, 2016

Target group:	Poorest 10%				Poorest 20%			
Mechanism:	FET	FTO	VDT	Retirees	FET	FTO	VDT	Retirees
Access ratio	0.41	0.41	0.41	0.41	0.62	0.62	0.62	0.62
Coverage ratio	1.23	1.69	2.05	0.93	1.24	1.68	2.16	0.95
Consumption ratio	0.53	0.54	0.62	0.63	0.56	0.48	0.66	0.57
Per-unit subsidy	1.13	0.93	1.01	1.01	1.10	0.89	1.02	0.98
TPI	0.31	0.35	0.53	0.24	0.47	0.45	0.90	0.33
Target group:	Poorest 30%				Poorest 40%			
Mechanism:	FET	FTO	VDT	Retirees	FET	FTO	VDT	Retirees
Access ratio	0.75	0.75	0.75	0.75	0.82	0.82	0.82	0.82
Coverage ratio	1.19	1.55	1.92	0.97	1.16	1.44	1.72	0.98
Consumption ratio	0.62	0.54	0.73	0.61	0.66	0.60	0.76	0.65
Per-unit subsidy	1.06	0.90	1.02	1.00	1.05	0.91	1.02	1.00
TPI	0.58	0.56	1.06	0.44	0.66	0.65	1.09	0.52

Source: World Bank calculations using SEDLAC (CEDLAS and World Bank).
Note: FET = Fondo de Estabilización Tarifaria; FTO = Fondo Tarifario de Occidente; VDT = volume-differentiated tariff.

The VDT is more likely to be received by low-income households and, along with the FET, to pay these households higher per unit subsidy amounts. This reduces the regressivity of the overall system. Among those connected to the power grid, approximately a third of households in the wealthiest decile are excluded from receiving subsidies, as well as 7 percent of the poorest decile and 12 percent of the second decile (figure 5.19). On the other hand, the amount of subsidized electricity that the wealthiest decile consumes (257 kWh per month) is more than 100 kWh more per month than what the poorest decile consumes (144 kWh per month) (figure 5.20).

Figure 5.19 Electrification and Subsidy Coverage Rates, by Income Decile, Panama, 2016

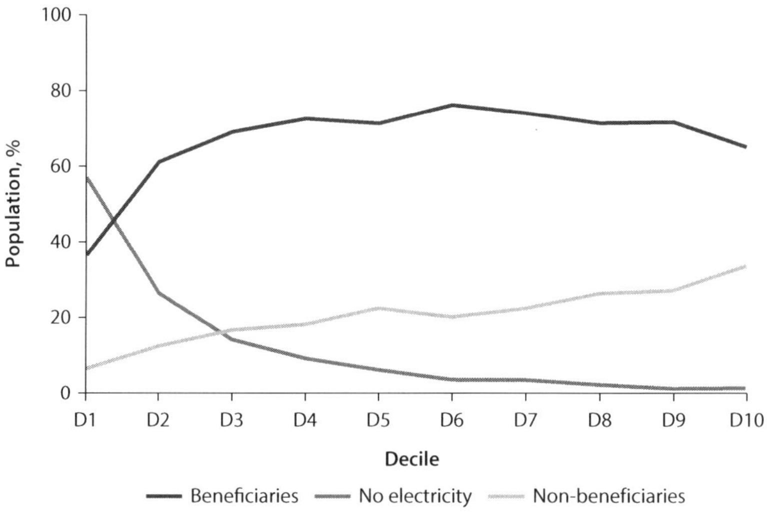

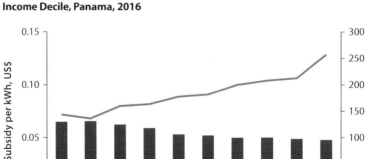

Source: World Bank calculations using SEDLAC (CEDLAS and World Bank).

Figure 5.20 Subsidy per kWh and Consumption of Subsidized Electricity, by Income Decile, Panama, 2016

Source: World Bank calculations using SEDLAC (CEDLAS and World Bank).

Annex 5A: Derivation of the Targeting Performance Indicator

Following the framework presented in chapter 5 and developed by Komives et al. (2007), the targeting efficiency of subsidies is determined according to four factors:

C' = access to electricity

E' = coverage of subsidies

K' = quantity of subsidized electricity consumed

S' = subsidy per unit consumed

Let

S_G = total electricity subsidies that group G receives

C_G = number of individuals in group G connected to the electricity grid

E_G = number of individuals in group G who receive electricity subsidies

K_G = quantity of subsidized electricity, measured in kWh, that individuals in group G consume

$$C'*E'*K'*S' = \left(\frac{C_G}{G}\right)\left(\frac{E_G}{C_G}\right)\left(\frac{K_G}{E_G}\right)\left(\frac{S_G}{K_G}\right) = \frac{S_G}{G}$$

where

$\dfrac{S_G}{G}$ = per capita electricity subsidy that group G receives

$\dfrac{C_G}{G}$ = electrification rate of group G (proportion connected to the electricity grid)

$\dfrac{E_G}{C_G}$ = coverage rate of group G (proportion with access to electricity grid that receive electricity subsidies)

$\dfrac{K_G}{E_G}$ = consumption rate of group G (average quantity of subsidized electricity consumed by subsidy beneficiaries)

$\dfrac{S_G}{K_G}$ = per-unit subsidy of group G (average subsidy amount per kWh of subsidized electricity)

Let T designate the target population for a given subsidy and A designate the total population. The share of subsidies that the target population receives can be written as

$$\left[\frac{\frac{S_T}{T}}{\frac{S_A}{A}}\right] = \left[\frac{\left(\frac{C_T}{T}\right)}{\left(\frac{C_A}{A}\right)}\right]*\left[\frac{\left(\frac{E_T}{C_T}\right)}{\left(\frac{E_A}{C_A}\right)}\right]*\left[\frac{\left(\frac{K_T}{E_T}\right)}{\left(\frac{K_A}{E_A}\right)}\right]*\left[\frac{\left(\frac{S_T}{K_T}\right)}{\left(\frac{S_A}{K_A}\right)}\right]$$

Which can be rewritten as:

$$\left(\frac{S_T}{S_A}\right)\bigg/\left(\frac{T}{A}\right) = \text{targeting performance indicator}$$

Fiscal and Welfare Impacts of Electricity Subsidies in Central America
http://dx.doi.org/10.1596/978-1-4648-1104-3

where

$$\frac{T}{A} = \text{Proportion of population in the target group}$$

$$\frac{S_T}{S_A} = \text{Proportion of subsidies that the target group receives}$$

Annex 5B: Targeting Performance Indicator (TPI) Results for Target Groups from Poorest 10 Percent through Poorest 40 Percent, 2016

	Costa Rica	El Salvador	Guatemala	Honduras	Nicaragua	Panama
Poorest 10%						
Access ratio	0.96	0.92	0.79	0.76	0.65	0.41
Coverage ratio	1.20	1.36	1.12	1.02	1.11	1.15
Consumption ratio	0.62	0.58	0.68	0.42	0.51	0.53
Per-unit subsidy	1.07	1.09	1.16	2.24	1.08	1.20
TPI	**0.77**	**0.79**	**0.70**	**0.73**	**0.40**	**0.30**
Poorest 20%						
Access ratio	0.98	0.93	0.80	0.79	0.74	0.62
Coverage ratio	1.14	1.32	1.12	1.02	1.04	1.13
Consumption ratio	0.68	0.65	0.68	0.42	0.55	0.53
Per-unit subsidy	1.06	1.07	1.19	2.29	1.06	1.17
TPI	**0.80**	**0.85**	**0.73**	**0.77**	**0.45**	**0.44**
Poorest 30%						
Access ratio	0.99	0.94	0.84	0.83	0.80	0.75
Coverage ratio	.14	1.28	1.13	1.02	1.05	1.11
Consumption ratio	0.71	0.69	0.71	0.48	0.61	0.59
Per-unit subsidy	1.05	1.06	1.18	1.97	1.04	1.14
TPI	**0.84**	**0.88**	**0.79**	**0.79**	**0.54**	**0.55**
Poorest 40%						
Access ratio	0.99	0.96	0.87	0.87	0.83	0.82
Coverage ratio	1.12	1.24	1.14	1.01	1.04	1.09
Consumption ratio	0.76	0.73	0.74	0.54	0.66	0.63
Per-unit subsidy	1.03	1.04	1.14	1.73	1.02	1.11
TPI	**0.86**	**0.91**	**0.83**	**0.81**	**0.59**	**0.63**

Source: World Bank elaboration based on SEDLAC (CEDLAS and World Bank) and data obtained from country authorities.

Notes

1. Although this framework was developed specifically for electricity subsidies, the same logic can be used to assess the targeting efficiency of any transfer or tax.
2. In previous studies (e.g., Komives et al. 2007), this factor was divided into two separate factors: the electrification rate and the uptake rate (how many households

chose to connect). These two factors are combined in this study because poverty levels typically determine both—at the community level or at the household level. In addition, household surveys do not generally differentiate between reasons for not having electricity.

3. A quantitatively similar approach has been taken in the literature, for example, in Komives et al. (2007), where the targeting performance indicator is referred to as Ω.

4. See annex 5B for TPI decomposition results for the four target groups.

5. To compare the contribution of each component to total TPI, a log transformation was applied to each component, resulting in an additive relationship between components. Any component less than 1 is transformed into a negative contribution, and components greater than 1 yield a positive contribution.

6. The consumption ratio has the same value in these two countries (0.68), but because the other factors differ, they yield different contributions.

7. Figure 5.2 should be interpreted with caution because the figure does not represent the relative magnitude of each component across countries.

8. This is a result of the ratio being limited to subsidized electricity, which has different implications in an IBT system. See the last section of this chapter for more details about the results for Costa Rica.

9. For the TPI calculations based only on positive subsidies, the level of subsidy received per unit of subsidized electricity does not vary significantly depending on the income decile (ranging between US$0.018 and US$0.019 per kWh), even as the amount of subsidized electricity consumed increases from 137 kWh per month for the poorest 10 percent to 172 kWh for subsidy recipients in the richest 10 percent.

10. This is in part because households that consume less are already included in the lower consumption block. Removing this block would imply higher coverage rates by the other consumption blocks for the poorest deciles.

11. Because of a lack of recent data on electricity consumption at the household level, these rates are based on projections from the 2007 household survey (see annex 4A for details on how this was estimated), the most recent data source that contains information on electricity consumption by income level.

12. Adjusted for cost of living (purchase price parity), Honduras's 2015 GDP per capita is US$5,085, compared with US$15,377 in Costa Rica and US$22,192 in Panama (Source: World Development Indicators).

13. The depth of the cross-subsidy is 30 percent of the tariff for the first 100 kWh per month, 2 percent for 100 to 300 kWh, 0 percent for 300 to 500 kWh, and −10 percent for additional kWh consumed. Because this mechanism is an IBT, the cost of the negative subsidy surpasses the benefits from the positive subsidies only at levels of 840 kWh per month.

14. There are no official figures for what the cost-reflective tariff per kWh is in Nicaragua. To estimate it, we used the average price per kWh for the residential sector in 2014 published in official figures. Based on this value, the cross-subsidy is slightly unbalanced, and the implicit threshold is 150 kWh.

15. The discount per kWh increases with the consumption block, ranging from 4.4 cordobas per kWh for the first 25 kWh consumed per month to 25.8 cordobas per kWh for consumption between 101 and 150 kWh per month (see chapter 2).

Bibliography

Angel-Urdinola, D., and Q. Wodon. 2007. "Do Utility Subsidies Reach the Poor? Framework and Evidence for Cape Verde, São Tomé, and Rwanda." *Economics Bulletin* 9 (4): 1–7.

Coady, D., M. Grosh, and J. Hoddinott. 2004. "Targeting Outcomes Redux." *World Bank Research Observer* 19 (1): 61–85.

Komives, K., J. Halpern, V. Foster, Q. Wodon, and R. Abdullah. 2007. "Utility Subsidies as Social Transfers: An Empirical Evaluation of Targeting Performance." *Development Policy Review* 25 (6): 659–79.

Komives, K., V. Foster, J. Halpern, Q. Wodon, and R. Abdullah. 2005. *Water, Electricity, and the Poor: Who Benefits from Utility Subsidies?* Washington, DC: World Bank.

CHAPTER 6

Simulating Policy Options

Marco Antonio Hernández Oré, Leopoldo Tornarolli, Laura Olivera, and Liliana D. Sousa

This chapter illustrates the trade-offs involved in different reform strategies by simulating the fiscal and welfare effects of five prospective reform scenarios for electricity subsidies. The results show that, in every country in the region, reforming residential electricity subsidies could significantly lower fiscal costs and improve the efficiency of targeting, without negatively affecting the welfare of lower-income households and with only minor budget implications for higher-income households. For instance, combining electricity consumption with other eligibility criteria, such as participation in a cash-transfer system, can reduce errors of inclusion and exclusion, increasing the share of subsidy benefits that reaches lower-income households.

The preceding chapters examined the fiscal cost of electricity subsidies in Central America and the limited extent to which they advance these countries' poverty reduction, distributional equity, and macroeconomic stability objectives. In all six Central American countries, residential electricity subsidies have a demonstrably positive effect on the welfare of households across the income distribution, particularly poor households. But because of their high fiscal cost and inherent targeting limitations, electricity subsidy regimes are not the most efficient tool for reducing poverty, promoting distribution equity, or reinforcing macroeconomic stability.

Residential electricity subsidy regimes have a number of weaknesses that can be at least partially addressed by adapting existing subsidy mechanisms. First, no targeting system based on electricity consumption can perfectly reflect differences in household income levels, so electricity subsidies will inevitably suffer from errors of inclusion and exclusion. Subsidizing electricity (as opposed to other goods) is especially problematic, because low electrification rates in rural poor households can exacerbate errors of exclusion. Second, because all subsidies artificially reduce the price of the subsidized good, subsidizing electricity provides incentives for wasteful power consumption. Encouraging excessive electricity consumption has particularly negative implications for Central America, where oil accounts for an expanding share of each country's energy mix. Third, using public policy to determine residential electricity prices can increase the opacity of fiscal policy, generate administrative inefficiencies, create opportunities for rent seeking, and undermine the financial stability of electric utilities. Although these concerns are not thoroughly explored in the analysis, any reform that reduces subsidy spending or attenuates political influence over electricity prices would have positive spillover effects in these areas.

Given their limitations, ending subsidy regimes in favor of more traditional redistributive fiscal policies would be a better option for achieving poverty reduction, distributional equity, and macroeconomic stability objectives in all six Central American countries. Any poverty or equity objective that can be accomplished by subsidizing electricity consumption can be accomplished more efficiently through more traditional redistributive economic policies, including targeted fiscal transfers. Cash transfers, for example, can shift resources from wealthier to poorer households with greater accuracy than electricity subsidies. Similarly, if the goal is to stabilize household budgets against electricity price shocks, cash transfers can accomplish this without distorting electricity prices.

Limitations notwithstanding, electricity subsidies are well-established elements of economic policy in all Central American countries, and they enjoy strong support among powerful constituencies. As a result, abolishing subsidies outright may prove politically infeasible, and policy makers should consider reform strategies that enhance the effectiveness of electricity subsidy regimes while leaving their essential structure in place (Inchauste and Victor 2016).

This chapter explores reform options designed to manage the cost of subsidy regimes without harming the welfare of lower-income households. Any shift in the distribution of subsidy benefits—even if it serves to make the system more progressive and pro-poor—will have negative implications for certain households, and policy makers need to be sensitive to these concerns and strive to address the costs of reforms. To illustrate the trade-offs involved in reforming electricity subsidy schemes, five alternative scenarios are simulated for each Central American country.

The outcome of each simulated reform scenario is judged according to three criteria: fiscal savings, targeting efficiency, and its effect on welfare. The fiscal savings criterion reflects the savings, as a proportion of GDP, that each set of reforms generates. The targeting efficiency criterion assesses the distributional equity of spending, as measured using the targeting performance index (TPI) for households in the bottom 40 percent of the income distribution, and identifies the share of subsidy benefits "leaked" to upper-income households, defined in all countries as those in the top 20 percent of the income distribution. The welfare criterion assesses the effect of the reforms on poverty, as measured according to the poverty rate using the international poverty line of US$4 per person per day, and according to the impact of the budget on middle-class households.[1]

The simulations reflect the initial conditions in every country, including income levels, degree of access to electricity, the relationship between income and electricity consumption, and the structure of existing pricing mechanisms.[2] The analysis is based on a static model and does not attempt to project adjustments in household behavior that may result from the reforms. The scenarios simulated in this chapter represent a fraction of the available reform options. Their purpose is to highlight several key, crosscutting issues involved in reforming electricity subsidies.

The simulation results reveal that restructuring electricity subsidy regimes could generate both substantial fiscal savings and significant efficiency improvements without harming the welfare of lower-income households and with only limited effects on the middle class. Replacing current electricity subsidy mechanisms with a progressive cross-subsidy augmented by cash transfers could yield simultaneous improvements in the fiscal cost, distributional equity, and pro-poor effect of subsidy policies across Central America—although, under some scenarios, these gains come at the expense of lower-income households, which experience a substantial decrease in benefits. Rising poverty rates under these scenarios underscore the harm to households near the poverty line. Other scenarios use cash transfers to offset this effect, successfully shielding lower-income households from negative welfare effects while still generating significant fiscal savings and improvements in distributional equity.

Reform Scenarios

This section outlines the five reform scenarios and an overview of the results. Country-by-country results are reported in the next section. Because of the nature of Costa Rica's subsidy regime, which is based on a balanced incremental block tariff (IBT) cross-subsidy, it is treated differently in the simulations than the other five Central American countries and is hence excluded from this section.

Reform Scenario 1: Residential Electricity Subsidies Are Eliminated

Under the first scenario, all electricity subsidies are eliminated, and all consumers pay a cost-reflective tariff. The primary purpose of this scenario is to establish a frame of reference against which to judge the effect of alternative policies. As in all five simulation scenarios, it is assumed that households will not alter their consumption patterns in response to changes in electricity prices. Applying a cost-reflective tariff to all consumers does not imply that every household will pay the same rate. Costa Rica, El Salvador, Guatemala, and Panama all have multiple distribution companies, each with its own cost structure. Moreover, for any given electricity company, the cost of supplying electricity to households with different consumption volumes may differ.

Shifting to a cost-recovery tariff yields fiscal savings equal to 100 percent of the cost of its subsidy regime. In all cases, eliminating electricity subsidies also curbs leakages to households in the top 20 percent of the income distribution. Although upper-income households bear a larger share of the total cost increase, the move to cost-reflective tariffs imposes a greater cost increase on lower-income households relative to their household budgets. As a result, in all countries, the cessation of subsidies increases the poverty rate. Ending subsidies also raises electricity costs for middle-class households.

Reform Scenario 2: Electricity Subsidies Are Fully Financed through a Progressive Cross-Subsidy

Under the second scenario, each country's current subsidy regime is adjusted so that it becomes fully self-financing through cross-subsidies. High-volume consumers are charged above-cost tariffs, and low-volume consumers are charged below-cost tariffs, but the structure of each country's subsidy system is left broadly unchanged. This threshold is set at 100 kWh; tariff rates are held constant for all households consuming up to 100 kWh a month,[3] and tariffs on households with consumption levels above this threshold are increased to the level necessary to balance the cross-subsidy. This does not imply that all households consuming more than 100 kWh pay above-cost tariffs, although they all experience an increase from their current tariff rate. For instance, Nicaraguan households that consume up to 150 kWh are currently heavily subsidized, and even after the simulated rate increase, they continue to pay a below-cost tariff. Because the cross-subsidy is fully self-financing, the reform generates a fiscal savings equal to 100 percent of total subsidy spending.

In each case, the simulation improves the progressivity of the subsidy regime; households in the bottom 40 percent of the income distribution receive a larger share of the benefits, and households in the top 20 percent receive a smaller share, but some lower-income households face an increase in electricity costs, and the result is a moderate rise in the poverty rate. Meanwhile, the middle class experiences a relatively large cost increase because many households begin paying above-cost tariffs to finance the cross-subsidy.

Reform Scenario 3: Public Spending on Electricity Subsidies Is Reduced by 50 Percent and Is Augmented by a Cross-Subsidy

Scenario 3 uses the same assumptions as scenario 2, but instead of completely eliminating the fiscal cost of electricity subsidies, it reduces it by 50 percent. By construction, the fiscal savings that this reform generates are equal to half of the original cost of the subsidy regime. The increase in tariffs on households consuming more than 100 kWh reflects the amount necessary to cover the remaining cost of subsidies to households consuming less than 100 kWh.

Similar to scenario 2, the cross-subsidy yields a more progressive distribution of benefits and reduces leakages to the top 20 percent. Also similar to scenario 2, the reduction in subsidy spending has a negative effect on lower-income households and leads to an increase in the poverty rate, albeit by less than in the second scenario. Under this scenario, the harm to middle-class households is smaller but still substantial. This scenario can be interpreted as a hybrid subsidy system, or as the halfway point in a gradual transition toward a fully self-financing cross-subsidy.

Reform Scenario 4: Electricity Subsidies Are Fully Financed through a Progressive Cross-Subsidy and Are Complemented by Targeted Cash Transfers to Protect the Welfare of Low-Income Households

The fourth reform scenario combines the same cross-subsidy used in scenario 2 with targeted cash transfers. These transfers are designed to fully off-set the negative welfare effects on lower-income households that result from the shift to a cross-subsidy. Two subscenarios are used to gauge the effect of different transfer-targeting criteria. In the first, the transfer is provided to all households in the bottom 40 percent of the electricity consumption distribution. In the second, the transfer is provided to all households that already receive benefits under each country's existing cash-transfer program.[4] These households do not need to be connected to the electricity grid to receive the transfer. Because, in the real world, due to limited information, subsidy benefits cannot be precisely, directly targeted to households according to income level, these subscenarios rely on proxy indicators that would be available to program administrators.

The objective of this scenario is to protect the welfare of lower-income house-holds, reflecting the principle of shared prosperity, whereby development policies should focus on promoting the welfare of households in the bottom 40 percent of the income distribution. This is accomplished by estimating the total subsidy benefit that households in the bottom 40 percent of the income distribution receive and then delivering an equivalent benefit through one of the two subscenario targeting mechanisms. In each subscenario, the total subsidy benefit is divided equally among households in the target group. Because both subscenarios use proxy indicators to identify beneficiaries, in each case the target group may include some households not in the bottom 40 percent of the income distribution and exclude some households in the bottom 40 percent.

Overall, complementing the cross-subsidy with cash transfers successfully eliminates negative welfare effects for the average lower-income household while yielding significant net fiscal savings. In most cases, the cash transfers also decrease poverty. Because the transfers are executed through each coun-try's existing cash-transfer programs, the magnitude of their poverty and equity effects depends highly on the targeting efficiency and coverage of those systems. Because of differences in the size of the transfers necessary to offset negative welfare effects, the amount of fiscal savings also varies greatly accord-ing to country, ranging from as little as 12 percent of total subsidy spending in Guatemala under the first subscenario to as much as 73 percent in Panama under the second subscenario.

Reform Scenario 5: Electricity Subsidies Are Fully Financed through a Progressive Cross-Subsidy and Are Complemented by Targeted Cash Transfers Equal to 50 Percent of the Fiscal Cost of the Original Subsidy Regime

Whereas scenario 4 attempts to estimate fiscal outcomes while holding welfare effects on low-income households constant, scenario 5 holds the fiscal outcomes constant and estimates welfare effects. Instead of setting a transfer amount that attempts to preserve the existing subsidy benefit to lower-income households, the transfer amount is set to half of the fiscal cost of the original subsidy regime. The same targeting mechanisms are used to create two subscenarios: one in which the transfer goes to all households whose electricity consumption is in the bottom 40 percent, and one in which it goes to all households receiving transfers through an existing cash-transfer program. In each case, the amount of the subsidy is 50 percent of each country's current subsidy spending divided equally among all households in the beneficiary group.

The simulated reforms improve the targeting efficiency of electricity subsidies, with positive or neutral effects on poverty. Scenario 5 is also less administratively complex than scenario 4, because all the information needed to select the beneficiary households and estimate the amount of the transfers is already available to the government.

Simulations by Country

Costa Rica

The simulation scenarios for Costa Rica differ from those used for the other five countries, because Costa Rica already uses a fully self-financing IBT cross-subsidy. As a result, it is also the only country in which the replacement of the current subsidy regime with cost-reflective tariffs yields no fiscal savings, because its current regime already imposes no fiscal cost. Eliminating the IBT cross-subsidy (scenario 1) has negative implications for lower-income households, but because of the small size of the subsidy, its effect is modest. Under this scenario, poverty rises by 1 percent, and electric costs for vulnerable households increase by 0.12 percent of their average household budget (table 6.1).[5] In all scenarios, the reforms have a negligible impact on the budgets of middle-class households.

Table 6.1 Fiscal and Welfare Impacts of Subsidy Reform Scenarios in Costa Rica

Scenario	Fiscal savings as a percent of GDP	TPI	Leakage to top 20%	Change in Poverty %	Change in Poverty N	Impact on household budget Vulnerable (US$4–US$10) (%)	Impact on household budget Middle class (US$10–US$50) (%)
Baseline		*0.859*	*21.6*	*12.0*			
Scenario 1 (cost-recovery, flat tariff)	0.00			1.0	4,970	−0.12	0.01
Scenario 2 (cost-recovery, lower threshold—180 kWh)	0.00	0.873	−1.6	1.3	6,660	0.01	0.00
Scenario 3 (cost-recovery, from IBT to VDT)	0.00	0.923	−10.8	1.8	9,160	0.05	−0.03
Scenario 4 (cost-recovery, from IBT to VDT + lower threshold—180 kWh)	0.00	0.905	−5.1	2.0	10,220	−0.02	−0.01

Note: Baseline values for leakage and poverty refer to leakage rates estimated using 2016 tariffs and poverty rates estimated for 2014.
IBT = incremental block tariff; TPI = targeting performance indicator; VDT = volume-differentiated tariff.

Under scenario 2, the IBT cross-subsidy remains in place, but the threshold at which tariff rates reach full cost recovery falls to 180 kWh. The results of the simulation highlight the trade-off between errors of inclusion and exclusion. Lowering the cost-recovery threshold reduces errors of inclusion, cutting leakages to households in the top 20 percent of the income distribution by 1.6 percent, but it also increases errors of exclusion, causing poverty to rise by 1.3 percent as more low-income households pay above-cost electricity prices. The reform has a positive net effect on the share of benefits that households in the bottom 40 percent of the income distribution receive, and the TPI rises from a baseline of 0.859 to 0.873, although the distribution of subsidy benefits remains regressive under all scenarios. The impact on the budgets of vulnerable and middle-class households is negligible.

Under scenario 3, the cross-subsidy remains in place, but the mechanism changes from an IBT to a volume-differentiated tariff (VDT). The resulting cost structure is still balanced at the same cost-recovery threshold, but the tariff structure increases much more steeply as electricity consumption rises. Although this has a moderately negative impact on poverty, which increases by 1.8 percent, it has a highly positive effect on leakages to high-income households, which fall by 10.8 percent. This simulated reform has the most positive effect on targeting efficiency of any scenario, and the TPI rises to 0.932. The effect on vulnerable households is positive, and the impact on middle-class households is negative, but both are marginal. Overall, scenario 3 yields the greatest net improvement in targeting efficiency and distributional equity, but with an increase of more than 9,000 households living on less than US$4 per day.

Scenario 4 combines the reforms simulated in scenarios 2 and 3. The IBT mechanism is replaced with a VDT, and the cost-recovery threshold falls to 180 kWh. This scenario improves targeting efficiency and reduces leakages to high-income households more than scenario 2 but less than scenario 3. It also results in the greatest increase in poverty, although this change is still modest, at 2 percent (the equivalent of 10,220 people). Once again, the reforms have a negligible effect on the budgets of vulnerable and middle-class households.

El Salvador

There are five electricity distribution companies in El Salvador. The simulations are based on the tariff rates that the three largest distribution companies use (CLESA, CAESS, and Del Sur). The current tariff structures for these three companies and the structures that would result from each of the simulated reform scenarios are presented in table 6.2.

Under scenario 1, households in the lowest consumption ranges (0–99 kWh) bear the entire burden of the elimination of the subsidy scheme, experiencing rate increases of 104 percent on average. Under scenario 2, by construction, households that consume more than 99 kWh finance the cross-subsidy, and achieving equilibrium requires raising tariff rates on these households by 44 percent. Under scenario 3, public spending on electricity subsidies is reduced by 50 percent, and thus a 22 percent tariff increase for households that consume

Table 6.2 Tariff Structure for El Salvador under Baseline and Reform Scenarios

kWh per month	Baseline Current tariff 04/2016	Cost-recovery Flat tariff Tariff	Cost-recovery Flat tariff % difference	Cost-recovery Progressive tariff Tariff	Cost-recovery Progressive tariff % difference	Partial recovery Progressive tariff Tariff	Partial recovery Progressive tariff % difference
0–49	0.082	0.167	104	0.082	0	0.082	0
50–99	0.085	0.167	95	0.085	0	0.085	0
100–200	0.165	0.165	0	0.238	44	0.202	22
201+	0.167	0.167	0	0.241	44	0.204	22

Source: Based on data from country authorities. This table presents estimates averaged across the three largest distribution companies.

Table 6.3 Fiscal and Welfare Impacts of Subsidy Reform Scenarios in El Salvador

Scenario	Fiscal savings as a percent of GDP	TPI	Leakage to top 20%	Change in poverty rate %	Change in poverty rate N	Impact on household budget Vulnerable (US$4–US$10) (%)	Impact on household budget Middle class (US$10–US$50) (%)
Baseline		0.912	20.7	31.4			
Scenario 1: Cost-recovery (flat tariff)	0.49			2.1	38,040	−0.88	−0.32
Scenario 2: Cost-recovery (progressive)	0.49	0.912	0.0	1.0	18,040	−0.64	−0.77
Scenario 3: Partial recovery (progressive)	0.25	0.912	0.0	0.3	6,460	−0.32	−0.39
Scenario 4: Scenario 2 + cash transfers with the transfer amount based on welfare needs							
1. Quantity-targeting	0.10	1.014	−11.8	−4.5	−83,020	0.02	−0.58
2. Cash transfer programs	0.22	1.180	−23.8	−4.2	−77,730	−0.29	−0.71
Scenario 5: Scenario 2 + cash transfers equivalent to 50% of fiscal savings							
1. Quantity-targeting	0.25	0.989	−8.9	−3.7	−67,480	−0.23	−0.65
2. Cash transfer programs	0.25	1.164	−22.5	−4.1	−74,840	−0.32	−0.72

Note: Baseline values for leakage and poverty refer to the leakage rates estimated using 2016 tariffs and poverty rate estimated for 2014. TPI = targeting performance indicator.

more than 99 kWh is sufficient to cover the cost of the cross-subsidy. The effects of these scenarios in terms of fiscal savings, targeting efficiency, and distributional equity (measured by the TPI and subsidy ratios) are presented in table 6.3.

By construction, scenarios 1 and 2 reduce fiscal spending on subsidies by 100 percent, the equivalent of 0.49 percent of GDP, and scenarios 3 and 5 reduce it by half. In scenario 4, the amount of fiscal savings varies based on the endogenously defined beneficiaries and transfer amounts. The first subscenario of scenario 4, in which transfers target households whose consumption is in the bottom 40 percent, yields a fiscal savings of 0.10 percent of GDP, and The second subscenario of scenario 4, in which transfers are targeted to beneficiaries of an existing cash-transfer system, yields a fiscal savings of 0.22 percent of GDP.

The TPI reflects the distributional equity and targeting efficiency of spending. No TPI is calculated for scenario 1, because it involves no subsidies. In scenarios 2 and 3, households that consume less than 100 kWh continue to receive the same distribution of benefits as under the current system. The TPI for these scenarios does not differ from the baseline. In scenario 4, the cross-subsidy combined with either of the two targeting mechanisms yields a progressive distribution. The improved targeting under this scenario reduces the amount that leaks to the top 60 percent, so households in the bottom 40 percent receive a larger share of total subsidies.

Transfers further improve the progressivity of the distribution, and differences in the TPI between The first and second subscenarios of scenario 4 reflect the relative targeting accuracy of the two mechanisms used. These results indicate that both targeting mechanisms are relatively efficient means of transferring resources to the bottom 40 percent of the income distribution while reducing leakages to the top 60 percent. The results of scenario 5 are mixed, but the distribution is more progressive in The second subscenario of scenario 5, in which the transfer targets households that already benefit from a cash-transfer system. As with scenario 4, the shift to a cross-subsidy also improves progressivity by reducing leakages to wealthier households, although scenario 5 yields a greater increase in fiscal savings; and because these resources are not transferred to lower-income households, the TPI is lower than under scenario 4.

By design, the amount of fiscal savings is predetermined under all scenarios except scenario 4. In El Salvador, as in every other country, providing transfers to all households in the bottom 40 percent of the consumption distribution (the first subscenario of scenario 4) yields less fiscal savings than targeting transfers to households that already qualify for a cash-transfer program (the second subscenario of scenario 4).

Because electricity subsidies are progressive in relative terms—meaning they represent a larger share of household budgets in households at lower income levels—the removal of subsidies under scenario 1 affects household budgets in lower-income groups more adversely. The establishment of a cross-subsidy in scenarios 2 and 3 causes households near the top of the income distribution, the middle class, to bear the largest cost increase. In scenarios 4 and 5, which augment the cross-subsidy with targeted transfers, households in the middle class bear most costs, and vulnerable households bear lower costs—although the net cost to higher-income households is lower under scenarios 4 and 5 than under scenario 2, because these households receive a share of the transfers.

Poverty indicators display a similar pattern. In the first three scenarios, poverty increases as the reforms negatively affect household budgets in the lowest deciles. In scenario 1, an estimated 38,000 people would fall below the poverty line. In scenarios 2 and 3, an increase in errors of exclusion would cause somewhat smaller increases in poverty. Scenarios 4 and 5 decrease poverty, especially when the transfer targets beneficiaries of existing cash-transfer systems. Under both scenarios, the poverty rate drops by approximately 4 percent, as about 70,000 people escape poverty. The first subscenario of scenario 4 has the greatest effect on poverty reduction, and under this scenario, an estimated 83,000 people would exit poverty.

Guatemala

Guatemala has three electricity distribution companies: EEGSA, DEOCSA, and DEORSA. The average current and simulated tariff structures for these three companies are presented below.

Under scenario 1, Guatemalan households that consume less than 100 kWh per month experience an average rate increase of 76–203 percent, far higher than in El Salvador (table 6.4). Under scenarios 2 and 3, households that consume more than 100 kWh finance a cross-subsidy through a tariff increase of 37 percent and 19 percent, respectively.

The fiscal savings generated under scenario 4 are lower than under scenarios 3 and 5; within scenario 4, using the quantity-targeting approach decreases savings more than using the cash-transfer program (0.04 percent and 0.08 percent, respectively) (table 6.5). In Guatemala's case, the TPI improves and approaches 1, although the distribution remains regressive. Under scenarios 4 and 5, using the cash-transfer programs yields the highest TPI score, confirming that identifying beneficiaries through the country's existing cash-transfer system effectively increases the targeting efficiency of the subsidy regime.

The removal of subsidies under scenario 1 adversely affects lower-income households more than those at the top of the income distribution, as reflected in increased poverty rates and a bigger reduction in the budgets of vulnerable households than of middle-class households. Despite the more progressive distribution of benefits under scenarios 2 and 3, the reform still negatively affects the budgets of poor and vulnerable households, suggesting that some of the poorest households in Guatemala consume more than 100 kWh, making them subject to errors of exclusion. Under scenarios 4 and 5, which include a targeted transfer, households living in poverty or near the poverty line receive a substantial increase in total benefits. The budgets of vulnerable and middle-class households are reduced, but in all cases by less than 0.5 percent.

Table 6.4 Tariff Structure for Guatemala under Baseline and Reform Scenarios

| | Baseline | Cost-recovery | | | | Partial recovery | |
| | | Flat tariff | | Progressive tariff | | Progressive tariff | |
kWh per month	Current tariff 04/2016	Tariff	% difference	Tariff	% difference	Tariff	% difference
0–60	0.065	0.196	203	0.065	0	0.065	0
61–88	0.097	0.196	102	0.097	0	0.097	0
89–100	0.111	0.196	76	0.111	0	0.111	0
101+	0.196	0.196	0	0.269	37	0.232	19

Source: Based on data from country authorities.

Table 6.5 Fiscal and Welfare Impacts of Subsidy Reform Scenarios in Guatemala

Scenario	Fiscal savings as a percent of GDP	TPI	Leakage to top 20%	Change in poverty rate %	Change in poverty rate N	Impact on household budget Vulnerable (US$4–US$10) (%)	Impact on household budget Middle class (US$10–US$50) (%)
Baseline		0.833	22.0	59.8			
Scenario 1: Cost-recovery (flat tariff)	0.31			0.5	45,960	−0.37	−0.13
Scenario 2: Cost-recovery (progressive)	0.31	0.833	0.0	0.6	56,550	−0.44	−0.43
Scenario 3: Partial recovery (progressive)	0.16	0.833	0.0	0.3	27,290	−0.22	−0.21
Scenario 4: Scenario 2 + cash transfers with the transfer amount based on welfare needs							
1. Quantity-targeting	0.04	0.888	−10.1	−0.9	−81,760	−0.15	−0.35
2. Cash-transfer programs	0.08	0.983	−26.9	−0.8	−74,260	−0.25	−0.40
Scenario 5: Scenario 2 + cash transfers equivalent to 50% of fiscal savings							
1. Quantity-targeting	0.16	0.872	−7.2	−0.7	−61,090	−0.27	−0.38
2. Cash-transfer programs	0.16	0.952	−21.2	−0.7	−65,460	−0.31	−0.41

Note: Baseline values for leakage and poverty refer to the leakage rates estimated using 2016 tariffs and poverty rate estimated for 2014. TPI = targeting performance indicator.

Poverty indicators follow a similar pattern. Both subscenarios under scenario 4 and the second subscenario under scenario 5 are the most effectively targeted and have the greatest effect on poverty reduction. Under scenario 1, an estimated 46,000 people fall below the poverty line. By contrast, scenarios 4 and 5 help to reduce poverty, with an estimated 81,760 people escaping poverty under the first subscenario of scenario 4. These results suggest that a substantial number of Guatemalans are close to the poverty line and that small changes in their household budgets can have a significant effect on the poverty rate.

Honduras

Honduras has six consumption ranges and subsidizes almost all electricity consumers; only households that consume more than 840 kWh pay a cost-reflective tariff.[6] Although, in the other countries, only the lowest-volume consumers face higher tariff rates under scenario 1, in Honduras tariffs increase in all consumption ranges (table 6.6). Although tariffs increase more for low-volume households, the results reveal how heavily the Honduran electricity subsidy scheme depends on government funding.

Under scenarios 2 and 3, households consuming less than 100 kWh maintain their current tariff rates, and all other consumers experience a rate increase of 24.4 percent and 12.2 percent, respectively, although not all households that experience a tariff increase are financing the cross-subsidy; only those that

Table 6.6 Tariff Structure for Honduras under Baseline and Reform Scenarios

| | Baseline | Cost-recovery | | | | Partial recovery | |
| | | Flat tariff | | Progressive tariff | | Progressive tariff | |
kWh per month	Current tariff 04/2016	Tariff	% difference	Tariff	% difference	Tariff	% difference
0–75	0.000	0.146	–	0.000	–	0.000	–
76–100	0.102	0.146	43	0.102	0	0.102	0
101–150	0.110	0.146	33	0.136	24	0.123	12
151–300	0.123	0.146	19	0.153	24	0.138	12
301–500	0.133	0.146	10	0.165	24	0.149	12
500+	0.142	0.146	3	0.177	24	0.160	12

Source: Based on data from country authorities.
Note: These tariff figures are averages for households in each consumption range. Because of the nature of the incremental block tariff, individual tariff rates vary. – = The percent difference cannot be estimated for increases from a tariff of 0.

Table 6.7 Fiscal and Welfare Impacts of Subsidy Reform Scenarios in Honduras

| | Fiscal savings as a percent of GDP | TPI | Leakage to top 20% | Change in poverty rate | | Impact on household budget | |
| | | | | % | N | Vulnerable (US$4–US$10) (%) | Middle class (US$10– US$50) (%) |
Scenario							
Baseline		0.806	26.3	58.1			
Scenario 1: Cost-recovery (flat tariff)	1.07			0.6	27,780	−0.64	−0.28
Scenario 2: Cost-recovery (progressive)	1.07	1.334	−54.1	0.5	21,380	−0.87	−0.70
Scenario 3: Partial recovery (progressive)	0.54	1.334	−35.1	0.2	10,810	−0.44	−0.35
Scenario 4: Scenario 2 + cash transfers with the transfer amount based on welfare needs							
1. Quantity-targeting	0.37	1.273	−51.8	−0.6	−26,320	−0.61	−0.64
2. Cash-transfer programs	0.42	1.344	−66.4	−0.4	−19,370	−0.70	−0.67
Scenario 5: Scenario 2 + cash transfers equivalent to 50% of fiscal savings							
1. Quantity-targeting	0.54	1.280	−52.1	−0.5	−20,620	−0.67	−0.66
2. Cash-transfer programs	0.54	1.345	−65.5	−0.4	−16,570	−0.73	−0.67

Note: Baseline values for leakage and poverty refer to the leakage rates estimated using 2016 tariffs and poverty rate estimated for 2014. TPI = targeting performance indicator.

consume more than 150 kWh in scenario 2 and more than 300 kWh in Scenario 3 finance the cost of the subsidy scheme.

As in the previous cases, fiscal savings are predetermined for all scenarios except scenario 4. Under this scenario, fiscal savings on subsidies fall to 0.37 percent of GDP in the first subscenario and to 0.42 percent in the second subscenario (table 6.7). Under scenarios 2 and 3, Honduras's subsidy threshold drops from 840 kWh to 150 and 300 kWh, respectively. In Guatemala and El Salvador, the original threshold was much lower, at 100 kWh. As with Guatemala and El Salvador, the second subscenarios under scenarios 4 and 5 yield the best equity results, underscoring the extent to which delivering benefits through the existing cash-transfer system improves targeting efficiency.

Lower-income households are the most adversely affected under scenario 1, as reflected in a poverty increase of 0.6 percentage point and a bigger decrease in the household budgets of vulnerable households than middle-class households (0.64 percent vs 0.28 percent). Although the distribution of benefits is more progressive under scenarios 2 and 3, the simulated reforms would also increase poverty. Under scenarios 4 and 5, lower-income households receive a net benefit, and poverty falls, and those in the top income deciles face cost increases as a percentage of household income of similar magnitude as that of vulnerable households.

Nicaragua

A single electricity distribution company, Dissur-Disnorte, serves approximately 95 percent of Nicaraguan households. Small regional companies that have tariff structures similar to that of Dissur-Disnorte serve the remaining 5 percent. Table 6.8 reports baseline and simulated tariffs for Dissur-Disnorte.

Under scenario 1, tariff rates would increase significantly for low-volume consumers, and households that consume more than 150 kWh would have their tariff rates reduced by 29 percent. Under scenarios 2 and 3, tariffs would increase by 33 percent and 16.5 percent, respectively, in all households that consume more than 100 kWh, but only households that consume more than 150 kWh would finance the cross-subsidy.

Because Nicaragua does not operate a large cash-transfer program, relying instead on a number of smaller programs, scenarios 4 and 5 have only one subscenario. The fiscal savings under scenario 4 are close to 0.49 percent of GDP, the highest share of any country because of the simulated reduction in errors of inclusion from reducing the subsidy threshold from 150 kWh to 100 kWh (table 6.9). Nicaragua's TPI results are similar to those of Guatemala;

Table 6.8 Tariff Structure for Nicaragua under Baseline and Reform Scenarios

kWh per month	Baseline Current tariff 04/2016	Cost-recovery				Partial recovery	
		Flat tariff		Progressive tariff		Progressive tariff	
		Tariff	% difference	Tariff	% difference	Tariff	% difference
0–50	0.061	0.152	149	0.061	0	0.061	0
51–100	0.065	0.152	134	0.065	0	0.065	0
101–150	0.075	0.152	103	0.100	33	0.087	17
151+	0.216	0.153	-29	0.287	33	0.252	17

Source: Based on data from country authorities.

Fiscal and Welfare Impacts of Electricity Subsidies in Central America
http://dx.doi.org/10.1596/978-1-4648-1104-3

Table 6.9 Fiscal and Welfare Impacts of Subsidy Reform Scenarios in Nicaragua

Scenario	Fiscal savings as a percent of GDP	TPI	Leakage to top 20%	Change in poverty rate %	Change in poverty rate N	Vulnerable (US$4–US$10) (%)	Middle class (US$10–US$50) (%)
Baseline		0.618	29.2	35.9			
Scenario 1: Cost-recovery (flat tariff)	1.07			2.3	51,432	−1.22	−0.64
Scenario 2: Cost-recovery (progressive)	1.07	0.703	−6.1	1.4	31,640	−0.92	−1.15
Scenario 3: Partial recovery (progressive)	0.53	0.634	3.0	0.6	14,380	−0.46	−0.62
Scenario 4: Scenario 2 + cash transfers with the transfer amount based on welfare needs							
1. Quantity-targeting	0.49	0.891	−25.8	−4.1	−92,788	−0.38	−1.01
2. Cash-transfer programs	n.a.	n.a.	n.a.	n.a.	n.a.	n.a.	n.a.
Scenario 5: Scenario 2 + cash transfers equivalent to 50% of fiscal savings							
1. Quantity-targeting	0.53	0.883	−24.9	−3.5	−78,718	−0.42	−1.02
2. Cash-transfer programs	n.a.	n.a.	n.a.	n.a.	n.a.	n.a.	n.a.

Note: Baseline values for leakage and poverty refer to the leakage rates estimated using 2016 tariffs and poverty rate estimated for 2014. TPI = targeting performance indicator.

total TPI is generally progressive, and positive TPI is regressive in all scenarios. This reflects the low levels of household electricity consumption in Nicaragua relative to the simulated subsidy threshold of 100 kWh. This threshold was determined arbitrarily for the purposes of the simulation, but a lower threshold might be more appropriate to Nicaragua's electricity consumption patterns. As in Guatemala, scenario 2 yields the highest total TPI score, but unlike Guatemala, total and positive TPI are regressive under scenario 3.

The results for the household budget indicator are consistent with those of the other countries. Under the first three scenarios, all households would be adversely affected. The poverty rate rises by 2.3 percent under scenario 1, and scenarios 2 and 3 have a more modest but still negative effect on poverty. scenarios 4 and 5 each reduce the poverty rate by 3.5 to 4.1 percent, enabling between 78,000 and 93,000 people to escape poverty.

Panama

Panama's three distribution companies, ELEKTRA, EDECHI, and EDEMET, provide electricity to different regions of the country. Tariff rates vary modestly but significantly between these three distributors. Like Honduras, Panama's tariff structure has seven consumption ranges.

Table 6.10 Tariff Structure for Panama under Baseline and Reform Scenarios

kWh per month	Baseline Current tariff 04/2016	Cost-recovery Flat tariff Tariff	% difference	Cost-recovery Progressive tariff Tariff	% difference	Partial recovery Progressive tariff Tariff	% difference
0–50	0.088	0.184	109	0.088	0	0.088	0
51–100	0.085	0.163	92	0.085	0	0.085	0
101–150	0.129	0.159	24	0.158	23	0.143	11
151–200	0.127	0.157	23	0.156	23	0.142	11
201–300	0.140	0.156	11	0.172	23	0.156	11
301–500	0.162	0.186	15	0.199	23	0.180	11
501+	0.177	0.201	13	0.218	23	0.198	11

Source: Based on data from country authorities.

As in other countries, under scenario 1, low-volume consumers bear most of the burden of the elimination of the subsidy scheme. For example, the tariff rate for EDECHI consumers in the range of 0–50 kWh rises by 132 percent (table 6.10). Similar to El Salvador and Nicaragua, all households in consumption ranges that experience a tariff increase finance the subsidy mechanism by paying above-cost rates. Under scenarios 2 and 3, tariffs on high-volume consumers increase by 22.8 and 11.4 percent, respectively.

The amount of fiscal savings under the second subscenario of scenario 4 in Panama is estimated at 0.23 percent of GDP, or more than half of current spending on subsidies for residential electricity consumers (table 6.11). As in the other countries, all simulated reforms improve the progressivity of Panama's subsidy system, but only the second subscenarios of both scenarios 4 and 5 result in a progressive distribution, as indicated by TPI scores greater than 1. This is in large part because of Panama's low initial TPI score of 0.72. The subsidy ratios are consistent with the TPI results, with the second subscenarios of both scenarios 4 and 5 producing the most equitable distribution of benefits.

Changes in Panama's household budget indicator are generally consistent with those of the other countries, although the negative effect under the first three scenarios extends to the top deciles as well and is not solely concentrated at the bottom of the income distribution. In scenarios 4 and 5, households at the bottom of the income distribution receive a substantial net benefit.

In large part because of Panama's relatively low poverty levels, the simulated reforms have a limited effect on the poverty rate. The poverty rate increases by 1.2 percent under scenario 1, but changes under scenarios 2 and 3 are negligible. Both subscenarios of scenario 4 reduce the poverty rate by approximately 2.5 percent but the second subscenario of scenario 5 reduces the poverty rate by 3.1 percent, lifting an estimated 17,370 people above the poverty line.

Table 6.11 Fiscal and Welfare Impacts of Subsidy Reform Scenarios in Panama

	Fiscal savings as % GDP	TPI	Leakage to top 20%	Change in poverty rate		Impact on household budget	
				%	N	Vulnerable (US$4–US$10)	Middle class (US$10–US$50)
Baseline		*0.624*	*31.8*	*14.6*			
Scenario 1: Cost-recovery (Flat tariff)	0.39%			1.2%	6,810	−0.74%	−0.38%
Scenario 2: Cost-recovery (Progressive)	0.39%	0.727	11.7%	0.6%	3,200	−0.53%	−0.39%
Scenario 3: Partial recovery (Progressive)	0.19%	0.668	4.8%	0.2%	1,090	−0.26%	−0.19%
Scenario 4: Scenario 2 + Cash transfers with the transfer amount based on welfare needs							
1) Quantity-targeting	0.12%	0.826	26.2%	−2.4%	−13,510	0.18%	−0.16%
2) Cash-transfer programs	0.23%	1.086	44.1%	−2.6%	−14,860	−0.03%	−0.32%
Scenario 5: Scenario 2 + Cash transfers equivalent to 50% of fiscal savings							
1) Quantity-targeting	0.19%	0.812	23.8%	−2.0%	−11,230	−0.02%	−0.22%
2) Cash-transfer programs	0.19%	1.135	48.6%	−3.1%	−17,370	0.10%	−0.30%

Note: Baseline values for leakage and poverty refer to leakage rates estimated using 2016 tariffs and poverty rates estimated for 2015.
TPI = targeting performance indicator.

Conclusion

The simulations presented in this chapter reveal that improving the design of electricity subsidy policies can yield substantial fiscal gains while maintaining or even enhancing their contribution to poverty reduction and distributional equity. In all cases, replacing the existing subsidy regime with a cross-subsidy enhances its progressivity but raises electricity costs for lower-income households. Combining the cross-subsidy with a targeted transfer can shield these households from negative welfare effects or even increase the benefits they receive. Targeting transfer beneficiaries through existing cash-transfer systems is not only administratively efficient; it also yields the most progressive pro-poor distribution of benefits.

Nevertheless, even with the most favorable scenario, errors of inclusion and exclusion limit the gains from electricity subsidy reform. Although this chapter has examined only a small fraction of all potential reform options, it is difficult to conceive of a scenario in which higher-income households would not benefit from electricity subsidies or in which those subsidies would reach every single low-income household. Moreover, country characteristics that extend beyond the scope of subsidy reform drive errors of exclusion, in part. These include the electrification rate and, when transfers are used to complement subsidy benefits, the accuracy of each national cash-transfer system. Although further refinements in the targeting methodology—such as the use of multiple beneficiary criteria drawn from each country's social protection framework—could reduce errors of exclusion, it is unlikely that these errors could be fully eliminated.

The persistence of targeting errors reflects one of the intractable weaknesses of electricity subsidies as a means of reducing poverty and promoting distributional equity: electricity consumption patterns do not perfectly align with household income levels. In the simulations, the addition of targeted transfers greatly enhances the progressivity and pro-poor effect of subsidy regimes because such transfers are independently more effective at achieving poverty and equity goals than the subsidy policies they complement.

Even the most well-designed and conscientiously executed subsidy reform program that continues targeting based on energy consumption will be unable to fully address errors of inclusion and exclusion. Electricity consumption is an imperfect proxy for household income level, and no subsidy regime based on electricity consumption will be able to accurately target beneficiaries according to income group. Moreover, even in relatively wealthy Central American countries, a significant number of households are not connected to the electricity grid, and these households are almost always among the poorest. As a result, even in the most optimistic reform scenario, some share of subsidies will accrue to wealthy households, and a fraction of poor households will be unable to benefit from the subsidy regime. Although refining the targeting methodology and complementing subsidies with cash transfers could reduce these errors, they cannot be fully eliminated.

The analysis of Honduras's direct-transfer VDT subsidy for low-volume consumers presented in chapter 5 corroborates this conclusion. This is the only subsidy policy in the region that uses a nominal cash transfer rather than a discounted tariff rate, and it is also the only subsidy policy in the region to yield a progressive distribution of benefits. Because this transfer is allocated on the basis of electricity consumption and is executed through Honduras's existing cash-transfer system, it bears important similarities to the second subscenarios of both reform scenarios 4 and 5—the most progressive and most pro-poor of the simulated reforms.

Developing a more thorough understanding of the cost of electricity subsidies is especially crucial in light of national and global commitments to provide more affordable electricity. For example, the United Nations' 7th Sustainable Development Goal is to expand access to "clean and affordable energy." Although subsidies can effectively reduce household spending on electricity, consumer prices are only one dimension of affordability; lowering electricity tariffs without paying attention to precise targeting encourages inefficient and unsustainable patterns of production and consumption and generates high and unpredictable fiscal costs, weakening macroeconomic foundations and risking serious environmental consequences. The difficulties in reaching poor households using the instruments currently in place in Central American countries has to be taken into account. This study shows that these limitations can be addressed through policy reform to some extent. But significant improvements in effectiveness will require clearer policy objectives and better criteria for eligibility, including working in coordination with similar programs to support poor households.

Fiscal and Welfare Impacts of Electricity Subsidies in Central America
http://dx.doi.org/10.1596/978-1-4648-1104-3

Notes

1. Technically, increasing the cost of electricity would not increase poverty rates because poverty is measured based on income. Instead, this exercise estimates the share of households whose income *after* paying electricity expenses would fall below the poverty line. Following other literature in the region, the middle class is identified as households with daily per capita income between US$10 and US$50.

2. The simulations reflect the electricity tariff and subsidy regimes in place in April 2016. See annex 4A in chapter 4 for a technical description of the data and estimation methodology for each country.

3. This was 99 kWh in the case of El Salvador.

4. These include Comunidades Solidarias in El Salvador, Mi Bono Seguro in Guatemala, Bono 10 Mil in Honduras, and Red de Oportunidades in Panama. Nicaragua does not have a single, prominent cash-transfer program, relying instead on a number of smaller programs.

5. Vulnerable households are defined as those whose per capita income is between US$4 and US$10 per day.

6. Because Honduras's most recent household survey was conducted in 2007, electricity consumption data from 2007 were updated to reflect coverage patterns in 2014 (see annex 4A in chapter 4).

Bibliography

Inchauste, G., and D. Victor. 2017. *The Political Economy of Energy Subsidy Reform.* Washington, DC: World Bank.

Environmental Benefits Statement

The World Bank Group is committed to reducing its environmental footprint. In support of this commitment, we leverage electronic publishing options and print-on-demand technology, which is located in regional hubs worldwide. Together, these initiatives enable print runs to be lowered and shipping distances decreased, resulting in reduced paper consumption, chemical use, greenhouse gas emissions, and waste.

We follow the recommended standards for paper use set by the Green Press Initiative. The majority of our books are printed on Forest Stewardship Council (FSC)–certified paper, with nearly all containing 50–100 percent recycled content. The recycled fiber in our book paper is either unbleached or bleached using totally chlorine-free (TCF), processed chlorine-free (PCF), or enhanced elemental chlorine-free (EECF) processes.

More information about the Bank's environmental philosophy can be found at http://www.worldbank.org/corporateresponsibility.